The New
Democratic Professional
in Education

The New Democratic Professional in Education

Confronting Markets, Metrics, and Managerialism

GARY L. ANDERSON

MICHAEL IAN COHEN

TEACHERS COLLEGE PRESS

TEACHERS COLLEGE | COLUMBIA UNIVERSITY

NEW YORK AND LONDON

Published by Teachers College Press, 1234 Amsterdam Avenue, New York, NY 10027

Library of Congress Cataloging-in-Publication Data

Names: Anderson, Gary L., 1948– author. | Cohen, Michael Ian, author.
Title: The new democratic professional in education : confronting markets, metrics, and managerialism / Gary Anderson, Michael Ian Cohen.
Description: New York, NY : Teachers College Press, [2018] | Includes bibliographical references and index.
Identifiers: LCCN 2018025523| ISBN 9780807759424 (acid-free paper) | ISBN 9780807759431 (hardcover) | ISBN 9780807777275 (ebook)
Subjects: LCSH: Teachers—Professional relationships—United States. | Public schools—United States. | Democracy and education—United States.
Classification: LCC LB1775.2 .A55 2018 | DDC 371.102—dc23
LC record available at https://lccn.loc.gov/2018025523

ISBN 978-0-8077-5942-4 (paper)
ISBN 978-0-8077-5943-1 (hardcover)
ISBN 978-0-8077-7727-5 (ebook)

Printed on acid-free paper

Manufactured in the United States of America

25   24   23   22   21   20   19   18   8   7   6   5   4   3   2   1

For
Kathryn and Maya
Amy, Fischer, and Jade

Contents

Acknowledgments   ix

Introduction   1

1. **Privatizing Professionals:**
   Teaching and Leading under New Public Management   7

   What's Behind the Attack on the Public Sector
   and the Public-Sector Professional?   10

   Are Teaching and Administration Professions?   12

   Professional Work in an Audit Culture   14

   New Capitalism and the New Corporate Workplace   17

   New Governance and New Public Management   21

   New Public Management and the Activist State   23

   Toward a New Democratic Professional in Education   24

   Conclusion   25

2. **The Historical and Political Construction of the New Professional**   27

   How Did We Get Here?   28

   Early Business-Inspired Reforms   29

   Professionalism in the Bureaucracy   32

   Bureaucracy Versus Community   42

   Early Business Policy Players   45

   Conclusion   48

3. **The Second Wave of Business Influence**
   and the Appeal of New Managerialism   51

   The Failure of New Public Management Reforms in Education   53

Corporations, Managerialism, and the Role of Business Schools   55

New Managerialism and the Failure of the American Business Model   58

A Brief History of the American Corporation   61

The Appeal of New Public Management: Political Spectacle,
   Cross-sector Borrowing, and Cognitive Framing   63

Conclusion   68

4. **New Policy Actors and Networks Design
      the New Teacher and Leader**   **69**

Strange Bedfellows: Who Supports New Public Management Reforms?   71

New Policy Actors: The Emergence of Issue Networks   77

The Growing Role of Privatization, Contracting, and "Edubusinesses"   83

Training the New Education Professional   85

Conclusion   87

5. **Responding to NPM and New Professionalism**   **89**

How New Public Management and New Professionalism
   Became the New Normal   91

Resisting New Public Management and New Professionalism   96

From Resistance to Democratic Professionalism   108

Conclusion   110

6. **The New Democratic Professional:
      Building New Alliances for Change**   **111**

Characteristics of a New Democratic Professional   114

Building on Existing Democratic Practices and Policies   123

Building Counter-Networks: New Alliances for Change   137

Conclusion   138

References   **141**

Index   **163**

About the Authors   **177**

Acknowledgments

We'd like to acknowledge the many scholars who are peering behind the (discursive and material) curtain to view the machinations that are shaping a "new" professional around a neoliberal logic of action. Many of these scholars are cited in this book. We'd also like to acknowledge Brian Ellerbeck of Teachers College Press for seeing value in a book on the new entrepreneurial professional in education even before we felt prepared to produce it. In the mean and lean world of publishing today, in which even copyediting is a luxury, we also want to thank Lori Tate and Myra Cleary for their careful readings and suggestions. Finally, we want to thank our students, most of whom are school professionals who share with us their daily struggles with markets, metrics, and managerialism. These are struggles we recognized as former school professionals and currently as university professionals.

Introduction

The United States is witnessing a revival of teacher activism. Wildcat strikes and walkouts in states like West Virginia, Oklahoma, Kentucky, Colorado, and Arizona have challenged austerity policies as teachers are demanding better wages, but also more voice and respect as professionals. In postausterity and posthurricane Puerto Rico, teachers are fighting a bill that would turn all of their schools into charters, much like New Orleans after Katrina. Teachers are fed up, not only with degraded salaries, but also with a degradation of their professional identities. And the public seems to support them. An April 2018 AP-NORC poll asked 1,140 adults their views of teacher pay and recent protests advocating for more school funding. Seventy-eight percent of adults said that teachers are underpaid for the work they do, and 52% approved of teachers striking to protest low teacher pay and cuts to school funding. While giving a host of tax breaks to business, Arizona has cut education spending per student by 36.5% since 2008.

Unfortunately, the threat to teachers is deeper than low wages and attacks on teachers' pensions. As schools and districts increasingly are absorbed into a market, profit, and efficiency logic, the professional identities of teachers and leaders are being radically reshaped (Ball, 2001; Gillies, 2011). While professionals have always been "managed" to some extent, they are experiencing a "new managerialism" that relies on the discipline of the market and high-stakes outcomes measures. In education, a new generation of teachers, counselors, and principals has already been largely incorporated into this new professional identity. The same could be said for nurses, doctors, social workers, police officers, and other public-sector professionals. Private-sector professionals in the new mean, lean corporations and the gig economy also are being reshaped in similar ways. This book seeks to understand how this has occurred, who made it happen, and how collective resistance to this new managerialism might forge a new democratic professional.

In education, the list of reforms that this new managerial logic has spawned is long: high-stakes testing regimes, school choice, vouchers, charter schools, mayoral control, schools and districts as profit centers, and professional deregulation through alternative pathways to teaching and administration, to name just a few. Many of these reforms are targeting not schools that serve the middle class, but rather those that serve low-income communities of color (Scott, 2011). On the surface, they may seem like disconnected reforms, each responding to different problems or offering unique solutions. However, as an assemblage, they are linked by a new managerialist logic, or what we will refer to as New Public Management (NPM), which transfers a market and corporate logic to the public sector (Ward, 2011).

These pro-market reforms of public education do more than shape policy and curriculum; they also influence educators' understanding of themselves as professionals, driving at the very core of what it means to be a teacher or a leader (Ball, 2001; Poole, 2008). And this trend is not limited to the United States. Globally, we are seeing the creation of a "new professionalism" and the replacement of an ethos of public service with the discipline of the market (Denhardt & Denhardt, 2011; Exworthy & Halford, 1999). According to Seddon, Ozga, and Levin (2013), education reforms across the globe "have endorsed market mechanisms and technical rational learning, but without affirming moral and political principles that orient learning towards citizenship" (p. 5).

This book explores current scholarship in the sociology of the professions on the "new professionalism" that is emerging in virtually all service sectors, from medical professionals, to teachers, to police officers. Regardless of what service sector professionals work in, they are encountering market-based reforms; high-stakes, outcomes-based measures of performance; entrepreneurialism; decentralization; and discourses of professional "autonomy" and fiscal expediency (Evetts, 2009; Exworthy & Halford, 1999; Radin, 2006). As educators, we will focus mainly on education professions, but we will include some examples from other professions as well. It is crucial that public-sector professionals understand that they are not alone in their struggles with new professionalism. While our focus is on the United States, the trends we describe are global, and we include scholarship from beyond the United States as well.

Both of us have been teachers and administrators in K–12 schools, so we bring a "from the trenches" perspective and a deep respect for education professionals. Although some may find the book biased against NPM reform policies, we believe that there is overwhelming evidence that this business and market mindset not only has failed to increase academic achievement, but has introduced perverse incentives into the system and promises to further damage our already threadbare democracy. Throughout the book, we provide both scholarly evidence of this and anecdotal evidence from our own experience.

This book will describe the corporate characteristics of this new professionalism as it is manifested within schools and districts as well as in university-based certification programs and alternative pathways, especially "fast track," online programs. We also will explore the historical and corporate origins of the new professionalism and why it has a bipartisan appeal in spite of logical and empirical evidence that it has not improved schooling or led to more socially just outcomes (Adamson, Astrand, & Darling-Hammond, 2016; Lubienski & Lubienski, 2014). Ultimately, we will demonstrate how we might not merely resist the new professionalism, but also use this moment to forge a more democratic professional who can advocate for community empowerment and work for a common good.

While the book will highlight the negative influences of the corporate sector on education, it is not anti-business. Many local businesses have partnered with public schools to fund educational activities and help build civic capacity, and many local businesspeople have served honorably on school boards. Business owners are part of our civil society, and we need the business community to support public schools. At local levels, this is often the case. Moreover, there are many examples of progressive corporations promoting corporate responsibility (Blowfield & Murray, 2014), and democracy has entered the workplace in a number of worker-owned and worker-managed enterprises (Wolff, 2012). But corporate leaders need greater humility about the boundaries of their own professional knowledge and the boundaries of their own profit-seeking (Cuban, 2004).

While not anti-business, the book will, however, argue that the system world and the lifeworld of our public organizations are out of balance (Habermas, 1987; Sergiovanni, 2000). This was the case with the factory-model school and, more recently, the over-regulation of many professionals through markets and metrics. In this sense, we are fighting against two kinds of excess, that of the first wave of business influence that over-bureaucratized schooling and that of the second wave that uses new technologies of power (markets, high-stakes testing, etc.) that discipline from a distance.

We will document how these reforms, largely developed by elite, White males, are disproportionately affecting low-income students and students of color (Achinstein, Ogawa, & Speiglman, 2004), marginalizing multicultural and civic education (Sleeter, 2012; Veltri, 2010), and making it harder to recruit and retain teachers of color (Achinstein & Ogawa, 2012). The goal of some reformers is to create a parallel system for low-income students that is privatized, promoted by new advocacy networks, funded by venture philanthropists, and increasingly delivered online (Mungal, 2016; Nespor & Voithofer, 2016; Zeichner & Pena-Sandoval, 2015).

But teachers, leaders, parents, and students are reappropriating or resisting such reforms both individually and collectively. Resisting new professionalism should be seen as advocating not for a return to some idealized "old professionalism," but rather for the creation of "third spaces," within schools and outside schools, that seek alternative definitions of professional identity (Bhaba, 1994; Martin, Snow, & Franklin Torrez, 2011; Soja, 1996) that are more equitable, democratic, and student- and community-based.

Creating this new democratic professional will mean creating new alliances of educators, students, parents, and communities to harness their burgeoning concerns around excessive testing, school closings, funding inequalities, too few teachers of color, and diminishing community input. The good news is that many policies and practices that the democratic professional can build on are already in existence and will be examined in Chapter 6 (e.g., community schools, alternative assessment, restorative justice, culturally responsive teaching, peer assistance and review, social movement unionism, etc.).

This new alliance also must extend beyond education and even beyond the public sector. Public-sector unions are actively under attack, and the terrain is being prepared for privatized, nonorganized, and deskilled professionals within an increasingly privatized public sector. While public-sector professionals are feeling the brunt of New Public Management, many private-sector service workers are experiencing comparable shifts. Global education reformers working to privatize public education have learned the art of networking and building alliances. Educators will need to do so as well, seeking allies across social sectors and in their own school communities.

The current wave of teacher strikes and walkouts stands on the shoulders of previous teacher activism in Wisconsin in 2011, when teachers fought the end of public sector collective bargaining (Yates, 2012), and in Chicago in 2012, when a reformed union struck to gain greater voice in education policy (Nunez, Michie & Konkol, 2015). Teachers' unions are often playing "catch-up" to grassroots teacher activists who are sometimes more critical than the unions themselves. Educators and other public-sector professionals are fed up with being denigrated, cut out of policy influence, and underpaid. This book provides a political and historical diagnosis of the problem and documents the emergence of a new democratic professional.

Chapter 1 provides an overview of the emergence of the "new professional" within the private and public sectors. We draw on research from the sociology of the professions on how changes in the corporate workplace are being transferred into the public sector and describe how they are transforming teaching and administration. We also provide an overview of New Public Management and its effects globally within a restructured public sector.

In Chapter 2, we explore some historical examples of business-inspired reforms in public education, how they influenced the professionalism of teachers and school leaders for much of the 20th century, and how they laid some of the groundwork for today's "new professionalism." The idea that business should serve as a model for the way our school systems are organized and governed, and that it should even set the standards for what children are learning, is an old and durable one in the United States. In fact, the schools we have today are in many ways the products of business-oriented reforms initiated more than a century ago.

In Chapter 3, we describe the more recent, second wave of business-influenced education reforms. These reforms, which have extended markets beyond the private sector and used high-stakes outcomes measures to steer the system from a distance, can be traced to the rise of business schools and a business mindset in the past several decades. We also discuss how discourse and framing strategies (Lakoff, 2008) are used by think tanks and the media to produce what Edelman (1988) called a political spectacle that undermines the public sector, laying the groundwork for privatization.

In Chapter 4, we explore who the political actors are who have successfully promoted NPM reforms in education and how these policy entrepreneurs have galvanized a diverse network of fellow advocates for current reforms. The construction of the new public-sector professional is a complex phenomenon that is promoted by different groups with different interests. We explore why neoliberalism and New Public Management reforms, despite their lackluster performance, are so appealing both to major political parties and to such disparate groups as hedge fund managers and many members of low-income communities of color.

In Chapter 5, building on our discussion of the widespread appeal of the new professionalism and NPM reforms, we explain why they are so difficult to resist, even for those educators who work within the system and are frustrated daily with market-driven reforms. Foucault's theoretical work on power and identity helps us see that education policy does more than change educators' practices; it also can change the way they understand themselves as educators, how they relate to other stakeholders, and—more broadly—how they conceptualize the purpose of public education. We propose a new framework of resistance that builds upon what educators have attempted thus far but takes a longer view, one that sees resistance as a crucial collective step toward a democratic professionalism.

In Chapter 6, we discuss the characteristics of a democratic professionalism. While we will present a vision of a new kind of democratic professionalism, we are not simply theorizing it or offering vague prescriptions. We draw on current promising practices that might form a basis for a new assemblage of policies and practices that could provide a context for a democratic professional. As the Every Student Succeeds Act (ESSA) brings more flexibility to states, developing these and other approaches can promote a professionalism grounded in participatory communities of practice, as well as advocacy for and input from school communities.

CHAPTER 1

Privatizing Professionals

Teaching and Leading Under New Public Management

Most public-sector professionals today are accustomed to working within a marketized, accountability-driven environment in which recruiting clients, developing "revenue streams," engaging in public relations, contracting with the private sector, competing for merit pay, developing their "brand," fundraising, striving or "gaming" to meet high-stakes outcomes, and polishing their CVs have become central to their work. Public-sector professionals now belong to what Shipps (2012) calls a market regime in which public bureaucracies are restructured around a particular conception of *corporate* principles of efficiency and accountability, and entrepreneurial principles of competition and choice. This slow, but persistent, colonization of the public sector by the private was accomplished with almost no public discussion and with little organized resistance. How this growing privatization of the public sector has been accomplished and the prospects for reclaiming and rethinking both a more democratic professionalism and a democratic public sphere is the focus of this book.

While this book is primarily about teachers and school administrators in the public sector, we believe it is important to emphasize that the economic, political, and cultural shifts we are seeing are affecting both private-sector professionals and professionals across the public sector, not just in public education. In this chapter, we address some shifts in professionalism in the for-profit, corporate sector, but professionals in a growing nonprofit sector are experiencing similar effects (Baldridge, 2014; Gilmore, 2007).

The transfer of business principles to the public sector has been exacerbated by a withdrawal of the state from funding public services, in accordance with the neoliberal notion that many public services should be financially self-supporting like a private business. In education, these policies of disinvestment are seen most starkly in higher education. According to the State Higher Education Executive Officers Association (2017), "Adjusted for inflation, states spent $5.7 billion less on public higher education last year [2016] than in 2008, even though they were educating more than 800,000 additional students" (p. 1).

This disinvestment from higher education has increased the already growing corporatization of universities. Barrow (2018) argues that faculty have become entrepreneurs, in many cases expected to earn their own salaries. In fact, he argues that universities no longer merely act like corporations as others have documented (Slaughter & Rhoades, 2009), but rather have essentially become corporations. Corporate practices include market-based allocation of resources, deferring to management to develop institutional goals, using benchmarking and productivity measures, treating academic departments as profit centers, shifting to marketing and customer service orientations, seeking new revenue streams, and creating a professional entrepreneurial ethos.

But disinvestment is also occurring in K–12 education, especially during the post-2008 recession and the austerity policies imposed by both political parties. This has created a teacher gap—more students, fewer teachers—as the population continues to grow, but the public sector doesn't. According to Elise Gould (2016) of the Economic Policy Institute, since 2008, there has been a shortfall of 372,000 jobs for teachers in the United States. Hitting low-income areas the hardest, the teacher gap has resulted in larger class sizes, fewer paraprofessionals, and fewer extracurricular activities. The same is happening across the public sector, resulting in a reduction in services and a deteriorating public physical infrastructure, which represents a broader policy of disinvestment (Adamson et al., 2016).

While a business-led market and accountability-driven policy environment has created *policy alienation* among public professionals in general (Tummers, Bekkers, & Steijn, 2009), this book will focus primarily on the education sector, and how a market regime has reshaped the professional dispositions and behaviors of teachers and school and district administrators.* Increasing numbers of educators, including the authors of this book, have grave concerns about how their work is being redesigned through high-stakes accountability systems, privatization, and, increasingly, profitization of the public sector.

Public-sector professionals are experiencing heightened levels of stress. A 2014 Gallup poll found that 46% of teachers report high daily stress during the school year. This is tied with nurses for the highest rate among all occupational groups. There is also a growing consensus among education scholars that this accountability-driven policy environment has introduced perverse incentives into the U.S. education system (Adamson & Darling-Hammond, 2016; Cuban, 2004; Gewirtz, Mahony, Hextall, & Cribb, 2009; Ingersoll, 2006; Lubienski & Lubienski, 2014; Ravitch, 2014; Scott, 2011; Zeichner, 2010).

The language that is used to talk about the changes we will discuss in this book can be confusing, so we will take a moment to orient the reader to how we will be using some key terms. The broad historical shift from a Keynesian welfare state (1930s to 1970s) to a Milton Friedman–inspired, neoclassical or neoliberal model (1970s to present) often is discussed as a shift within capitalism from "embedded" or regulated capitalism to free-market capitalism. Friedman's model was called "neoclassical" economics, but "neoliberalism" often is preferred because it captures not only the economic, but also the political and cultural dimensions of

---

* According to Tummers et al. (2009), *policy alienation* is defined as a "general cognitive state of psychological disconnection from the policy programme being implemented by a public professional who regularly interacts directly with clients" (p. 686).

the shift away from the Keynesian, welfare state. The political dimensions refer to the model's effects on freedom and democracy, and the cultural effects refer to how it changes the way public-sector professionals, like teachers and administrators, think about themselves and their commitment to working for a common good.

An aspect of neoliberalism that pertains to how institutions and organizations have been affected is *managerialism*, which denotes the historical tendency of owners of capital to hire managers, thus creating a new level of leadership more responsive to profits and shareholders than to the companies they manage (Locke & Spender, 2011). While the management of organizations has a longer history, managerialism as ideology posits that all organizations are essentially the same and that performance can be optimized by the application of generic management skills and practices (Klikauer, 2013). As Quiggin (2003) notes, "To a practitioner of managerialism, there is little difference in the skills required to run a college, an advertising agency or an oil rig" (p. 1).

Managerialism, when transferred to the public sector, also changes how we think about things like accountability, which used to be known as professional responsibility and being answerable to our stakeholders and the public. As Biesta (2004) points out, "accountability" used to refer only to financial documentation. However, as the managerial meaning was transferred to the public sector, it was expanded to mean the demand for auditable accounts of all of an organization's activities. Being responsible or answerable and being accountable (i.e., auditable) are not the same thing and yet, "the rhetoric of accountability operates precisely on the basis of a 'quick switch' between the two meanings, making it difficult to see an argument against accountability as anything other than a plea for irresponsible action" (Biesta, 2004, p. 235). We will return to this issue of professional *responsibility* later.

New Public Management (NPM) refers to the transfer of managerial and market principles to the public sector, much like the example of "accountability." NPM as public-sector managerialism includes a strong focus on the use of outcomes measurement and mathematical models for decisionmaking, what corporations call the statistical control of product quality.

While big data and predictive analytics claim to hold great promise for improving professional practice in many fields, when high stakes are attached, Campbell's law tends to predict the result. According to Campbell (1976), "The more any quantitative social indicator is used for social decision-making, the more subject it will be to corruption pressures and the more apt it will be to distort and corrupt the social processes it is intended to monitor" (p. 85). Furthermore, big data are only as good as the algorithms that are used, the values of the people who created them, and the level of transparency and public oversight of their use. In her book, *Weapons of Math Destruction: How Big Data Increases Inequality and Threatens Democracy*, Cathy O'Neil (2016) provides a sobering overview of the dark side of data-driven decisions in areas ranging from teacher evaluation to employment recruiting and credit ratings.

The problem of managerialist reforms is less the transfer of language, concepts, and practices between the private and public sectors, than the lack of serious and rational discussion of the appropriateness of the transfer and the possible "side-effects" when it is driven more by managerialist ideology or the bottom line than by the equitable social provision of human needs. Clearly, a certain amount of borrowing between sectors is inevitable and desirable. The public sector has weaknesses that could be informed by new ideas, and social provision sometimes can be appropriately supplemented by private organizations or in the form of partnerships (Minow, 2002). Private corporations also have much to learn from the public sector, for instance, about their civic responsibilities to the public good or, ironically, how to be more entrepreneurial (see Mazzucato, 2015, on the entrepreneurial state).

But serious study and attention to cross-sector borrowing has been conspicuous by its absence. The marketization of the public sector was a hallmark of Milton Friedman's (1962) proposal in *Capitalism and Freedom*, and it has been promoted ideologically or accepted largely through a set of unwarranted assumptions about the alleged greater efficiency, effectiveness, and innovativeness of the private sector (Goodsell, 2004; Mazzucato, 2015).

Furthermore, with a growing for-profit sector eyeing the public sector as a profit center, the risks entailed in private companies providing public services have been laid bare by the recent scandals of for-profit prisons, private military contractors like Blackwater (P.W. Singer, 2007), loosely regulated charter schools (P. Green, Baker, Oluwole, & Mead, 2016), and unscrupulous for-profit universities, even one owned by the President of the United States (Breneman, Pusser, & Turner, 2006). Global networks of profit-seeking "edu-businesses" are selling their wares to vulnerable and often corrupt governments in developing countries (Riep & Machacek, 2016; Robertson & Verger, 2012). Given the labor-intensive nature of public education, teachers ultimately must be further deprofessionalized and de-unionized in order to increase edu-business' profits.

WHAT'S BEHIND THE ATTACK ON THE PUBLIC SECTOR AND THE PUBLIC-SECTOR PROFESSIONAL?

In what he refers to as a "neoliberal project," Harvey (2005) argues that in the post–World War II years, the corporate community was mobilized by what it considered an attack on business. Corporations were not happy with high taxes to fund the growth of a welfare state, "big government," and the power of unions, which were a result of the labor movement of the 1930s. Harvey saw this neoliberal project as both ideological and economic.

The *ideological* project was summed up by an infamous memo written by Lewis Powell in 1971 to the Director of the U.S. Chamber of Commerce, just before he was appointed to the Supreme Court by Richard Nixon. At the time, Powell served on 11 corporate boards and was chief counsel to the U.S. Chamber of Commerce. The Powell memo laid out an agenda for business executives and their organizations to engage in activism, founding think tanks and institutes within and outside universities, writing books, endowing professorships, and renewing a focus on the courts. This memo helped mobilize the Chamber of Commerce and the Business Roundtable and spurred the creation of a plethora of conservative think tanks (McLean, 2017).

Another aspect of the ideological project was to discursively undermine the public sector and marketize it in order to make it behave more like a private enterprise. NPM was inspired, in part, by public choice theory in the 1950s and 1960s, and was implemented in many countries in the 1990s (Ward, 2012).

The *economic* side of the neoliberal project involved (1) curbing the power of labor by outsourcing jobs and increasing automation; (2) a trend toward financialization and speculation as fast and jobless paths to easy profits; (3) deregulating capital; and (4) slashing corporate and individual income tax rates. Through the mid-1970s, wages, profits, and productivity rose in parallel fashion. This ended by the late 1970s when wages leveled off and profits and productivity continued to rise. This surplus value of labor that was not paid out in wages, combined with a new, less progressive tax code, contributed to the creation of the current billionaire capitalist class that has gained both economic and political power (Harvey, 2005).

How does this relate to the public sector? Capital accumulation has always been the legitimate goal of capitalist enterprises, but some see us entering a new phase of capitalism that Harvey (2005) refers to as "accumulation by dispossession." This means that capital is seeking profit in areas that previously were not seen as profit centers, such as the public sector, which potentially represents trillions of dollars in profit. Burch (2009) has documented various industries that seek profit in the education sector, although there is perhaps even more money to be made in other sectors such as public services and transportation, health care, prisons, and the military.

Because labor costs are high in education, reaching 85% of operating costs in many cases, profits in education often require a reduction in labor costs, which include salaries, benefits, and pensions. This is why teachers' unions are a major target of corporate-led organizations like the American Legislative Exchange Council (ALEC) (G. L. Anderson & Montoro Donchik, 2016). As was the case in the private sector, where unions were sidelined by "right to work" laws and benefits and pensions are now rare, unions once again find themselves targeted as corporations seek profit in the public sector (Weiner, 2012). As Scott and DiMartino (2009) have documented, profit-seekers are just one part of a larger network of reformers that target public schools and the teachers and leaders who work in them. We will discuss these other groups in more detail in Chapter 4.

We have provided here a far too reductionist overview of the neoliberal project—sometimes referred to as "late capitalism," "fast capitalism," or "supply-side economics"—but an in-depth analysis of global shifts in the political economy is beyond the scope of this book. Rather, our concern is how these economic and political shifts are reshaping our work lives and our very understandings of what it means to be a public-sector professional. The emergence of public school teaching and administration as professions is a relatively recent 20th-century phenomenon, beginning with normal schools that evolved into teachers' colleges and eventually into universities. Most commentators who are critical of what they see as privatizing and deprofessionalizing tendencies also critique many aspects of how professionalism has been defined and is taught in universities (G. L. Anderson, 2017; A. Brantlinger & Smith, 2013; Zeichner & Pena-Sandoval, 2015).

While professionalism is being reshaped in a direction that we will critique in this book, it is also necessary to critique aspects of how schooling, and consequently professionalism, has developed during the 20th century. Historians have documented how public schooling and the development of professionals have been largely a White male project (J.D. Anderson, 1988; Rousmaniere, 2013; Watkins, 2001). Anyone who reads histories of U.S. education should be struck by the extent to which White men were the architects of education not only for White students, but also for women and people of color (D. Goldstein, 2014; Scott, 2009; Watkins, 2001). These influential men also tended to be from the privileged classes.

The notable historical exceptions prove the rule: Molefi Asante, Mary McLeod Bethune, Edward Alexander Bouchet, Charlotte Hawkins Brown, W.E.B. Du Bois, Margaret Haley, Dolores Huerta, Helen Keller, Lucy Sprague Mitchell, Booker T. Washington, Emma Willard, and Carter Woodson, to name a few. We will address this issue in more detail in subsequent chapters, but, while we don't want to fall into historical presentism—judging the past by today's values—it is important that we understand the history of professionalism in education as partly a gendered, classed, and racial enterprise.

In fact, the neoliberal project was in many ways a reaction not only to the economic factors we enumerated above, but also to the progress that women and people of color were making by the 1970s. In Chapter 4, we will elaborate in more detail on the strategic alliances that were forged among neoliberals, neoconservatives, religious groups, and middle-class professionals from both political parties to roll back the gains of the labor and civil rights movements (Apple, 2006).

ARE TEACHING AND ADMINISTRATION PROFESSIONS?

At a time when certification requirements for teachers and administrators are being rolled back in many states, the question of whether teaching and administration are skills, crafts, or professions is taking center stage. While there are enough definitions of what constitutes a profession in education to fill this entire book, according to a U.S. Department of Education report on teacher professionalism, the five criteria of professionalism had to do with (1) credentialing, (2) induction, (3) professional development, (4) authority over decisionmaking, and (5) compensation (Ingersoll, Nabeel, Quinn, & Bobbitt, 1997).

In education, most of these criteria had been achieved by the second half of the 20th century. While credentialing requirements are being rolled back in many states, most not only require credentials for teachers, but often require a master's degree.[†] With unionism came better compensation. And while public school and district bureaucracies had complex legal frameworks and compliance systems, most teachers had control over decisionmaking in their classrooms. Professional development by the 1980s had transcended teacher isolationism and "talking head" inservices. Teachers had more input into their professional development and increasingly engaged in professional learning communities and action research (Cochran-Smith & Lytle, 2009; Lave, 1988).

But in 1983, *A Nation at Risk* (National Commission on Excellence in Education) introduced a new paradigm into public education (Mehta, 2013). It claimed that students were human capital, that the primary goal of schooling was to contribute to global economic competitiveness, and that our public schools were the reason why Germany and Japan were outperforming us economically. Before long, countries were being ranked by test scores, as were states, schools, and later teachers and students. Soon, teachers, principals, and schools frequently were being "audited" through outcomes measures of various kinds.

Not only teachers and principals, but nurses, doctors, police officers, and even UPS truck drivers were being monitored from a distance through various high-stakes outcomes measures (J. Goldstein, 2017). Notions of professionalism were changing globally as professionals became increasingly "managed" by a growing "audit culture" (Power, 1999; Shore & Wright, 2015; Strathern, 2000). This audit culture increasingly was taking decisionmaking out of professionals' hands or making it conditional on achieving quantitative outcomes, and professional standards were created and measured by those outside the profession (Apple, 2004; Codd, 2005).

Evetts (2011) conceptualized the shift in professionalism as one from "notions of partnership, collegiality, discretion and trust to increasing levels of managerialism, bureaucracy, standardization, assessment and performance review" (p. 407). This new professionalism is largely the result of a transfer of private-sector logics into the public sector and the replacement of an ethos of public service with the discipline of the market and outcomes-based external accountability (Denhardt & Denhardt, 2011; Evetts, 2009; Exworthy & Halford, 1999; Radin, 2006).

Scholars of the new professionalism argue that while there are some continuities from the "old" professionalism, a shift has occurred as the work of professionals increasingly is controlled by managers external to the occupational group, a tendency that Evetts (2011) refers to as *organizational professionalism* or professionalism "from above" (p. 407). She contrasts this with *occupational professionalism* or professionalism "from within" (p. 407) and documents a shift from professional to new managerialist values. Woods (2011) characterizes the shift as one from bureau-professional governance toward an emerging "bureau-enterprise culture" (p. 32).

This shift suggests a decrease in professional autonomy and control over one's profession through the exercise of professional judgment, professional associations, and unions, and an increase in control by managers in work organizations

---

† Some states are passing legislation that requires only a bachelor's degree, and no other training, to become a teacher (Strauss, 2017).

and beyond. This control is characterized by traditional forms of rational-legal control and standardized work procedures and practices, along with new external forms of regulation and accountability measures, or what some have called governing or *steering* from a distance (Denhardt & Denhardt, 2011; Kickert, 1995; Rose, 1993). While teachers may retain some autonomy in the classroom, and principals, some school-level autonomy, this autonomy is constrained by external pressures, such as pressures to emphasize only tested subjects like language arts and mathematics (Forsey, 2009; Wills & Sandholtz, 2009).

In addition to being steered from a distance by outcomes data, professionals are disciplined by the market, as they are forced to compete with their colleagues both within and outside their units or organizations. One result of these reforms is that most professionals are experiencing work intensification as they are expected to reach ever-higher levels of productivity, enforced by outcomes measures and competition. Across the private and public sectors, the advent of 24/7 availability via the Internet, pressures for quick work turnarounds, the ability of bosses to monitor employees' computer keystrokes, students' standardized test scores, and cargo-truck-tracking devices makes escape seem impossible (Crary, 2014).

PROFESSIONAL WORK IN AN AUDIT CULTURE

Another way to approach this shift from occupational (from within) to organizational (from above) professionalism is to conceive of it as an imbalance between the system world and lifeworld of schools. Briefly, the system world is the set of rules, procedures, accountability measures, and other structures required for the effective and efficient functioning of an educational organization. The lifeworld is made up of the lives of the students, their relationships with one another and with adults in the school, and the teaching and learning that occur in classrooms and throughout the school and community. While promoted as an antidote to bureaucracy, current high-stakes accountability systems have resulted in the cancer-like growth of the system world, and the shrinking of the lifeworld of schools (Habermas, 1987; Sergiovanni, 2000). At present, in too many schools, these two dimensions are out of balance, causing an impoverishment of authentic activities in classrooms and of authentic relationships among students, teachers, and communities.

Authentic schools that serve low-income children have a developed sense of internal accountability that functions within the lifeworld of the schools. According to Carnoy, Elmore, and Siskin (2003), these internal forms of accountability include:

> individual teachers' and administrators' beliefs about teaching and learning, their shared understanding of who their students are, the routines they develop for getting their work done, and the external expectations from parents, communities, and administrative agencies under which they work. (p. 5)

This lifeworld level of accountability is where authentic forms of accountability operate, because they are the spaces in which a group of professionals, parents, and community members come to agreement about the well-being of their students/children. Achieving this common agreement has always been the central challenge of educational leadership, especially given the racial and class segregation of our public schools. There have always been external or formal forms of accountability as well: policy handbooks, union contracts, state department regulations, legal procedures, report cards, supervisors, and even a certain amount of standardized testing. Good schools have always been those that bring coherence to these various forms of accountability, and the best leaders have known how to maintain balance and coherence among them.

The current reform movement has added new external forms of accountability, including high-stakes testing, the discipline of the market, school closings, pay-for-performance, and the threat of public humiliation if annual targets are not achieved. This new system world of high-stakes formal accountability measures has made achieving coherence and balance among the various forms of accountability more difficult. Teaching staffs, principals, and often parents are finding that their shared understandings of good teaching and learning and other aspects of the lifeworld of the school clash with the demands of the formal accountability system. While it is true that authentic schools are hard to sustain over time, sustainability depends on a certain amount of stability. The current frenetic churn of policy changes and teacher turnover make sustaining good schools more difficult. While high-stakes accountability targets underperforming schools in an attempt to "motivate" teachers to teach better, it does so with punitive, zero-tolerance policies that lack an understanding of what motivates professionals. Numerous studies have documented the way teachers' classroom autonomy and job satisfaction have diminished in the post-NCLB era (Crocco & Costigan, 2007; Wright, Shields, Black, Banerjee & Waxman, 2018).

What does this look like in practice? In 2008, the New York City Department of Education (DOE) mandated that every school have an inquiry group composed of school professionals. On the surface, this appeared to be an attempt to open up a space to engage in the kind of professional sharing and inquiry that could build professional capacity in the lifeworld of schools. During the 1980s and 1990s, such professional learning communities or "critical friends' groups" were quite common (Lieberman & Miller, 2008). But with the advent of NCLB these spaces for teacher inquiry were slowly co-opted by an emphasis on big data and "data utilization" (Wayman & Springfield, 2006). An account by one of our graduate students is typical of anecdotes widely shared by teachers who were frustrated at how tightly controlled and monitored these inquiry groups tended to be in practice.

She reported that the members of the inquiry group in her school observed that their most pressing problem was the alarming number of their students who were dropping out between 9th and 10th grades. They decided to select 15 ninth-graders and conduct interviews and focus groups to better understand the issues the students were facing to see whether some of the issues might be school- or classroom-related and therefore amenable to intervention by the school. After all, they reasoned, in order to help students achieve, they needed to better understand how to keep students in school.

When the data coach from the central office attended the next inquiry group meeting, she told the group members that they didn't seem to quite understand how the inquiry group was supposed to work. They were to focus on instruction and use testing data to identify deficits in their students' achievement and to provide remediation. This meant using spreadsheets of student test scores to identify which skills needed re-teaching.

These inquiry groups, it turns out, were put in place largely as part of a plan to get teachers to utilize a certain type of data to make instructional decisions. The DOE had just purchased the $80 million Achievement Reporting and Innovation System (ARIS) database, and the inquiry groups were part of a "data-driven decisionmaking" apparatus largely borrowed, like many of Mayor Bloomberg's educational policies at the time, from the business sector. It turns out that the "inquiry groups" were less about inquiry and more about combining technology and data utilization (Wayman & Springfield, 2006).

It made a certain amount of sense to provide teachers and principals with a database that they could manipulate to make better instructional and schoolwide decisions based on issues they identified through professional deliberation. After all, previously they had to request this kind of data from the district's evaluation office. Contracts the district signed with vendors included not only the database itself, but data warehousing and ongoing data management services. Now everything was all together in one place and accessible to teachers and parents, at least those parents who had computers. The problem was the top-down way the district tried to implement and structure use of the data. It hired "data coaches" and mandated that each school have an inquiry group, but the groups too often had limited autonomy to engage in authentic inquiry.

Like any reform, increasing data use for school-based inquiry ultimately can be a positive development, but if it is mandated from above and the wrong types of data predominate, it can result in an audit culture in which professional judgment atrophies and teaching becomes more scripted as teachers are accountable to standards and criteria that they had no part in developing. Under such conditions, relationships among teachers devolve into contrived collegiality (Datnow, 2011; Hargreaves, 1994), making authentic forms of inquiry more difficult. Further, an over-emphasis on test data also can distort and further narrow the curriculum, deprofessionalize teachers, and perpetuate unequal school outcomes.

To the extent that students are seen as numbers on spreadsheets, a relational, holistic, multicultural, and critical education becomes less likely (Au, 2016). Some also have argued that this often-exclusive attention to individual student data encourages a meritocratic view of schooling and undercuts a more complex understanding of sociocultural, socioemotional, and out-of-school factors that impact children (Berliner, 2009; Bronfenbrenner, 1979).

This brief anecdote and others throughout the book illustrate the ways professionalism is diminished by reforms that seek compliance and fidelity and provide so-called "evidence-based" answers rather than honor the complex dilemmas that professionals face. And this diminishment is being experienced in all social sectors. In most professions and occupations, accountability measures with high stakes attached, whether ComStat data for police officers in New York, *U.S. News & World Report* rankings for higher education faculty, or high-stakes testing for teachers, are narrowing professional discretion and encouraging gaming the system and, in extreme cases, outright cheating (Amrein-Beardsley, Berliner, & Rideau, 2010).

Scholars of new professionalism acknowledge that the new versus old professional binary is overly simplistic and that some aspects of NPM can be appropriated in ways that have the potential to enhance professionalism. They understand that there is overlap between the old and new and that new forms of professionalism are emerging in spite of or through reappropriations of NPM (Sachs, 2003). There is a growing body of scholarship that explores these more nuanced ways in which professionals respond to NPM.

Stone-Johnson (2014) uses "parallel professionalism" to indicate that the concept of the new professional is too monolithic. She argues that the standards movement and high-stakes testing have affected new teachers differently than veteran teachers (see also Wilkins, 2011), and that the effect might depend on the nature of the discipline that is being taught. Heffeman (2017) makes a similar case with regard to school administrators, and in a study of "no excuses" charter schools, Torres and Weiner (2018) found that novice teachers didn't mind being told *what* to teach, or their school's highly structured environment, if they felt they retained some discretion over *how* to teach. Finally, Moore and Clarke (2016) suggest that teachers may cling to old professionalism as an affective and idealistic discourse even while implementing NPM policies they otherwise might consider "irresponsible."

Although our focus is on public-sector professionals, we should not assume that those professionals who work in the private, for-profit or nonprofit sectors are exempt from these tendencies. On the contrary, these reforms were experienced first by private-sector professionals, before they were transferred into the public sector through NPM. We will discuss these new forms of *managerialism* and the influence of business schools further in Chapter 3. But an understanding of how changes in corporate culture have affected the work lives of private-sector professionals is helpful, since it is this very logic that has been transferred into the public sector.

NEW CAPITALISM AND THE NEW CORPORATE WORKPLACE

In 1972, Sennett and Cobb published their classic book, *The Hidden Injuries of Class*, in which they interviewed blue-collar workers during the welfare state of the 1960s. Years later, Sennett (1998) returned to interview the adult children of these workers, many of whom were now employed in white-collar mid-level corporate jobs. This follow-up study provides a description of how managerialism has transformed work in the new flexible corporation.

Sennett (1998, 2006) uses the term "new" or "fast" capitalism to describe the shift from Keynesian to Friedmanian economic models. While most people think of neoclassical or neoliberal economics as a purely economic model, it has important social and cultural consequences that we are only beginning to understand. Sennett (2006) provides an eloquent account of the ways that shifts in our economic model have resulted in cultural shifts in our workplaces and in the ways in which we live our lives. Since the corporate workplace is increasingly the model for schools and other public-sector organizations, Sennett's work has important implications for 21st-century educators. In his qualitative study of several corporations, Sennett has identified characteristics of work in the new capitalism.

Sennett (2006) traces the recent phenomenon of global neoliberalism back to the breakdown in 1973 of the 1944 Bretton Woods controls over the global circulation of money. Sennett argues that this breakdown of controls, coupled with wage stagnation in spite of rising profits and productivity, left large amounts of new capital seeking short-term investments. Later, stock prices began to replace profit as a goal for many businesses. Money was made not by owning and producing, but by trading, and later speculation. This new speculative and flexible approach to capital, sometimes called financialization, has changed work life and institutional structures, particularly in sectors of capitalism such as finance, insurance, real estate, media, communications, and high technology, where short-term exchange replaces long-term relationships. In order to fit into this new "fast" capitalism, individuals have to give up notions of stability of employment and become flexible, mobile workers in a constantly changing global economy.

Furthermore, workers become disposable as owners of capital continuously seek to cut labor costs through automation, outsourcing, and union-busting. Popular management books like the bestseller *Who Moved My Cheese?* (S. Johnson, 1998) used a childlike allegory about entrepreneurial mice who embraced change to prepare the ideological terrain for the new entrepreneurial worker. The lesson is that it is better to see losing one's job as a chance for some better opportunity that surely lies around the corner. The new entrepreneurial culture that is promoted in all sectors of society prepares employees for this new world of unstable employment in the new "risk" society (Beck, 1992). Calling the new corporate workplace "white collar sweatshops," J. A. Fraser (2002) argues that along with this new instability of work comes intensification, leading to longer work hours and greater levels of stress and anxiety.

However, Sennett (1998) argues that such trends are not only bad for workers, but actually counterproductive for business, since the cost to business of the resulting short-term employment is a reduction in employee loyalty and organizational memory. Moreover, with shorter contracts, work in flexible teams, and a highly competitive internal work environment, authentic relationships are less likely to form because of short timelines. This continual employee turnover and the tendency to use temporary workers and outside consultants weaken institutional knowledge. Sennett argues that these new tendencies are good for the bottom line and stock prices in the short term, but are not good for the long-term health of businesses, national productivity, or the building of relationships and personal character. In fact, he titled one book in his trilogy *The Corrosion of Character: The Personal Consequences of Work in the New Capitalism* (Sennett, 1998).

The creation of authentic human ties cannot occur easily in transient workplaces and communities. A similar phenomenon occurs in education, especially in urban districts, where principals are moved from school to school, teacher turnover grows, and schools are closed for low standardized test scores. Flexible organizations in a choice environment means that teachers, administrators, and students will be more mobile, leading to less stability and a weakening of organizational learning. New, younger teachers may tolerate increased intensification and standardization of work for a while, but many experienced teachers with families and a strong professional culture are tending to change careers or retire early in part because of the organizational conditions of their work (Ingersoll, 2006). The very notion of teaching or administration as a lifelong career may be a thing of the past. In the long run, this may have devastating effects on the quality of schooling, especially in schools that low-income students of color attend.

Sennett (2006) also identifies other personal deficits associated with this new managerial culture. The first is the demise of the work ethic. Only a fool would delay gratification in the new flexible workplace. Employees report feeling a sense of personal betrayal as companies trade loyalty to workers for short-term profits. Second, this loss of long-term employment, with its associated benefits and pensions, makes it more difficult for newer generations of employees to create life narratives and produces a sense of nihilism toward the future. While much unionized, welfare state employment was neither exciting nor available to everyone, it provided people with a life narrative in which they could pay a mortgage over 30 years, look forward to a pension and Social Security, and plan for vacations. In the new risk society, there is an absence of any way to think strategically about one's life, one's sense of purpose, future goals, and economic security (Beck, 1992).

In flattened hierarchies or network organizations, pyramidal hierarchy is replaced by a horizontal elite core and a mass periphery, with minimal mediation and communication between the two. This structure represents a new concentration of power without centralization of authority. According to Sennett (1998), "This absence of authority frees those in control to shift, adapt, reorganize without having to justify themselves or their acts. In other words, it permits the freedom of the moment, a focus just on the present. Change is the responsible agent; change is not a person" (p. 115).

Internal units are created to compete with one another for contracts. Outside consultants are brought in to do the dirty work that management used to do. Senior management can claim they are taking their cue from the expert consultants who come in and leave quickly. (For the role of consultants in education, see Gabriel & Paulus, 2014; Gunter, Hall, & Mills, 2015.) In this impersonal environment, no relationships are built, as no one has to take responsibility for decisions. Upper management, with its stronger networks, moves more often as new opportunities arise. Personnel records take the place of humans who are being standardized so "performance" can be compared (just as high-stakes testing in education allows students, teachers, and schools to be compared as a prerequisite for a marketized system).

Impression management increasingly replaces substantive change. News reports of a restructuring can lead to gains in stock price, regardless of whether the change is good for the company. Principals, superintendents, and university administrators are following suit as they manage the media and build and market their "brands" (DiMartino & Jessen, 2016; Oplatka, 2007).

Flexibility to adjust to changes in the market is gained. This is perhaps good news for stockholders seeking short-term profits, upper-level executives, and consultancy firms, but it isn't clear who else benefits, or what it contributes to the common good. This new model and its logic are being implemented in public-sector organizations across the country. Upper-level public administrators are contracting out to private companies or taking private-sector positions in the burgeoning education services industry. Public–private partnerships are often a vehicle for this shift in work culture (Robertson & Verger, 2012). This restructuring of the institutional environment has dramatically changed the work culture of schools.

We now have over 3 decades of experience with a rise of corporate culture in education. A 2012 MetLife Survey of Teachers found that job satisfaction for teachers was at a 25-year low, with only 39% indicating they were "very satisfied" with teaching. Over half of teachers reported feeling under great stress several days a week, an increase of 70% from 1985 (Markow, Macia, & Lee, 2013). If Sennett's analysis of the new corporate culture is any indication, we should continue to see less employee loyalty, more work stress, more automation, and a performance culture in professional organizations like schools and universities. Much like the automobile industry in which robots replaced many workers, automation in education increasingly views teaching as "facilitating" online curricula educators have little role in producing or choosing (Burch & Good, 2014).

Fast forward, and the new startup culture simply has intensified and normalized the trends that Sennett identified 20 years ago. Lepore (2014) describes the more recent millennial version: "The upstarts who work at startups don't often stay at any one place for very long. (Three out of four startups fail. More than nine out of ten never earn a return.) They work a year here, a few months there—zany hours everywhere" (p. 18). She suggests that entrepreneurs like Josh Linkner

> tell them that the world is a terrifying place, moving at a devastating pace. . . . His job appears to be to convince a generation of people who want to do good and do well to learn, instead, remorselessness. Forget rules, obligations, your conscience, loyalty, a sense of the commonweal. If you start a business and it succeeds, Linkner advises, sell it and take the cash. Don't look back. Never pause. Disrupt or be disrupted. (p. 18)

We see this culture creeping into public education as idealistic millennials join corporate-funded nonprofits like Teach for America, New Leaders for New Schools, Education Pioneers, and Presidio Institute, or want to do charter school startups, not build careers in public education. New capitalism has transformed public-sector professionals in similar ways to their corporate counterparts. In the following section, we will provide an overview of NPM and how—to quote Richard Sennett—it has resulted in the "corrosion of character" among education professionals and school reformers.

NEW GOVERNANCE AND NEW PUBLIC MANAGEMENT

NPM became popular in the delivery of public services in the 1990s and has evolved over the years (Hood & Peters, 2004). As a new form of governance, NPM contains an assemblage of specific shifts in discourse, policies, and practices. The following is a list of the most common ideas and practices transferred from the corporate sector into education reform (Bottery, 1996; Hood, 1991; Ward, 2012). For many teachers and principals, these reforms are the only reality they have ever known, but the reforms are relatively recent and threaten to become the new common sense of schooling in the United States.

- The introduction of markets and quasi-markets within and between public organizations
- An emphasis on explicit standards and high-stakes measures of performance
- Greater emphasis on outcomes and their measurement using quantitative data
- Greater use of standardization and "scaling up" of practices
- Contracting out public services to vendors in the private sector and the increased use of consulting companies
- A trend toward temporary and short-term workers and against unionization
- A trend toward for-profit education and viewing school districts as profit centers
- Administrative decentralization and bounded autonomy
- Greater discipline and parsimony in resource use in a context of austerity and disinvestment in the public sector
- Closing low-performing organizations and creating "startups" that are non-union and often outside of local democratic control (e.g., charter schools)

Any one of these practices perhaps could be justified as an attempt to bring a more flexible or dynamic approach to education. But it is the overlapping accumulation of these practices that is transforming the ethos and character of public-sector professionals and their workplaces.

NPM reforms are promoted globally with the argument that a new global knowledge economy requires that countries ramp up their education systems, and that outcomes measures like the Program for International Student Assessment, better known as PISA, hold them accountable. But as Hargreaves (2003) has noted, "The very profession [teaching] that is often said to be of vital importance for the knowledge economy is the one that too many groups have devalued, more and more people want to leave, less and less want to join, and very few are interested in leading" (p. 11).

There is also some evidence that benchmarks on many exams in the United States are set so high that most students will fail. This is particularly true of the National Assessment of Educational Progress (NAEP), commonly known as the "nation's report card." The results often are used to disparage public education, teachers, and teachers' unions and to support privatization. Yet, a report by the National Superintendents Roundtable (2018) concludes that very few students in most nations would clear the NAEP proficiency bar the United States has set for itself in reading, math, and science.

Nor does educational research evidence support NPM (Haney, 2000; Valenzuela, 2004). In fact, there is growing evidence that NPM reforms have neither reduced the achievement gap nor even produced the narrow quantitative outcomes they promote (Center for Research on Education Outcomes, 2015; Gleason, Clark, Tuttle, & Dwyer, 2010; Lubienski & Lubienski, 2014; Mickelson, Giersch, Stearns, & Moller, 2013).

Such concerns seem increasingly quaint though as NPM enters a new phase in which the public sector is largely viewed as an obstacle to the privatization and marketization of education. Some argue that we are in a more extreme form of NPM that Harvey (2005) calls capital "accumulation by dispossession," in which making profit off the public sector is the ultimate goal. It no longer seems to be the goal of NPM to restructure the public sector by making it more innovative, efficient, and flexible, but rather to eliminate it as much as possible as part of what Steve Bannon called the deconstruction of the administrative state.

In the United States, school administrators are increasingly trained in business schools. Countries are outsourcing their beleaguered public education systems to for-profit corporations (Reip & Machacek, 2016). An entire private parallel system to public education has been created in the United States with its own teachers (e.g., Teach for America), its own charter schools, and its own teacher preparation programs (e.g., Relay Graduate School) (Mungal, 2016).

Others believe we are in a new stage of NPM that focuses on platform capitalism and the digitalization of NPM or "digital-era governance" (Dunleavy, Margetts, Bastow, & Tinkler, 2005), in which faceless online systems dominate. There is also an important research agenda that attempts to understand how NPM recontextualizes itself as it enters different districts, states, or countries. For instance, in Europe, systems of education are affected differently (or not at all in some cases) by NPM in post-communist as opposed to social democratic or neoliberal states (Gunter, Grimaldi, Hall, & Serpieri, 2016).

Within the United States, NPM entered public education through a combination of discourses of excellence and equity. In the 1980s, neoliberals were promoting the notion that the welfare state, the war on poverty, and attempts at achieving equity had failed and that there was insufficient attention to *excellence*. Many educational leaders were reading books like Peters and Waterman's bestseller, *In Search of Excellence: Lessons from America's Best-Run Companies* (1982), and the discourse of excellence caught on among education reformers and many professors of educational leadership, as books on Total Quality Management in education proliferated (Sallis, 1993).

For school leaders, these new reforms sometimes instilled an entrepreneurial ethos and greater autonomy in budgeting, contracting, and hiring, while the core elements of instruction and curriculum were largely steered from the top (Gobby, Keddie, & Blackmore, 2017). Moves to provide greater autonomy for middle managers were often part of a trend toward work intensification. For instance, in New York City, where autonomy and markets were central to Mayor Bloomberg's reforms between 2002 and 2013, school principals reported being more beleaguered than empowered (Shipps, 2012).

NEW PUBLIC MANAGEMENT AND THE ACTIVIST STATE

NPM is not only a new form of governance at the institutional and organizational level; it also represents a new relationship with the state. The neoclassical economics of Milton Friedman (1962) were anti-government and anti-regulation, calling for a withdrawal of the state from involvement in most aspects of society. Yet rather than withdraw or shrink, the state has shifted its role to an activist one of promoting market forces throughout society and privatizing many of the services the state offers. To some extent, the state has become the handmaiden of the market.

But NPM thrives on a public that is largely unaware of these larger forces. NPM requires a new type of depoliticized professional who can be counted on to unproblematically accept these new policies and dispositions. Boggs (2000) argued that a depoliticized public has five broad features in common:

> An unmistakable retreat from the political realm; a decline in the trappings of citizenship and with it the values of democratic participation; a narrowing of public discourses and the erosion of independent centers of thinking; a lessened capacity to achieve social change by means of statecraft or social governance; and the eventual absence of a societal understanding of what is uniquely common and public, what constitutes a possible general interest amidst the fierce interplay of competing private and local claims. (p. 22)

How these forms of new governance have manifested themselves in educational organizations and reshaped teachers and leaders is the subject of this book.

Although we will discuss this in more detail in the following chapter, it is important to note that the previous bureaucratic form of organizing and managing schools also was borrowed from corporate leaders who promoted organizing efficient schools around a bureaucratic, factory model. However, as public, professional organizations, schools contained—in theory, at least—a strong professional and public ethos. In this current second wave of neoliberal corporate influence in education, it is this professional and public ethos and the commitment to a common good that are being eroded.

TOWARD A NEW DEMOCRATIC PROFESSIONAL IN EDUCATION

Our response to the "new professional" is not to defend the "old professional" or to "take back" professionalism. Teaching and school administration as professions, as well as the bureaucratic organizations teachers and administrators work in, have been under attack for a long time, and some of the criticisms have merit (Friedrich, 2014; Levine, 2006). Traditional bureaucracies and the older model of professionalism were notorious for resisting change and failing to meet the needs of many children (Meier, 1995; Payne, 2008; Rogers, 1968/2006). Furthermore, claims to professionalism by school personnel often have marginalized the voices of low-income parents and communities (Driscoll, 1998; Podair, 2002). The task ahead is not to reassert "traditional" professionalism, but rather to better understand how to engage in what Achinstein and Ogawa (2006) call "principled resistance" to the most egregious assaults on professionals, while acknowledging the weaknesses of the old professionalism and constructing a vision of a new democratic professionalism (Zeichner & Pena-Sandoval, 2015). At a minimum, such a vision would insist on a professional ethos with the public good at its center.

We live in precarious times in which it is easy to become discouraged. "Alternative facts" and ideologically motivated think tanks seem to have more influence on policy and practice than do science and serious scholarship. We transfer business models into the public sector with little thought or analysis of their congruence with the social goals and core purposes of public service. Our democracy and our media are threatened by unlimited corporate money. Longstanding American principles such as the separation of Church and State and the Voting Rights Act are being rolled back. Our society has become more economically unequal and racially segregated than at any time in the past 100 years. And globally, religious fundamentalism, nationalism, racism, patriarchy, and classism are all making a comeback. And if none of that is cause for concern, human life on our planet may not survive another century.

More relevant to the purpose of this book, our public schools and the public sphere in general are under assault. The slow demise of the public sector has been the result of a bipartisan group of sometimes well-intended reformers and the popularity of NPM schemes to use business principles to "modernize" it. We are not talking just about political conservatives. Many of these "pragmatic" reformers are neoliberal, "new" Democrats who cluster around the Progressive Policy Institute and Democrats for Education Reform. More recently, they have been joined by an education industry that sees the public sector as an emerging profit center. Our military, our prisons, our schools, our health care system, our Social Security, our pensions, our national parks, and, under the Trump administration, our own government have all become profit centers for entrepreneurs.

And yet, there is a growing grassroots resistance to all of these tendencies, and many public-sector professionals and low-income communities of color are engaged in these struggles. The current neoliberal reform model in education is encountering increasing resistance. The mainstreams of both political parties were rejected in the 2016 U.S. elections, suggesting that the American public is seeking profound change.

The new democratic professionals that we describe in Chapter 6 already exist and are increasingly organized. These emerging professionals understand that the solution to inequality and equal opportunity does not lie in Teach for America or franchise charter schools or markets and high-stakes testing. Rather, it lies in public investment in education by the State and in committed public-sector professionals who understand that the problem is not saving individual kids only, but rather supporting social policies that lift up poor and working-class families and children, who are disproportionately of color (J. Anyon, 2014).

This is a difficult time to be an educator for those who view their job as keeping their head down and allowing the reformers to define them professionally. But for those who are committed to their students, families, communities, and democratic public schools, and are willing to struggle to change policies and practices inside schools and join with those trying to make changes outside schools, these are exciting times to be an educator.

CONCLUSION

In the rest of the book, we will provide an historical and sociopolitical analysis of how New Public Management has emerged from previous managerial regimes influenced largely by private-sector elites. However, it is important to note that in every period of the ascendency of business models, influential educators have, to use a colloquial expression, "drunk the Kool-Aid," which is a powerful recipe of efficiency, effectiveness, meritocracy, metrics, and markets, and too often has mixed in heavy doses of classism, racism, sexism, xenophobia, and homophobia. Many administrative progressives of the early 20th century were enamored of the new bureaucratic efficiency, in part because it sought to eliminate politics by replacing political corruption and nepotism with instrumental rationality (Callahan, 1962). Unfortunately, as is so often the case, in solving one set of problems, the administrative progressives created new ones. But there also have always been educators who have struggled against running schools like businesses, from John Dewey and the pedagogical progressives to George Counts and social reconstructionists who saw the potential for education to make society more democratic and equitable (Apple, 2013; Cuban, 2004).

In Chapter 5, we will take up the issue of how educators are responding to NPM both individually and collectively. In Chapter 6, we describe how a new democratic professional is emerging in the shadow of powerful venture philanthropists and corporate attempts to make public education their new profit center. We will explore this emerging democratic professional in three overlapping dimensions: (1) a democratic dimension focused on *inclusion* in governance, in opportunity, and in a public sphere, (2) a dimension of professional *responsibility*, or what current reformers call "accountability," and (3) an *activism and advocacy* dimension, or how professionals advocate for more just practices and policies. But the next two chapters will provide a brief history of the two waves of business reforms that dominated the 20th century and continue today as NPM, but with a different discourse and in a different form.

CHAPTER 2

The Historical and Political Construction of the New Professional

Doubtless many educators who had devoted years of study and thought to the aims and purposes of education were surprised to learn that they had misunderstood their function. They were to be mechanics, not philosophers. (Callahan, 1962, p. 84)

One afternoon in the fall of 2013, after leading a professional development session at a high school in Denver, Colorado, I (Michael Cohen) noticed a bumper sticker on a car in the teachers' parking lot that read: "Those who *can*, teach. Those who *can't*, pass laws about teaching." The sticker was a play on an older saying, disparaging toward teachers: "Those who can, do. Those who can't, teach." I thought the new version was clever and particularly suitable for the times. After all, I had just led a session about implementing the most controversial feature of recent school reform legislation in the State, the requirement that at least 50% of teachers' evaluations be based on quantifiable measures of their students' learning. Given the long list of compelling reasons to disagree with the mandate on a philosophical basis—not to mention the myriad practical difficulties of implementing the law when fewer than 25% of the city's teachers taught grades or subjects for which state tests were administered—it wasn't difficult to conclude that our legislators were out of touch with the realities of teaching and learning. As teachers and principals frequently would say, if only these senators would try teaching, not only would they see how hard it was, but they also might begin to appreciate its complexity.

And yet, I also thought, if teachers and principals directed their ire solely toward state legislators and the governor, they'd be neglecting the role of some of the most powerful players in the policymaking arena: business leaders and their philanthropic organizations. In Denver, the Bill & Melinda Gates Foundation had already invested tens of millions of dollars in the new teacher evaluation system, and a number of other philanthropies—associated with the high-tech industry (the Susan and Michael Dell Foundation), major retailers (the Walton Foundation), and private equity firms (Bain Capital)—were making their mark on state legislation and the practices of our district. Sure, policymakers in our state should be held accountable for what they had legislated. At the same time, however, the wealthiest 0.1% of the nation, and the policy advocacy networks they steered, were using sophisticated lobbying and policy-framing strategies to gain an outsize influence on our legislators. They were setting the very terms of debate about education policy.

But business leaders and venture philanthropists didn't stop at the State Capitol Building; they managed to get really close to the work happening on the ground in local school districts. The Bill & Melinda Gates Foundation, through its grants, funded a substantial portion of my team's work in the assessment department—particularly our work in coaching teachers to develop new formative assessment practices. And so, on a few memorable occasions, when representatives of the Foundation flew into Denver to get updates on our work, I found myself sitting across a conference table from one of them, having to justify the work of my team and make a compelling case that it matched the goals of Bill and Melinda Gates. To make matters more complicated, these goals would change from time to time, typically without a satisfying explanation. For example, when the Gates Foundation said it no longer would support the work of teachers developing their own formative assessments, we had to give up this practice and reprioritize our team's efforts. Although many teachers seemed rather used to this kind of sudden, unexplained change in the district's initiatives, those who found value in this kind of assessment support expressed disappointment. It was clear that the district wasn't in charge.

After my first meeting with the Gates Foundation, I recognized—with more clarity than ever—that questions of who was responsible for new education reforms, and whose interests were being served, were getting ever-more complicated. I had already known that powerful business leaders were influencing education policy—just as they influenced many other kinds of legislation—and then funding much of its implementation. What I hadn't expected was that business leaders would set the goals of the work I had been professionally educated to do, would pay the salaries of some of the district employees I supervised, and would send visitors to check on my progress and let me know whether they approved or disapproved of it all.

HOW DID WE GET HERE?

We certainly have entered a new era of big business influencing public education, as indicated by many critics who have adopted the phrase "corporate reform" to describe the sort of changes that Gates and others have been imposing on cash-strapped districts and schools (Hursh, 2015; Saltman, 2013; Shipps, 2006). But it is not the first time in the history of American public schooling that business leaders have enjoyed such influence. The idea that business should serve as a model for the way our school systems are organized and governed, and that it should even set the standards for what children are learning, is an old and durable one in the United States. In fact, the schools we have today—the very ones that business-minded reformers have been working to overhaul—are in many ways the products of business-oriented reforms initiated more than a century ago. The reforms of the late 19th and early 20th centuries, which focused on establishing an orderly, stable, and efficient school system responsive to the needs of a growing population, an increasingly complex life in urban centers, and a rapidly expanding industrial economy, resulted in the vast, centrally governed bureaucracies and factory-model schools typical of city school systems throughout most of the 20th century. Indeed, business gave public education the very system that business has been working to dismantle and replace with newer models—derived, once again, from business.

In this chapter, we explore some of the earlier examples of business-inspired reforms, how they influenced the professionalism of teachers and school leaders for much of the 20th century, and how they laid the groundwork for the educator professionalism we know today. The current reforms of public education in the United States grow out of a long tradition of business-inspired reforms, dating back to the late 19th century. However, while there are important commonalities between the current wave of business reforms and those of earlier eras, we also will show that today's reforms constitute much more than a new chapter in a book of old themes. In many ways, the reformers of today are attempting to write a brand-new book—replete with a new set of characters, including education professionals who will, if the reformers have their way, bear little resemblance to their counterparts in the old story.

EARLY BUSINESS-INSPIRED REFORMS

Historians of education have already contributed a rich body of research investigating earlier waves of school reform based on business ideas, and we do not intend to provide a detailed rendition of that literature here. Instead, we want to provide some general background for our closer examination of the way concepts of educator professionalism have shifted in recent decades under NPM.

Centralized Governance and Bureaucracy

The centrally governed bureaucracy, which became the dominant form of urban public school districts in the late 19th and early 20th centuries (roughly between the 1870s and 1920s), is perhaps the most substantial example of business influence in public education. Historians have demonstrated that the bureaucratic organizational form, modeled after successful business corporations, became the preferred model among urban superintendents and many lay educational leaders at this time because it seemed capable of addressing a variety of social concerns and practical administrative challenges. Enormous growth in population, including a diverse array of immigrants speaking foreign languages and bringing to the United States their home cultures and values; increases in poverty and the transience of wage laborers looking for steady work in the cities; the shift toward an industrial economy, which demanded norms of punctuality, regularity, and obedience to managers; the rise of radical political views, including communism and anarchism, which were viewed by some as a threat to "the American way"—these were just some of the major cultural shifts causing anxiety among elite citizens, political leaders, and educational administrators, all of whom worried about the health and economic viability of their society (Katz, 1987; Tyack, 1974).

Addressing such concerns in a uniform way was simply impossible in city systems lacking a structure of centralized control and supervision. Because industry in the late 19th century had already demonstrated success in "the coordination of large numbers of people in a complex enterprise . . . , it offered valuable lessons for public education" (Katz, 1987, p. 69). Early superintendents as well as lay reformers argued that without a corporate model of control, there was no way to ensure consistency across several hundred city schools in areas such as procedures for hiring, retaining, and dismissing teachers; implementing a standard curriculum that progressed logically from primary through grammar and secondary schools; or collecting data to evaluate the output of schools and facilitate comparisons among them (Tyack, 1974).

Indeed, the desire to collect performance data and evaluate output, although a central feature of today's NPM culture, can be seen even in the 1870s. After mandating a uniform curriculum across all the city's elementary schools in 1874, Portland, Oregon's first superintendent, Samuel King, not only required a standard examination for students, but also had students' individual results published in the newspaper alongside the names of their schools.

Tyack (1974) notes that in the Portland system, "parents could draw their own conclusions about the diligence of the child and the competence of the teacher, and they did" (p. 48). At that time, however, King's aggressive management proved too much; by 1877, outraged parents pushed him to resign. Over the course of the next few decades, King's successors, although more cautious, proved just as bureaucratic. According to a contemporary account, Frank Rigler, superintendent at the turn of the 20th century in Portland, "could sit in his office and know on what page in each book work was being done at the time in every school in the city" (as cited in Tyack, 1974, p. 48). In Portland and in many other cities, public school systems began to take on the organizational features of big business, aspiring in their operation to factory-like precision.

The obsession with uniformity and data-driven management in the new bureaucracies was not a strictly American phenomenon; nor was the tendency of teachers to become adept at "gaming" these systems. In his analysis of the British Revised Code of 1860, whose centerpiece was "payment by results," Welch (1998) documents the audit culture of the time, which, like today, resulted in creative compliance. According to Welch:

> Teachers 'stuffed and almost roasted' their pupils on test items once the teachers knew that the visit of the inspector was imminent. Other teachers secretly trained their pupils so that when they were asked questions they raised their right hands if they knew the correct answer but their left if they did not, thus creating a more favourable impression upon the visiting inspector. (p. 161)

Although the development of bureaucracy in school systems between the 1870s and 1920s was neither linear nor identical in configuration across U.S. cities, it tended to include some general features: centralized governance, standardized expectations for teachers as well as students, hierarchies of supervision and differentiation of roles, division of students by age, and consistent application of procedures. An orderly and stable system of management would enable schools to address key social issues of the era. The public school would facilitate the assimilation of immigrants through citizenship education, it would take children off the streets and away from bad influences, and it would teach students some of the skills and dispositions (e.g., docility, obedience) they would need to fill positions in factories. In this sense, the new public schools, with their close supervision, division of labor, and efficient operation on bell schedules, resembled factories in order to prepare students *for* the factories.

Scientific Management and Efficiency

In these decades, historians show, it became common for school administrators to make direct comparisons between their school districts and factories and machines (Callahan, 1962; Katz, 1987; Tyack, 1974). Two speeches at a National Education Association conference in 1904—one by Aaron Gove, the superintendent in Denver, and one by Margaret Haley, a leader in the Chicago Teachers' Federation—illustrated this tendency, albeit from opposing perspectives. Whereas Gove spoke of the work of school districts as "comparable to the turning out of work by an industrial establishment," Haley criticized "the increased tendency toward 'factoryizing education,' making the teacher an automaton, a mere factory hand, whose duty is to carry out mechanically and unquestioningly the ideas and orders of those clothed with the authority of position" (as cited in Tyack, 1974, p. 257). A clear division between management and workers—a division imported directly from business—had developed in districts and schools across the country.

The plight of the teacher as "mere factory hand," as described by Haley in 1904, would become the norm over the course of the first 2 decades of the 20th century. Raymond C. Callahan's classic 1962 text, *Education and the Cult of Efficiency: A Study of the Social Forces That Have Shaped the Administration of the Public Schools*, details the way business leaders successfully imposed on school districts a set of commercial principles and practices that would endure for much of the 20th century. Chief among these practices was Frederick Taylor's (1911/2009) scientific management, a system for eliminating waste and increasing productivity through standardization of work and tedious measurement of output in the private industrial sector. Some critical scholars in our current era have identified a number of striking similarities between Taylor's scientific management of the early 20th century and today's standards-based reforms, rife as they are with large-scale assessment, data-driven decisionmaking, scripted lesson plans, and systems of merit pay—a sort of neo-Taylorism (Au, 2011; Trujillo, 2014).

According to Callahan (1962), school administrators in the early decades of the 20th century were particularly vulnerable to pressures to adopt efficiency reforms. The perfect storm seemed to have arrived: rising populations, which led to higher taxes as schools expanded to accommodate new students; rising costs of living due to inflation; public discourse identifying wastefulness and corruption in municipal governments; intensifying concern for the outcomes of public schools; the business community's almost religious fervor for the new methods of scientific management; widespread admiration of the businessman in American culture, in spite of scandalous accounts in muckraking newspapers; and school administrators' need to please their local boards, which after 1900 tended to be composed almost entirely of businessmen.

Moreover, universities were just beginning to offer coursework in school administration, and the new professors in the field—including Ellwood Cubberley of Stanford University, who wrote the standard textbook for leaders, and Franklin Bobbitt of the University of Chicago, who became one of the nation's chief evangelists of efficiency—were under intense pressure to make their newly minted departments respectable within the university. For these professors, the "scientific label" (Callahan, 1962, p. 246) of the Taylor system offered the respectability they needed in order to survive.

Callahan (1962) offered a deeply critical assessment of the influence of scientific management in public education. In his view, efficiency had become the ultimate goal of school administration in the early 20th century, whereas it should have been only a means toward achieving more important educational ends. In the efficiency mindset, educational decisions, such as determining which courses should be offered in a high school, what resources should be provided to teachers for instruction, how much time to allot teachers for planning and preparation, or how many students should be assigned to a single classroom, would be made solely on the basis of financial calculation—that is, without serious consideration of espoused pedagogical values or children's needs. Callahan claimed that one of the most tragic consequences of the efficiency reforms was a drastic oversimplification of the teaching and learning process—a process that, he suggested, Bobbitt and other professors of educational administration appeared to neither acknowledge nor fully appreciate.

PROFESSIONALISM IN THE BUREAUCRACY

The teacher in the bureaucracy had become a sort of technician whose job wasn't so much to think creatively or critically, but to fulfill a set of goals developed by someone else (Callahan, 1962). The administrator was analogous to a factory foreman, accepting standards from outside the field of education the way managers of a steel mill accepted manufacturing standards from railroad corporations. Administrators, however, at least maintained the managerial prerogative, the ability to determine the *how* of the work if not the *what*. According to Callahan, administrators gained some professionalization in this process, but it was at the expense of teachers, who became, to adopt a phrase from Tyack (1974), "mere functionaries"

(p. 185). The role of a functionary, Callahan (1962) argued, conflicted with the role that many teachers expected for themselves: "Doubtless many educators who had devoted years of study and thought to the aims and purposes of education were surprised to learn that they had misunderstood their function. They were to be mechanics, not philosophers" (p. 84).

A Closed System and Professional Hierarchy

Early reforms based on business had substantial implications for the professionalism of educators. One of the key features of corporate management was the buffer it created between administration and outside influence. By 1920, centralized governance was the commonsense norm in cities across the United States, where small boards composed primarily of business leaders delegated the day-to-day management of the schools to their superintendent, who, in turn, managed a hierarchy of professional administrative staff at the district level and principals in individual schools (Tyack, 1974). The effect was to produce a system of management by experts, in stark contrast to an older system (prior to the 1870s) in which local wards elected part-time laypeople to supervise schools in their neighborhoods. Although elite reformers and school administrators saw clear advantages in the bureaucratic model, insulated as it was from the vicissitudes of local politics and the perceived parochialism of immigrant populations and the poor, not everyone saw themselves as beneficiaries of the model.

Teachers, occupying the lowest level of the professional hierarchy, and many community members, lacking voice in the decisionmaking apparatus of the school system, were marginalized. This was no accident. Early reformers, including superintendents and the new professors of school administration, argued that a modern public school system, fit for the demands of a complex urban society and an industrial economy, could not be administered democratically. Indeed, when corporate reformers touted the need to keep politics out of the schools so that experts could manage the system as necessary, critics in cities such as New York saw in this argument a self-serving effort to maintain a sort of aristocratic—and often Protestant—control of public education, unaccountable to ordinary working people (Tyack, 1974). The only politics that were removed from the schools were the politics of those who lacked easy access to policymakers and school district leaders. Meanwhile, business leaders and other elites influenced public school practices through their social networks and "via behind-the-scenes negotiations with school officials" (S. Cohen, 1964, p. 223).

The expert managers, of course, were the administrators, who gained a great deal of professional discretion in the early 20th century, albeit at the expense of democratic input from local communities and the professional status of teachers. The growing bureaucracy, which by the 1920s and 1930s increasingly included an array of nonteaching supervisory staff at the school level (e.g., principals, assistant principals, directors, deans) as well as in the district offices (Rousmaniere, 2007), served to solidify clear lines of authority extending from the superintendent through the principal and ultimately down to the teacher. Although the board of education remained a check on the superintendent's power, a new era of government by expert had been ushered in—not only in education, but also in municipal governments, universities, welfare services, and many other agencies serving the public (Tyack, 1974). As Tyack (1974) notes, "In the early twentieth century the faith of patricians in the charismatic and scientific captain of education mirrored their worship of the captains of industry and finance who were transforming the corporate economy" (p. 160).

Principals in the Bureaucracy

It is important to note that the modern principalship was in its formative stages at this time. Whereas in the late 19th century, when bureaucratic management was first developing, schools frequently were supervised by a head teacher or principal who maintained both teaching responsibilities and a set of mundane building management tasks, by the middle of the 1930s, 70% of the elementary principals in U.S. cities no longer had teaching responsibilities (Rousmaniere, 2007). This distinction between teachers and principals, along with a new tendency of state governments to require certain academic courses in administration, contributed to the professionalization of principals in these early decades. The principal, frequently occupying a separate office in the school, had become a sort of middle manager operating between the superintendent and the teachers.

Ellwood P. Cubberley (1923), the efficiency-minded Stanford University professor of educational administration, described the school principal as analogous to a business manager reporting to a company executive, or an army colonel reporting to a commanding general. In such a role, while principals had some discretionary power, it generally was confined to concrete matters of implementing in their specific schools the policies developed by the superintendent. The principal's functions were "more those of executing, in his own school or group of schools, plans which have been decided upon by authorities of larger scope, than of helping to formulate new plans and policies for the school system as a whole" (Cubberley, 1923, p. 344). Clear lines of managerial authority were as crucial in school districts as they were in other types of organizations: "On any other basis a business courts bankruptcy, an army disaster, and a school system disorganization and inefficiency," Cubberley (1923, p. 342) wrote. Furthermore, he added, a principal's refusal to comply with the policy mandates of senior officials

> represents a sort of bumptiousness running very close to actual disloyalty. Its exhibition ought to be clear notice to the superintendent and to the school board that the principal showing such characteristics is not one whom they can afford to advance further in the school system. (p. 344)

Thus, bureaucracy not only solidified the managerial imperative; it also created a professional career ladder within administration. So as bureaucracy grew, many professionals within it developed a vested interest in maintaining its structure.

Although in Cubberley's time it was customary to use the masculine pronoun generically, there is reason to believe that Cubberley (1923) meant no gender ambiguity when referring to the principal's functions "in *his* own school" (p. 344, emphasis added). In one of the few histories written specifically about the principalship in American public education, Kate Rousmaniere (2013) demonstrates that the development of bureaucracy and corporate styles of management in schools over the first half of the 20th century coincided with sharp declines in the numbers of female principals. Many early professors of educational administration focused their recruitment efforts specifically on men—typically high school teachers who aspired to become principals—because they believed that a modernized, efficient, and rational school system required a masculine sort of leadership. They also saw the male principal as a figure of stability, in contrast to female principals, who, in the eyes of some reformers, were prone to anxiety and typically would have to resign from their positions once married.

Furthermore, as states began to adopt licensing requirements for principals, which usually included some combination of teaching experience and university coursework in administration, men gained a very material advantage, since they had substantially greater access to higher education. Men gained even more advantage when some state departments and district hiring authorities granted more weight to university coursework than to teaching experience, enabling many young men to outcompete their more experienced female colleagues as principal positions opened (Rousmaniere, 2013).

In the cities, the trend toward male occupancy of the principalship could be traced even to the middle of the 19th century, contemporary with the rise of graded schools. Tyack (1974) famously characterized this organizational model as a "pedagogical harem" (p. 45), noting how children were classified by age in separate classrooms, each under the direction of a female teacher, while the collective of female teachers fell under the direction of one male principal (and sometimes his male assistant as well). And while this model was more prevalent in urban areas during the 19th century, it found its way into rural districts in the first half of the 20th century as well—particularly when schools were consolidated in order to pool resources and modernize their instructional programs (Rousmaniere, 2013). Reformers who pushed for consolidation tended to hire men as principals of the new larger schools, sending many female head teachers back into the classroom full time. By the middle of the century, the decline in the number of female principals was sharp: Rousmaniere (2007) notes that while women held more than 50% of the principal positions in the United States in 1940, they held only 25% of the positions by 1970. Indeed, organized groups of administrators sometimes based their advocacy for consolidation on the claim that only the new, larger schools would be attractive enough to men who sought principalships (Blount, 1998).

Bureaucratization and consolidation of schools had a similar effect on the racial composition of principals in the United States. Prior to the *Brown v. Board of Education* decision, the work of Black principals in the segregated schools of the South resembled the work of many White female head teachers before the formal principalship was introduced as part of the bureaucratization movement. For example, many Black principals held dual roles as teachers and administrators in their community-based schools—with the added stress of having to advocate for their perennially under-resourced buildings in a context of institutionalized white supremacy. After *Brown*, as schools in the South were desegregated and thousands of Black schools were closed, Black children were sent to school with White children in the newly consolidated schools. The latter were located outside of their communities and staffed overwhelmingly by White teachers and White principals. Many Black teachers lost their jobs, and Black principals would virtually disappear, their numbers dropping precipitously as desegregation gained momentum in the 1960s (Butler, 1974).

Thus, as school systems became larger and business models of governance and management became the order of the day in the early 20th century, the figure of the school principal became, on the whole, a White, male, middle manager in a corporate-style hierarchy. We should note, however, that notwithstanding the rhetoric of Cubberley and other business-minded reformers, who described the principal as a sort of branch manager whose job was to implement directives from district headquarters, many principals of the first half of the 20th century had much more complex relationships with the teachers they supervised. The image of military-style command-and-control, or of managerial despotism, while certainly a reflection of real power differentials in school hierarchies across the country, fails to account for principals who pushed against the norms of their day. For one thing, as states began to formalize licensing requirements in the early 20th century, principals usually were required to have served as teachers for several years. To the extent that some principals maintained empathy with classroom life in general, their prior experience afforded some common understandings between them and teachers (Rousmaniere, 2013).

Furthermore, the structure of large school systems, which housed upper administration in separate buildings from principals and teachers, sometimes at inconvenient distances from each other, enabled some principals to feel more kinship with teachers than with the officials above them—especially when principals and teachers shared frustrations about ill-conceived mandates from district administrators or boards of education. Indeed, many principals were fearful of possible termination if they did not comply with directives from the district office, and some of the bolder leaders among them met this fate. Still, there is historical evidence of principals finding creative ways to comply with mandates while buffering teachers from the onerous requirements of bureaucracy; pushing for various degrees of local, school-based autonomy; immersing themselves in community-based organizations, sometimes even in social activism on behalf of families in their schools when large-scale policies did not match their local needs; and advocating for teachers' instructional resources and improved working conditions so they could, in turn, best serve students (Johanek & Puckett, 2007; L. Johnson, 2017; Rousmaniere, 2013; Siddle Walker, 1996).

Much like principals of today, those of the early 20th century knew the tensions inherent in middle management, occupying that ambiguous space between classroom life and the business of district offices. Still, as the principalship came into its own over the course of the century, and principals accrued an ever-growing list of managerial responsibilities, principals would only grow more distant from the teachers they supervised.

Teachers in the Bureaucracy

While administrators at the school and district levels—particularly those who were White and male—gained professional status and authority in the new bureaucracies, teachers gained only a modicum of professionalization in the new organizational structures. The history of teacher professionalization, complex and nonlinear, cannot be described adequately in a few pages, but it is possible to point out a few key components of this professionalism, note how it differed from that of administrators, and then further contrast it with the new professionalism that would begin to develop with market based reforms toward the end of the 20th century.

Teachers made some gains in professional status early in the 20th century, particularly as they attained higher levels of education and states began to implement certification requirements that included diplomas from college-level teacher preparation programs. Whereas the state-run normal schools of the 19th century were roughly equivalent in level to a high school education, by the turn of the 20th century, many normal schools had increased the depth and breadth of their curricula, required a high school diploma for admission, and began to look more like colleges (Labaree, 2004). By the 1920s, almost every state in the United States required its teacher candidates to hold a diploma from one of these institutions, conveying a message that teaching was an occupation important enough to be regulated by the state. And as the demand for higher education grew in the 1940s, the teachers colleges would expand into general-purpose state colleges and even universities. This expansion would be something of a boon for the professional status of teachers, who were now earning their credentials from formal institutions of higher education (Labaree, 2004).

Once on the job, teachers in the new bureaucracies found themselves in relatively stable positions. Whereas teachers' employment in the decentralized ward systems of the 19th century had been subject to the whims of local politics and favoritism, by the 1920s, their jobs would be widely secured by tenure, which early unions had sought in order to protect their members from arbitrary termination. Many reformers, including some superintendents, also supported tenure in some form, in part because it would help them attract good teachers and retain them during the recurring teacher shortages of the time. In insulating teachers from outside political influence, tenure also enhanced the closed system of bureaucracy that superintendents valued.

Although teachers may have gained protections from outside political influences, they were hardly empowered within the bureaucratized schools and districts of the day. As we have noted, if principals could be compared with managers of business departments or foremen in factories, then teachers in the age of efficiency might be characterized as low-level clerks or factory workers on an assembly line. As early as the 1880s, Mary Abigail Dodge, an activist teacher in Hartford, Connecticut, claimed that teachers should have more professional autonomy, going so far as to assert that "teachers ought to run the schools exactly as doctors run a hospital" (as cited in J. Brown, 1992, p. 60).

There is plenty of evidence in the early 20th century of teachers resenting their principals and the new corporate style of management, especially among those steeped in the child-centered philosophy of Dewey and other pedagogical progressives. Arguing that teachers should have influence on important decisions concerning matters of curriculum and school policy, activist teachers spoke and wrote about the dangers of undemocratic rule in the schoolhouse. In 1920, for example, an organized group of female teachers in Buffalo, New York, advocating for professional autonomy in the workplace, produced a manifesto in which they characterized their pro-efficiency administrators as "self-appointed, autocratic demagogues" (as cited in W. B. Thomas & Moran, 1991, p. 399). Not surprisingly, the Buffalo teachers were dismissed from their positions for insubordination, later to be rehired on the condition that they renounce allegiance to the subversive group they had formed.

Limited autonomy. And yet, notwithstanding this general picture of managerial efficiency, of rigid hierarchies and clear lines of authority, teachers enjoyed a certain degree of professional discretion within their classrooms for the greater part of the 20th century—a fact that has frustrated education reformers of various stripes continuously (Cuban, 2013). To be clear, such discretion was never an intended outcome of the large-scale reforms we have described; rather, some have suggested that it was the necessary product of organizational structures and of the nature of classroom teaching itself (Labaree, 2010). Whether it was Franklin Bobbitt and Ellwood Cubberley making facile analogies between schools and business organizations; or Edward Thorndike and the proponents of intelligence testing and scientific curriculum describing teachers as mere deliverers of content; or the evangelists of vocational education, such as the National Association of Manufacturers, claiming that teachers ought to prepare students for future occupations; or even John Dewey and the child-centered progressives advocating for student-led inquiry, experiential learning, and democratic practices—anyone who wished to reform public education practices came up against what was arguably the stiffest barrier of them all: the classroom door.

It may be cliché nowadays to say that teachers of the 20th century were, for the most part, able to close their classroom doors and teach as they wished or deemed necessary, but this is a crucial point that distinguishes the old bureaucratic teacher professionalism from the new professionalism and NPM, and it is important to understand why this was so. Education historians, following Tyack (1974), traditionally have divided the reformers of the late 19th and early 20th centuries into two camps: the administrative progressives and the pedagogical progressives.

While the former are associated with bureaucracy, efficiency, business-like management, and vocational education, the latter are associated with child-centered modes of teaching, inquiry-based and experiential learning, democratic practices within schools, and the like. Historians have shown that while each camp has been able to influence public education in structure and rhetoric, neither group has had substantial influence on the way teachers teach and their students learn. Larry Cuban (1993) has likened the impact of curriculum and teaching reform efforts on classroom practices to that of a hurricane on an ocean floor: "Hurricane winds sweep across the sea, tossing up 20-foot waves; a fathom below the surface turbulent waters swirl, while on an ocean floor there is unruffled calm" (p. 2).

Although the administrative progressives were successful in changing the organizational structure of districts and schools between the 1870s and 1930s, and in shifting the rhetoric of education reform toward the discourse of business and human capital production, they had much less impact on everyday teaching and learning—what often is called the instructional core of schools. Labaree (2010) has argued that this failure was due, in part, to the administrative progressives' neglect of the teacher as a key component of the learning process. They were more focused on the work of psychologists such as Edward Thorndike, who in the 1920s broke new ground in intelligence testing and theories of learning (Kliebard, 1995). The administrative progressives saw in this research great potential for social efficiency: Students—particularly those deemed unfit for college—could be placed into specific learning tracks based on their tested ability and provided a curriculum that would prepare them for appropriate future occupations. In this view, then, what mattered was that the right curriculum was matched with the right students; the teacher was simply a person who delivered this curriculum. With their focus squarely on the structure and form of schooling and the content of the curriculum, the administrative progressives neglected the contributions of the teacher and ultimately had little influence on the everyday work of teachers in their classrooms, who would use their discretion to make day-to-day instructional decisions (Labaree, 2010).

Labaree (2010) argues that if the administrative progressives made the mistake of neglecting the role of the teacher in education reform, the pedagogical progressives made the analogous mistake of neglecting principals, district leaders, and governance structures. Instead, pedagogical progressives tried to go around the administration, working to effect change in teachers' work more directly. While this group did manage to shift some of the rhetoric of teaching over the course of the 20th century, influencing many to speak of such things as student inquiry, experiential learning, and the "whole child," they had relatively little impact on the way teachers taught (Zilversmit, 1993). As Larry Cuban (2013) has shown, for the greater part of the 20th century, classrooms leaned toward teacher-centered didactic approaches—especially at the secondary level—albeit with some gestures toward student-centered learning or fluid hybrids of the two.

While some teachers certainly engaged in principled resistance of reforms they saw as unsound or potentially dangerous, it is important not to romanticize most teachers' use of discretion or their various ways of resisting reforms within their own classrooms. Many teachers probably resisted change based on practical necessity. Labaree (2010) draws upon the work of Michael Lipsky (1980), who coined the term "street-level bureaucrats" in order to explain this point. For Lipsky (1980) and many others who have adopted this term, street-level bureaucrats are professionals, such as teachers, social workers, and police officers, who work in complex, unpredictable circumstances, serving the needs of clients who are, for the most part, involuntarily receiving services. Furthermore, the term *street-level bureaucrats* implies that such professionals are in the challenging situation of having to implement policies that were developed far from the action—for example, in the State Capitol Building or district offices. Of necessity, these professionals continuously adapt policies to the present circumstances, sometimes applying the "spirit" instead of the "letter" of a given policy as the individual situation demands (Weatherly & Lipsky, 1977) .

Teachers—who operate in the uncertain context of countless variables in classrooms of 20 to 30 children; who have the challenge not simply of conveying knowledge and skills, but of motivating their involuntary clients; and whose success depends on the development of positive relationships with individual students even as they maintain a necessary degree of order and discipline in their classrooms—arguably cannot function without the ability to adapt and shape procedures and policies (Cuban, 2013; Labaree, 2010). Following the "letter of the law" all the time (for example, following a scripted lesson plan or doling out discipline in exact accordance with school policies) would be simply ineffective and often counterproductive.

In this sense, then, teachers have always had to make some judgments regarding the appropriateness of particular materials, modes of instruction, or even schoolwide rules. Moreover, they have to gauge the extent to which their local administrators will tolerate such discretion—deciding, for example, whether they have to conceal their creative adaptations of curriculum or policy when principals "pop in" for observations. Whether such adaptations involved complying only superficially with directives or even ignoring them when possible, prior to the age of standards-based reform and NPM, teachers in many classrooms across the nation were able to maintain the relatively "unruffled calm" of Cuban's (1993) ocean floor.

Collective bargaining and teacher power. While teachers generally maintained some autonomy within their classrooms throughout much of the 20th century, it was a limited autonomy, punctuated by the efforts of various reformers to install prepackaged curricula, scripted lesson plans, basal readers, learning technologies, and countless other forms of pro-efficiency, "teacher-proof" materials. By the 1960s and 1970s, teachers throughout the nation had grown frustrated with bureaucratic management and their own lack of influence in the power structures of their schools and districts (Gelberg, 1997). Furthermore, with their members earning substantially lower salaries than other highly educated professionals in American society, and emboldened by the success of labor movements in the private sector, teachers' unions grew more militant, holding strikes and demanding the legal right of collective bargaining. Today, as teacher strikes and walkouts pro-liferate, we may be seeing the beginnings of a new teacher movement as wages have plummeted in many states since 2008, collective bargaining and pensions are under attack, and teachers seek more control over their profession.

It is crucial to note that while teachers wanted the right to bargain for higher salaries and the terms and conditions of their employment, they also wanted to influence managerial decisionmaking; they wanted to play substantial roles in de-cisions concerning curriculum, class sizes, and other policy matters affecting their work (Gelberg, 1997). In describing the development of collective-bargaining leg-islation in New York in 1967, which eventually would serve as the model for many other states, Gelberg (1997) points out that the architects of the legislation, George Taylor and Archibald Cox, essentially transferred a business model of bargaining to public education. Taylor and Cox, a business professor and a private-sector la-bor attorney, respectively, crafted bargaining laws that "focused exclusively on the labor aspect of teaching" (Gelberg, 1997, p. 97). While the laws "legitimized teach-er unions' goal of improving teacher welfare," they "did little to address the goal of teacher involvement in policymaking—a goal that was a prerequisite for the attainment of teacher professionalism" (p. 97). In this industrial style of collective bargaining, school-level administrators maintained what was called the "mana-gerial prerogative"—a point that was explicitly written into the laws in a number of states and later supported in judicial decisions (Gelberg, 1997). From the ad-ministrators' perspective, it was only logical for them to maintain decisionmaking power in areas of policy and governance. Unlike the teachers they supervised, ad-ministrators were subject to high levels of accountability, and they wanted to be able to make important decisions without having to consult teachers.

Collective-bargaining rights would only become more controversial over time. In limiting teachers' bargaining rights to compensation and employment terms and conditions—matters of "teacher welfare" (Gelberg, 1997, p. 97)—the laws not only rejected notions of shared governance; they arguably positioned teachers to appear driven by self-interest alone, a point that would become abun-dantly clear in the coming years, marked as they were by battles with local com-munities, economic downturns, and a general rightward shift in American politics (Podair, 2002).

The sort of bread-and-butter gains that teachers made in the fight for collec-tive bargaining point to the fact that bureaucracy was, in some respects, advanta-geous for teachers. While bureaucracies value standardization and hierarchy, often seeming to stifle the individual initiative and creativity of those who work within them, their centralized governance and value for uniformity afforded teachers a stable system of compensation and job security. Instead of having to negotiate with a series of independent neighborhood boards, a teachers' union in the bureaucra-cy would have to negotiate with only one central board of education. In fact, as collective bargaining in school districts became the rule across the nation in the 1960s and 1970s, empowering teachers' unions in unprecedented ways, it actually enhanced some of the features of bureaucracy (Gelberg, 1997). Teachers' contracts would now be loaded with details concerning the minutiae of what teachers and administrators could and could not do, tightening controls in a system already notorious for its rigidity. Thus, from an historical perspective, centralization and bureaucracy have not been unequivocal enemies of teachers; rather, they have afforded certain rights and protections that would have been difficult to obtain and coordinate within decentralized systems.

While union contracts may have contributed to bureaucracy, they are not, as is often claimed (Moe, 2011), responsible for the bureaucratic nature of schooling. The bureaucratic structure was the result of the business-inspired efficiency models described above. Unions helped defend teachers, who were mostly women, from being fired for getting married or, if married, for being pregnant. Unions also fought for equal pay between female and male teachers and for tenure, which guaranteed teachers the right to due process.

BUREAUCRACY VERSUS COMMUNITY

A major contention of this book is that the current deprofessionalization of teachers promises to degrade teaching as a profession and result in the kind of low-wage labor we are seeing in states where teachers are now fighting back. However, another major contention is that the response to deprofessionalization should not be to harken back to some previous era in which teachers were more respected and had more autonomy. In this section, we will problematize the ways that professionalism too often buffered teachers from the very communities they were supposed to be committed to (Driscoll, 1998). This dilemma of professionalism vs. community is one that must be resolved as part of a move to a new democratic professionalism.

While both administrators and teachers reaped material benefits from centralized bureaucratic systems over the course of the 20th century, many of the communities they served would not. In low-income neighborhoods of cities, people of color in particular would see centralized governance—of schools as well as other social service agencies—as an impediment to their communities' self-determination and their children's prospects of success, particularly in an increasingly post-industrial economy that demanded higher levels of education. In the 1960s, Black activists in cities such as Detroit and New York, seeing how difficult it was to remove teachers they deemed incompetent, insensitive to their children's needs, or even racist, from their neighborhood schools, would come to see the teachers' unions, administrators, and boards of education as their chief opponents in the struggle for equal educational opportunity (Mirel, 1993; Murphy, 1990).

For urban communities of color, bureaucracy was a mechanism for protecting an overwhelmingly White professional establishment, made up of teachers who harbored low expectations for their students and saw them as culturally deficient (Murphy, 1990). After failed attempts to integrate schools in the North, where policymakers had blamed segregation on *de facto* residential patterns (even though such patterns were usually the result of economic and housing policies and political favors extended to Whites), activists began to call for a radical decentralization of city schools. In New York City in the late 1960s, for example, Black activists started to demand community control, whereby local neighborhoods would be empowered to administer their schools as they saw fit, electing their own councils and controlling decisions in key areas such as hiring, firing, curriculum, and budgeting (D. Goldstein, 2014).

The struggle for community control in New York City would place minoritized communities in direct conflict with the teachers' union, the United Federation of Teachers (UFT). Having recently won its own struggle for collective bargaining and employment protections from the central board of education, the UFT had little interest in ceding control over personnel decisions to a series of community councils (Murphy, 1990). Despite the concerns of the UFT, led by Albert Shanker, the district piloted an experimental program of community control in a few neighborhoods. It wasn't long before the UFT's fears came true: In 1968, in the experimental district of Ocean Hill–Brownsville, the newly appointed local superintendent, Rhoady McCoy, sent 19 teachers and administrators back to the central district office to be transferred to schools in other neighborhoods, as he considered them unfit for teaching in his local district—a decision that would lead to a major teacher strike.

Crucially, the UFT had fought hard for protections against transfers, which historically had been used by administrators to punish teachers. The union also saw teachers' placement in "better" schools as a reward for longevity in the district. On the other hand, activists in Ocean Hill–Brownsville and other neighborhoods wanted real control over their schools. They wanted the right to teach a culturally relevant curriculum, one that would be more engaging than the City's Euro-centric instruction; they wanted to hire only teachers who had a social justice orientation, who were inspired to work with children whom the establishment had failed; they wanted parents to have a real voice in everyday school affairs; in short, they wanted the same kind of self-determination that White parents had asserted in their own neighborhoods and schools (Ferguson, 2013).

In the activists' struggle for self-determination, they had a rather unlikely ally. White executives from the Ford Foundation took an interest in the concept of community control, working side-by-side with Black community leaders—including the more radical Black separatists—as well as university researchers, to make a case for several key dimensions of the reform proposal: decentralizing the bureaucracy of the New York City schools, empowering parents through local democratic processes, and implementing a culturally relevant curriculum, to name a few (Ferguson, 2013). Furthermore, once the pilot plan was approved by district officials, the Ford Foundation would fund the operating costs of the three experimental school districts. In her book about the Ford Foundation's work with Black Power activists, Karen Ferguson (2013) explores the unlikely partnership between White philanthropists and the Black community in New York and other cities. Ferguson explains that the Foundation, led by McGeorge Bundy, saw community control and self-determination in Black neighborhoods as a relatively peaceful alternative to school desegregation, which had provoked ire in White communities and required disruptive strategies such as busing Black students to predominantly White schools where the local community was far from welcoming. And, like a number of other White philanthropists who had been involved in school reform in the late 19th and early 20th centuries, executives from the Ford Foundation in the 1960s were "driven simultaneously by the fear of urban unrest and Bundy's overweening confidence that he held the formula for a successful postcolonial transition" (Ferguson, 2013, p. 89).

In the Foundation's view, the success of community control ultimately would lead to the assimilation of Black people into the mainstream of American culture and economy (Ferguson, 2013). Furthermore, leaders at the Foundation and the progressive university professors with whom they partnered were ready to work with Black activists in taking on the UFT and the school bureaucracy, which they saw as part of an over-reaching and dysfunctional autocratic state. In the Cold War context of the time, the community control reformers positioned themselves as advocates of participatory democracy, while large bureaucratic institutions like the school system seemed capable only of blocking individual freedoms and opportunity (Ferguson, 2013).

The controversy surrounding community control in New York City would become the most high-profile example of similar battles between low-income community members and teachers' unions throughout the nation in the 1960s and 1970s, battles often fought along racial and ethnic lines. The teachers in New York and other cities eventually would win this battle, but it was a victory that exacted a heavy political price (D. Goldstein, 2014). While teachers throughout the country gained higher salaries and job protections through collective bargaining in the 1960s and 1970s, they would fall into disfavor among a variety of groups in the general public, who would come to see teachers' unions as primarily self-interested organizations that protected their members at any cost, effectively preserving the status quo of educational inequity (Mirel, 1993).

The work of the Ford Foundation in the struggle for community control and decentralization in New York City also marks an important turning point for the role of philanthropists in public school reform, a shift that the Foundation's leaders recognized. As one Foundation leader put it in a memo to Bundy, urging the latter to become directly involved in negotiations between the Black community and the Board of Education, rather than remain on the sidelines:

> It would stimulate certain members of our staff to assume a new modus operandi in which they actively "make things happen" rather than wait and reflect on proposals from the field. . . . It would give the Ford Foundation an unmistakable leadership role in the important problems of the day, a role that goes beyond merely making money available. (as cited in Ferguson, 2013, p. 98)

It is hard not to see, in such a statement, an early version of today's venture philanthropy, in which the funding organization sees its role extending far beyond support for a given initiative (Scott, 2011). As Kumashiro (2012) puts it:

Whereas traditional philanthropists view their giving as donations that support what others were doing, venture philanthropists view their giving as entryways into that work. That is, philanthropists are now getting involved in goal setting, decision making, and evaluating progress and outcomes to ensure that their priorities are met. This hands-on role allows venture capitalists to affect public policy more directly and substantially, particularly in a climate where their financial aid is so desperately needed. (p. 15)

With Kumashiro's distinctions between old and new (or venture) philanthropy in mind, it is no wonder that many teacher activists today are directing their protests not only to state and federal policymakers, but also to the venture philanthropists who fund a substantial portion of the market-driven and privatization reforms that are reshaping the profession. In 2013, for example, *The Washington Post* featured a group of activist bloggers who had published a series of teachers' open letters to Bill Gates, whom they accuse of using his "vast wealth and power to create corporate education reforms without the democratic process" (Strauss, 2013, June 14, para. 6).

EARLY BUSINESS POLICY PLAYERS

At the beginning of this chapter, we described the way business practices and ideas had a direct influence on school reforms in the late 19th and early 20th centuries. Such business-inspired reforms gave us the centrally-governed bureaucratic school district with its professional hierarchy, its factory-model schools, and its tendency to treat efficiency as an end in itself. It is also important to note that these large-scale reforms of public education did not arise *ex nihilo*. They had advocates from the wealthiest corners of society (Saltman, 2010).

Just as the business leaders and philanthropists of today are influencing public education policy and practice—from Bill Gates's work in the area of teacher evaluation, to Eli Broad's training of school district administrators through his Broad Academy, to foundations such as the New Schools Venture Fund, which invests in charter schools and edubusinesses—leaders from the business world were instrumental participants in the education reforms of the late 19th and early 20th centuries. The early reformers were well-networked—businessmen from cities as far apart as St. Louis and Boston shared strategies and ideas for overhauling their respective school systems—they enjoyed easy access to mass media outlets, and they had the finances necessary to organize persistent lobbying efforts at the state and national levels (Kantor, 1988; Tyack, 1974). A brief look at some early business policy players will help us understand the historical roots of today's policy ecology of issue networks, venture philanthropists, think tanks, and edubusinesses, all of which we discuss in Chapter 4.

Although the early wave of business reformers focused primarily on the structure and governance of school systems, they also advocated changes in curriculum. Over the course of the first 2 decades of the 20th century, business leaders and their organizations, including the National Association of Manufacturers

(NAM) and the U.S. Chamber of Commerce, successfully convinced Congress as well as legislatures in 29 states to fund vocational education in the public schools, which they saw as indispensable to the health of the nation's economy; without it, they argued, American industries would never be able to compete with Germany and Britain in world markets (Cremin, 1961; Kantor, 1988; Kliebard, 1995). In 1905, for example, NAM issued a report warning that Germany, with its highly developed system of vocational education, was outstripping the United States in the "world's race for commercial supremacy" (as cited in Lazerson & Grubb, 1974, p. 91). And 7 years later, NAM would claim that the United States was neglecting its development of "human capital"—a common term in today's discourse—and that it was the responsibility of a new generation of teachers to ensure that students would be prepared to contribute to a productive economy (as cited in Lazerson & Grubb, 1974, p. 92). Such concerns sound similar to the rhetoric of today's reformers, who see connections between a weak public school system and the United States losing its economic dominance in the world. What is less well known is that this rhetoric extends back much further than the 1983 *Nation at Risk* report, which is often seen as a watershed.

In his aptly titled book, *Learning to Earn*, Harvey A. Kantor (1988) argued that reformers from the business world achieved much more than their concrete goal of securing federal and state funding for vocational education. The reformers managed to "legitimate the idea that preparation for work was a primary function of public schooling" (p. 43), and that the public schools were "a key solution to the nation's economic ills" (p. 168). In this way, the reformers had a lasting effect on the rhetoric and ideology of public education in the U.S., despite objections from John Dewey and other child-centered progressives who had argued against the idea that the dominant purpose of schooling was to prepare students for future phases of their lives—a purpose they saw as an impoverished conception of learning and of childhood (Kliebard, 1995).

Influence on Racial Hierarchy: A Two-Tiered System

If the sort of socially efficient education that NAM and other business leaders advocated seemed narrow in purpose, or struck many as a brazen attempt by big business to serve its own interests, it paled in comparison to what was happening around the same time in the segregated South, where White northern philanthropists and local policymakers were designing vocational schools and curricula for Black children.

In his classic history of Black education in the South between the Civil War and the Great Depression, James D. Anderson (1988) details the role of White northern philanthropic organizations—most prominently the Rosenwald Fund—in working directly with southern city officials to design secondary schools for Black students. White northern philanthropists and White southern education reformers were alarmed by the massive migration of Black families from economically depressed rural areas to southern cities between 1916 and 1930. Although southern city officials had dragged their feet for decades when it came to providing secondary education for Black students, they now saw themselves approaching a crisis. The cities did offer more economic opportunity than rural areas at that time, but the labor market became saturated fairly quickly, and with no schools for Black adolescents to attend beyond the elementary level, "there was little else for them to do but roam the streets" (J. D. Anderson, 1988, p. 203).

At the same time, however, White city officials had no intentions of training Black students in skilled industrial trades—let alone in the traditional academic subjects—as such training conflicted with a racist ideology that demanded Black subservience; moreover, they feared the prospect of Black tradespeople competing with White laborers for jobs. In this context, "a coalition of southern white school reformers and northern industrial philanthropists . . . came reluctantly to support a brand of industrial secondary education designed to train Black children as a docile, industrial caste of unskilled and semiskilled urban workers" (J. D. Anderson, 1988, pp. 199, 202). Thus, they would be trained as maids, bricklayers, auto mechanics, laundry women, cooks, waiters, elevator operators, and similar unskilled or semiskilled vocations that posed no threat to the established racial hierarchy.

J. D. Anderson (1988) explains how the Rosenwald Fund—named for Julius Rosenwald, part-owner of Sears, Roebuck & Company of Chicago—and other philanthropists sponsored occupational surveys of southern cities such as Little Rock and New Orleans, where they were planning to build secondary schools for Black children. The surveys were intended to ascertain the current employment status of Black adults and the economic opportunities available to Black people in the city. Armed with this knowledge, the philanthropists and city officials would design schools and curricula that would prepare Black students to enter the kinds of vocations that their parents currently occupied. Indeed, philanthropists and local city officials explicitly acknowledged the socially reproductive nature of such projects, including in cases where surveys of students pointed out that most of them aspired to occupations more lucrative and prestigious than those of their parents.

The aspirations of Black adolescents were of no consequence to the White reformers who were funding the schools and planning their instructional programs. The words of Franklin Keller, a school administrator from New York City who served as the Rosenwald Fund's curriculum designer, are particularly telling in this regard. Commenting on the curriculum of a new Black high school in Columbus, Georgia, he wrote, "There is exhibited commendable courage in eliminating traditional subjects which have no value for the more hand-minded boys and girls and especially for the negroes whose opportunity to make use of such traditional subjects is much more limited" (as cited in J. D. Anderson, 1988, p. 222). As Anderson notes, Keller's "curriculum theory reflected a system of values and beliefs that subordinated the freedom and choices of Black children to the interests of an unequal and unjust southern society" (p. 223). Furthermore, and perhaps just as astounding, Keller saw his theory of curriculum as one that "met the needs of the child," although it was clearly serving the interests "of a racially segmented and repressive labor market" (p. 223).

The education of Black children in the South served not only the ideological interests of northern philanthropists, but also their business interests. Rosenwald may have been the most prominent of the White philanthropists who funded and designed Black education in the South, but a number of other wealthy White businessmen engaged in this work. William H. Watkins (2001) explores their influence in *The White Architects of Black Education: Ideology and Power in America, 1865–1954*. Through portraits of philanthropists such as William H. Baldwin (president of the Long Island Railroad), Robert C. Ogden (partner in major retail firms from Philadelphia), and the Rockefeller family (oil magnates from New York), Watkins (2001) explains the keen interest of White northern philanthropists in Black southern education. In the decades following the Civil War and extending into the early 20th century, such philanthropists

> knew full well of the Black American's key socioeconomic importance. For big business to operate effectively, an orderly South had to be maintained. A contained Black populace, providing cheap labor, was a key ingredient to an orderly South. (Watkins, 2001, p. 122)

Although corporate philanthropists' interests were often "cloaked in and associated with a kind of social humanitarianism" (Watkins, 2001, p. 152), the philanthropists were very clearly focused on increased profits and the maintenance of racial hierarchies—interests they saw as inseparable.

CONCLUSION

We have explored these early examples of education reform in order to demonstrate that business leaders have enjoyed a long history of influencing major education policy in the United States. But we also want to emphasize that in the process of advocating for new policies that served their own interests, business leaders have achieved not only a series of material changes in public schooling, such as new governance structures and shifts in curriculum, but also the establishment of an enduring set of ideological assumptions about public schools and their purpose.

It is also important to note that while business ideas and business policy players enjoyed massive influence on public education policy and practice in the late 19th and early 20th centuries, they were much less influential in the middle decades of the 20th century, roughly between 1930 and 1970. Indeed, we have shown that organizations like the Ford Foundation were immersed in the community control struggles, and business labor law served as the model for the collective-bargaining legislation introduced in these years. But these were somewhat discrete examples of business influence, especially when compared with earlier examples, such as the design of public schools and districts in the image of large industrial firms and the largely uncritical transfer of efficiency management principles from business to schools.

In the middle decades of the 20th century, much of the focus of education policy centered on equal education opportunity. The *Brown v. Board of Education* decision of 1954 and the Elementary and Secondary Education Act of 1965 were part of the broader struggle for civil rights and the crafting of policy programs aimed at providing wider access to the benefits of a mostly prosperous postwar economy. But when the recessions of the early 1970s put a halt to decades of economic growth, business leaders were quick to blame rapidly rising inflation and the general economic slowdown on what they saw as an inordinately powerful organized labor movement, excessive government spending on social programs, and a general attack on American businessmen and the free-market system (Phillips-Fein, 2009).

These sentiments would be captured in a memorandum Lewis Powell wrote and delivered to the U.S. Chamber of Commerce in 1971, a document that would serve as a political call to arms among business leaders. In the memo, Powell, who would become a U.S. Supreme Court justice only a few months after writing the memo, implored the business community to protect its rights and become as active in politics and legal struggles as civil rights advocates had been (Phillips-Fein, 2009). The memo's calls for fiscal conservatism in government and free-market policy in business would be widely influential, sometimes reappearing as political statements in the earnings reports of major corporations and in the speeches of prominent business leaders (Phillips-Fein, 2009). This rightward shift in American politics would lay the groundwork for several decades of deregulation in business and finance, but it also would lead to a resurgence of business influence in public education policy.

This influence was crystallized most famously in the 1983 publication of *A Nation at Risk* (National Commission on Excellence in Education) under the Reagan administration, a document that painted American public schools as a cause of the nation's economic ills—albeit with specious data and rhetorical flair as substitutes for balanced and sober research. The report's authors argued that without raising academic standards in the public schools, particularly in high schools, the United States would continue to fall behind international competitors such as Japan and Germany. Thus, the report intensified the notion, as NAM and the American Chamber of Commerce had previously, that the chief purpose of public schools was to produce human capital for the nation's economy, and it helped to shift the paradigm of public education policy toward standards-based reforms and high-stakes accountability, which would only escalate through the beginning of the 21st century with the passage of NCLB (Mehta, 2013). With market-based reforms and data-driven management practices also added to the reformers' toolbox in the late 20th and early 21st centuries, American business leaders would re-establish their outsize influence on the public schools.

Earlier business reformers and philanthropists, although deeply influential, generally planned and advocated their reforms at a distance from teachers and their students. They were not as involved in the minutiae of implementation as their counterparts today (Kumashiro, 2012; Lubienski, Brewer, & La Londe, 2016). Seeming to learn from the mistakes of their predecessors, the newest generation of business reformers have set their sights specifically on remaking education professionals. Through their support of a variety of alternative teacher preparation programs; their focus on dismantling structures that enable collective action, such as unions and traditional contracts; their development of new human resource management policies (often called "talent management" now), such as merit pay and performance evaluations tied to Byzantine observation protocols and value-added measures; and their influence on new governance structures, such as marketized systems, that promote a competitive ethos—through all of this and more, today's reformers are working to redesign the professional identities of teachers and school leaders.

CHAPTER 3

The Second Wave of Business Influence and the Appeal of New Managerialism

> The era of big government is over, having been replaced by the era of really-big government. But modern American government is differently big. . . . American governments at all levels have moved steadily in the direction of taking managerial and service-delivery functions out of the hands of civil servants and putting them in the hands of nonprofit and for-profit third-party contractors and grantees. . . . For every nonuniformed federal employee, there are now more than seven contract employees. . . . There are as many contract employees in Iraq and Afghanistan as there are GIs. Such are the realities of contemporary public life. (Frederickson, 2010, p. 241)

The privatization that Frederickson (2010) describes above is well underway in education. In the previous chapter, we provided an historical account of the first wave of business influence in education. In this chapter, we will describe the second wave of business influence and why and how reformers were so successful at transferring a particular kind of business managerialism or NPM into education and why, in the face of significant evidence of its failure, it retains the widespread support of both political parties. While Americans revolted against both political parties in the 2016 elections, seeking to "drain" the political and corporate "swamp" in Washington, the notion that the public sector should be run more like a business within a marketplace retains wide appeal. After all, Americans elected a businessman with no political experience to run the federal government.

We first lay out the evidentiary case for the failure of neoliberal education reforms of the past 3 decades and the seeming paradox that they still enjoy wide bipartisan support. We then provide a discussion of a shift within the business community in the 1980s toward new managerialism and the cross-sector borrowing that followed as policymakers in the public sector became enamored of business-sector managerialist discourses and practices, in spite of their mixed reviews in the private sector. We will then discuss how discourse and framing strategies

(Lakoff, 2008) are used by think tanks and the media to produce what Edelman (1988) called a political spectacle.

While our historical analysis may have digressed some from our focus on new professionalism, an historical understanding of the growth of a business mindset can help us understand where the audit culture and market regime that teachers work under have come from. It also can help us understand the apparently seamless movement of the training of educational leaders from colleges of education to business schools, a trend that is well underway. Finally, it can help us understand the bipartisan political support and general appeal of a business model of school reform that has performed poorly.

One reason for the widespread appeal of business models is that corporate support for the think tanks and policy networks, which we describe in the next chapter, has effectively created what Berliner and Biddle (1995) call a "manufactured crisis" to which these corporate-funded think tanks have provided their own ideological solutions.

But political spectacle (Edelman, 1988) and manufactured crisis alone cannot be blamed for the popularity of NPM. Part of the answer is that America's public schools have not lived up to their democratic potential, and, as Cuban (1990) and others documented, the constant reforms that preceded NPM were not sufficiently robust to improve public schools serving low-income students of color (J. W. Fraser, 1997). Some progress was made around what was then called "restructuring" schools around the principles of the effective schools research (Edmonds, 1979) and the many whole-school reforms of the era (Coalition of Essential Schools, Accelerated Schools, Comer Schools, etc.), but the progress was slow and uneven (Payne, 2008). Furthermore, the failure of efforts to promote more equitable funding and the 1974 *Milliken v. Bradley* decision, which shut the door to more authentic school integration (Horsford, 2016), meant that White, middle-class Americans rejected the notion of more equitable funding and real racial integration. In the absence of equitable structural reform and the slow progress of school improvement efforts, the political field was left open for the neoliberal, NPM reforms that followed, beginning with school choice and state-level systems of high-stakes testing in the 1990s, and leading to the passage of NCLB at the federal level in 2001.

Advocates of NPM saw the legitimate sense of indignation and urgency to improve public schooling and make it more equitable as an opening to promote their managerialist ideology. No need for more public investment or a more equitable distribution of resources. No need for a more authentic racial integration of schools. Schooling for "all" children, the advocates of NPM believed, could be achieved by a more efficient use of resources, replacing political democracy with that of the marketplace, and using a top-down, "get tough" approach to holding teachers and schools accountable—even blaming them for the poor economy.

Some who legitimately were frustrated with how public schools were complicit in the reproduction of social and racial inequalities ultimately allied themselves with neoliberals (Bowles & Gintis, 1976; Pedroni, 2007; Phelps, 2005; Skrla

& Scheurich, 2004). In this way, as we discuss in more depth in the following chapter, "new Democrats" (Bill Clinton, Barack Obama, Democrats for School Reform, etc.), Right-wing libertarians, neoconservatives, and the religious Right often found themselves on the same side when it came to promoting neoliberal education policies. NPM reforms were implemented in earnest in the 1990s with the advent of school choice, charter schools, and high-stakes testing, and have proliferated ever since, more recently being joined by a massive for-profit sector.

THE FAILURE OF NEW PUBLIC MANAGEMENT REFORMS IN EDUCATION

There is a growing consensus among educational researchers and school practitioners that NPM reforms in education largely have been unsuccessful. Based on a reform model that included the creation of markets and the high-stakes triad of autonomy–accountability–assessment, this model of top-down reform by noneducators has been a failure in the United States and wherever else it has been attempted (Adamson et al., 2016; Blanco Bosco, 2009; Saltman, 2013; Tucker, 2011). Not only have NPM reforms not achieved the quantitative outcomes hoped for (Lubienski & Lubienski, 2014), they have introduced unintended consequences and perverse incentives into the public sector (Mehta, 2013; Nichols & Berliner, 2007; J.E. Ryan, 2004; Settlage & Meadows, 2002).

Even the federal government had to waive NCLB requirements for states as the 2014 achievement targets came and went. States, rather than raise the bar, lowered it in order to increase their pass rates. Growth models were rushed into place to address this issue by providing measures of student progress attributed to individual teachers and schools (called value-added models), but these high-stakes tests were so lacking in internal and consequential or impact validity that the National Research Council, American Statistical Association, and American Educational Research Association all were compelled to come out with cautionary position statements. Many parents began voting with their feet. An opt-out movement led by parents has made these tests invalid in many states (Pizmony-Levy & Saraisky, 2016). In 2015 in New York State, 20% of designated test-takers—over 200,000 students—were opted out by their parents from standardized testing. When such a substantial number of students do not sit for a test, it becomes even more difficult to determine how individual schools and districts are performing.

Meanwhile, charter schools have failed to outperform public schools, in spite of serving fewer homeless or foster care students, English language learners, or students with disabilities, and being able to more easily expel students (Center for Research on Education Outcomes, 2009). In fact, because the test outcomes of charter schools, voucher schools, and virtual schools have not been impressive, the conservative American Enterprise Institute is starting to question whether test scores are an appropriate measure of quality, something educators have questioned for years (Lubienski & Brewer, 2018). Bancroft (2009) reports the following finding from her qualitative study:

I found that a charter school's difficulties with funds and students led to a desire to create a student body that would bring stability and success to the school's endeavors, by processes such as culling out the disruptive students, letting parents know that the school did not have special education services, and creating an application process so complex that only involved parents would undergo the process. (p. 275)

Nor have charter schools been the incubators of innovation their early supporters touted, and because in many states they are minimally regulated, they have been rife with financial scandals (Baker & Miron, 2015; Lubienski & Lubienski, 2014).

While some stand-alone charter schools (meaning charter schools that are not part of a chain) provided the potential for a more community-responsive approach and more curricular autonomy, this potential of charter schools was largely sidelined as charter management organizations (CMOs), funded by venture philanthropy, sought to scale up and reach a tipping point to influence or replace public schools. Ironically, these franchises created the same bureaucratic system as public schools, but, with their corporate headquarters often located out-of-state, individual schools had even less local control or autonomy. They also elevated influential and high-salaried noneducators

with interest and experience in entrepreneurial ventures in education, many of whom were brought on board through alternative channels. The influx of these individuals to the charter field created an emergent class of alternative educational professionals with strong links to the dominant business community and elites in multiple circles. In turn, these professionals served as a corps of advocates for the CMO form with connections to like-minded individuals situated in powerful political positions and with access to financial resources. (Quinn, Oelberger, & Meyerson, 2016, p. 32)

Nor are charter schools and other market reforms the result of popular demand. Vouchers, first proposed by Milton Friedman, have never enjoyed a groundswell of public support, and referenda to increase charter schools were voted down in the state of Washington three times (Corcoran & Stoddard, 2011). More recently, a ballot initiative to expand the number of charters was voted down in Massachusetts (O'Sullivan, 2016). Experiments in for-profit schools in both K–12 and higher education have led to corruption and greater inefficiencies (Abrams, 2016; Connell, 2016), and school choice policies have increased race and class segregation (Frankenberg, Siegel-Hawley, & Wang, 2011; Glazerman & Dotter, 2016; Reardon, 2013). In some districts, like Washington, DC, the combination of choice and "prestige" charter schools is making it easier for gentrifying parents to choose charter schools to segregate their children from those in local public schools (E. Brown & Makris, 2017; Mann & Bennett, 2016).

It has become increasingly apparent that public school privatization and NPM have little empirical warrant, but NPM is a powerful ideology that has a wide commonsense appeal in spite of its failure to produce results, even on its own terms. While the public may reject specific corporate-led policies, the idea that schools—and the country—should be led by business leaders with business models remains popular and is largely responsible for the creation of the new professional. We will take up this apparent contradiction in the following section on managerialism and business schools.

CORPORATIONS, MANAGERIALISM, AND THE ROLE OF BUSINESS SCHOOLS

As we discussed in Chapter 1, Sennett (1998) demonstrated how, in the post-industrial flexible corporation, workers are disposable, and the notion of a stable job or a long-term relationship with the company they work for is no longer seen as viable. He described the emotional and psychological toll that a lack of loyalty, trust, commitment, and stability takes on workers, leading to cynicism about their futures. In the era of the "gig" economy, this tendency is even more evident, although the new professional has learned to take it in stride, often not knowing any other reality. Many young professionals who move from gig to gig are not optimistic that social security, pensions, health care, or other inheritances of the welfare state will be there for them as they age. Many are barely aware that these social supports were hard-won victories of political activism. This depoliticization of the population and lowering of expectations are part of the austerity politics of neoliberalism.

Something similar has been happening to teachers and school leaders as the notion of building a career in education is viewed as less viable. Attempts to privatize public education have resulted in a triple assault on teachers. First, they are denigrated and blamed for student outcomes that are largely the result of out-of-school factors (Berliner, 2009) that are beyond their control. Second, their benefits, pensions, and unions are attacked because many private-sector workers no longer enjoy benefits, pensions, and unions. And as noted, this is part of a larger attempt to lower expectations in an economy in decline (Lafer, 2017). Third, their work is being standardized and "teacher proofed" so that for-profit technology companies can sell their "one size fits all" products more effectively.

> Applications are now being sold for almost everything—an app for student behavior management, an app for English language learners, an app for ninth-grade reading, an app to replace guidance counselors. Almost none of these have been tested by any education authority, and almost none are the products of teachers or education scholars. Their promotion and adoption are driven not by a need identified in the classroom but by a combination of venture capital and technology firms eager to tap an emerging market and unrivaled potential. (Lafer, 2017, p. 51)

When public education is viewed as more than a $4 trillion annual global market, education ceases to be a human right and instead becomes just another commodity in a marketplace, and the individual is responsible for the "choices" he or she makes within it. While the notion of *academic capitalism* (Slaughter & Rhoades, 2009) in higher education is widely recognized, these same trends have taken root in pre-K–12 education as well, leading to a broader *educational capitalism.*

The new professionals under educational capitalism, whether in private or public institutions, are experiencing a workplace that is changing around them, with largely unexamined moral, emotional, and psychological effects (Hochschild, 2003). While the hollowing out of loyalty, trust, and relationality in the corporate workplace is problematic for the reasons Sennett (1998) describes, it is even more problematic in education and other fields such as nursing and social work, where caring and relationality are central to the core activity of the field. According to Lynch, Grummell, and Devine (2015):

> New managerialism defines human relationships in transactional terms, as the means to achieving high performance and productivity within organizations. . . . Only counting what is measurable focuses attention on outputs and subordinates process; it subordinates the life world of care to the systems world of measurable productivity. . . . While care and developmental work have an outcome dimension (Lynch et al., 2009), it is generally not measurable in a specifiable short time frame. The gains and losses from having or not having care are only seen over time. (p. 199)

And yet, rather than move the preparation of teachers and leaders toward a greater understanding of the importance of process, caring, emotion, and relationality in schools and classrooms, we increasingly are taking the preparation of educators out of colleges of education or putting them online and turning them into "fast track" programs (Mungal, 2016).

A few years ago, some educational leadership programs in colleges of education, most notably at Harvard, began partnering with business schools to provide classes to certify school administrators. Today, business schools across the country are offering their own graduate degrees in educational administration, conveniently de-emphasizing instructional leadership. Andrea Hodge, the executive director of the Rice University Education Entrepreneurship Program at the Jessie H. Jones Graduate School of Business, stated:

> Our view is that our principals need to be more than instructional leaders on campus. The principal needs to be the chief executive. What we try to do is give principals exposure to more holistic organizational-management concepts that are not covered to the same degree in most schools of education. (Superville, 2015, para. 3)

According to Hodge, since the program started in 2008, nearly 224 school leaders have been trained to work in Houston-area schools.

> "Leadership is leadership is leadership," said LeAnn M. Buntrock, the director of the Woodrow Wilson MBA Fellowship in Education Leadership, which seeks to infuse the

education leadership training model with business principles. The Woodrow Wilson program, which targets educators, is in place at six universities in Indiana and Milwaukee, where it has partnered with the Milwaukee School of Engineering's business program, and New Mexico. (Superville, 2015, para. 5)

Such programs are proliferating, including programs at prestigious public universities, for example, the Bright New Leaders for Ohio Schools program based at the Fischer College of Business at Ohio State University.

It makes perfect sense that managerialist NPM models would lead to training education "CEOs" in business schools. This is the logical extension of NPM, as a managerialist logic has swept across the public sector. But what is managerialism and how did it begin within the private sector?

Managerialism refers to the emergence of shop-floor managers that represented a new organizational layer between the worker and the owner of an enterprise. The skills and strategies of this middle management were codified and described most notably by Frederick Taylor in *The Principles of Scientific Management* (1911/2009), in part based on his time-and-motion studies of workplace efficiency. As enterprises grew, managers involved in strategic decisionmaking became more and more distanced from managers overseeing daily operations. Top management no longer had to know engineering or understand the nature of the products being made. This led to the notion that top management, trained in accounting and finance, should focus mainly on issues of return-on-investment and decisions of a financial or commercial nature (Locke & Spender, 2011). It was only a small step from there to the idea that anyone with strong management skills could run any organization, regardless of its core purpose and practices.

This principle of managerialism is central to the notion that public service professionals do not necessarily require a deep understanding of teaching and learning or what it feels like to be a teacher, a nurse, a social worker, or a police officer, or how to value or resource them effectively. When I (Michael Cohen) was working in the assessment department of a large urban school district, a deputy superintendent who supervised 20 schools in the city made a remarkable comment during a meeting about measuring students' academic progress. Frustrated by the data showing slow growth, he claimed that until every teacher in the district "thinks like an accountant," our numbers would remain stagnant. The concern of the modern manager is the bottom line.

While managerialism is an old concept, many use the term *new managerialism* to describe the turn it took beginning around the 1980s, which we will discuss below. It also emerged more virulently in the United States and the United Kingdom than in countries like Japan and Germany, which were our main economic competitors during that time. It is ironic that public schools were blamed for the inability of the United States to compete effectively with Japan and Germany (National Commission on Excellence in Education, 1983), since the real culprit was the failure of American private-sector managerialism (Foroohar, 2016).

NEW MANAGERIALISM AND THE FAILURE OF THE
AMERICAN BUSINESS MODEL

Typically, business literature of the 19th century made reference to the business-person's "social duty" and the moral balance between private and social benefit. Even Adam Smith, one of the icons of market capitalism, was a moral philosopher. Early 20th-century American business schools followed suit. The Harvard School of Business Administration introduced the German-inspired "case method" in 1908 in which students read and analyzed hundreds of actual cases based on real business dilemmas, problems, and ethics. But in 1932, the Cowles Commission, made up of mathematicians and statisticians, many of whom were Europeans brought over to help with the Manhattan project that produced the atomic bomb, began to promote a new positivist science of management. This included mathematical economics, finance mathematics, statistics, and game theory.

In the postwar years, business school faculties began to adopt the latest trends in management science in order to make their field a respected scientific discipline—in much the same way that early professors of educational administration, under pressure to boost their prestige, had tried to ground their work in efficiency science, as described in Chapter 2. Faculty at business schools borrowed new mathematical models developed in part from the need for strategic planning, logistics, and the solving of operational problems during World War II (Locke & Spender, 2011). The Rand Corporation was founded by the military to do operations research and used mathematical and statistical models to make decision-making more scientific. By the 1960s, Planning, Programming, and Budgeting Systems were used widely in the private and public sectors.

This new management science was implemented in business schools with the help of the Ford Foundation just as business schools were growing enrollments. According to Locke and Spender (2011), "An explosive growth of graduate business schools and MBAs began. In 1960, some 4,814 of these qualifications were granted, 23,400 in 1970, 49,000 in 1980, 70,000 in 1990, with more than 200,000 plus per year at the century's end" (p. 16). This growth in business school enrollments is significant, not only because it intensified an already present business mindset within American culture (Abrams, 2016), but also because it reinforced a tendency to use mathematical models for decisionmaking in all contexts, with little regard for the local situation or ethical considerations. Unlike in Germany, where business schools have had little influence or prestige, it also created a large social and economic divide between management and labor.

The growing distance between management and the nature of products and work processes on the shop floor, in combination with the use of mathematical models divorced from those same realities, resulted in the poor performance of American industry compared with Germany and Japan. Locke and Spender (2011) describe in great detail how Japan's focus on relationships, trust, and loyalty in the workplace, and a focus on customers' needs, led to the production of high-quality cars that outsold those built in Detroit. The Germans had a similar relational workplace culture and job security, but added the notion of worker co-determination, in which workers and management shared formal power (Addison, 2009). While in the United States shared governance is at the discretion of management, in Germany it is a legal requirement and led to decisions that benefited workers as well as corporate and national interests.

The fundamental difference between the United States, on the one hand, and Germany and Japan, on the other, is that the yardstick of progress in the United States was not company sustainability or worker or customer satisfaction, but rather short-term profits and the price of publicly traded stocks (Davis, 2011). Mitchell (2007) describes a survey of more than 400 chief financial officers of major American corporations, in which they report that they would sacrifice the long-term health of their corporations to meet quarterly profit targets. According to the survey, they would cut the budgets for research and development, advertising, and maintenance, and would delay hiring and new projects. And the empirical evidence shows that publicly traded corporations have done just that—maximizing shareholder value at the expense of research and development—perhaps most stunningly in the pharmaceuticals industry, which we rely upon for innovations in medical treatments (Foroohar, 2016).

One more recent exception to the poor performance of American corporations is the venture-capital-financed IT startups of entrepreneurial Silicon Valley and the U.S. tech industry. However, Mariana Mazzucato's book *The Entrepreneurial State* (2015) demonstrates that virtually every innovation in the development of computers, smartphones, and tablets was funded almost exclusively by government agencies, mostly defense-related agencies, such as the Defense Advanced Research Projects Agency (DARPA). This includes the Internet, microprocessors, the multitouch screen, Siri, GPS, liquid-crystal display, lithium ion batteries, and many more. The vaunted entrepreneurialism of Silicon Valley is largely limited to creating apps and commercializing innovations produced by the federal government.

And this is not just the case in the IT industry; almost every major technology has been the result of large-scale and long-term investment by the state, something venture capitalists seldom have the patience for. The growth of the biopharmaceutical industry was not, as often is argued, the result of venture capital or other business finance promoting innovation in the private sector, but rather the result of government investment and ongoing support. Although the government often is accused of stifling private-sector innovation, according to Mazzucato (2015), the private sector, in fact, has a parasitic relationship to the State.

> 75 percent of the NMEs [new molecular entities] trace their research not to private companies but to publicly funded National Institute of Health (NIH) labs in the US . . . . While the State-funded labs have invested in the riskiest phase, the big pharmaceutical companies have preferred to invest in the less risky variations of existing drugs (a drug that simply has a different dosage than a previous version of the same drug). (p. 73)

While Silicon Valley and big pharma perhaps can be applauded for their entrepreneurialism in commercializing IT technologies and NMEs, the long-term investment, innovation, and risk are shouldered by the entrepreneurial state—the public sector (Mazzucato, 2015). The 2017 tax bill lowers statutory corporate taxes (what corporations pay in reality, via loopholes, is half that) from 32% (down from 52% in the post–World War II years) to 21%. Meanwhile, rather than invest in research and development or the creation of new jobs, U.S. corporations are holding $2.1 trillion abroad to avoid paying taxes. Mazzucato (2015) suggests the United States may want to follow the lead of countries like Finland and Israel, which retain equity in corporations that are recipients of government largesse in order to recoup the state's investment.

We dwell on these details in part to further debunk the popular myth that the private sector is more innovative than the public sector, but also to emphasize that the managerialism of the U.S. corporate sector was not inclined to take the long view, as was the case in Germany and Japan. Without the government-funded technological innovations that Silicon Valley piggy-backed on, there would have been no U.S. computer and cell phone industry, which gave the United States the competitive edge it lacked previously.

While these forms of managerialism were a factor in the lack of competitiveness of American corporations, the obsession with mathematical models and a turn in business schools toward finance had perhaps even more serious consequences. Fast forward to the 2008 Wall Street meltdown. Finance mathematicians had created models such as the capital asset pricing model (CAPM) that allowed stock market investors to build allegedly low-risk, high-return portfolios. No knowledge was needed about the stock itself, since CAPM was based on a mathematical model that assumed that "stock prices move, as mathematicians put it, in a 'random walk' in continuous time that allows investors to determine the relevant probabilities for volatility" (Locke & Spender, 2011, p. 161).

Business schools produced a plethora of products in mathematical finance that followed the same basic principle.

> You didn't have to know much about finance or stocks to build and sell models that allowed Wall Street to price trillions of dollars' worth of derivatives rationally in a market system thought of as an orderly, independent, continuous process. . . . But why turn actual trading in hedge funds and investment banks over to a bunch of mathematics geeks who knew almost nothing about finance? The answer is that the geeks' models made money, and lots of it. Quantification added volume, speed and spread to market trading. (Locke & Spender, 2011, p. 160)

The rest is history—Wall Street collapsed and was bailed out by the public sector, although the collapse of Wall Street was also due to other factors, such as the subprime loan debacle. In addition, Japan and Germany have been replaced by China and India as competitors, and global money flows have shifted. Yet, it was the managerialist faith in numbers and mathematical models and the obsession with short-term gain that made the collapse possible, and that may lead to yet another collapse.

But if, in fact, corporations have not been as innovative as the government and have enough power to bend Congress to their will, as we have seen in the tax bill of 2017, how did they amass so much power? How has the American corporation grown to compete with—some might say colonize—the government? Here it is necessary to distinguish *managerialism* from another common term, *corporatism*. Corporatism often is used similarly to managerialism, in the sense that public institutions behave more and more like corporations. But it also refers to how corporations have become so dominant in our society and how they have amassed the power to privatize the public sector in collusion with government.

A BRIEF HISTORY OF THE AMERICAN CORPORATION

Ironically, it was conservative economist Milton Friedman (1962) who warned that if government grew too big, it could be taken over by corporations. But what Friedman didn't say was that corporations had been amassing power since the 19th century. Few Americans are aware that the first corporations in America were chartered by the King of England. The notion widely held today that corporations are private enterprises would have appeared nonsensical to any American up to the end of the 19th century.

Corporations under the British monarchy were formed to promote the interests of the monarchy, and they were held on a short leash. Many of the original American colonies, such as the Massachusetts Bay Colony, were in fact British corporations chartered to stake claims in the New World. After the American Revolution, corporations were chartered by the American states in the interests of their citizenry, which at the time was limited to White propertied males.

At least legally, then, corporations were public institutions created by special charters of incorporation granted by state legislatures to serve the common good. Although many corporations chartered to build such things as canals or colleges also created wealth for individuals, the primary function of the corporation was to serve the public interest. People, through their legislature, retained sovereignty over corporations, and legislatures dictated rules for "issuing stock, for shareholder voting, for obtaining corporate information, for paying dividends and keeping records. They limited capitalization, debts, landholdings, and sometimes profits" (Grossman & Adams, 1995, as cited in Derber, 1998, p. 124).

However, popular sovereignty and legislative control over corporations began to unravel during the late 19th century. The Fourteenth Amendment to the U.S. Constitution, created to protect the rights of freed slaves, was used as a tool to provide corporations with the legal rights of a person. Much like today, conservative judges during the Gilded Age of the early 20th century were cynically allied with powerful corporate friends. These judges and corporate leaders colluded to turn public control over corporations into a violation of the Fourteenth Amendment, which holds that no state "shall deprive any person of life, liberty, or property, without due process of law." Thus, the courts of the Gilded Age broke with the state grant theory of public accountability over corporations and supported instead a conception of corporations as a voluntary contract among private people. In this way, a public institution, created and controlled by a sovereign people, became a private institution or "enterprise" whose existence was independent of the state *and largely immune from public accountability.*

More recently, under the Supreme Court case *Citizens United,* courts have used the First Amendment to the Constitution to view massive corporate contributions to political campaigns as an expression of free speech, thus supporting the notion that a corporation is the equivalent of a human being under the law. Also, corporations are amassing power globally, and in many instances they can sue countries that put laws in place that they don't like. This occurs through investor-state dispute settlement provisions that are featured in many trade agreements, including the North American Free Trade Agreement (NAFTA), nine U.S.–E.U. bilateral investment treaties, and the ill-fated Trans-Pacific Partnership (TPP) (Perez-Rocha, 2014).

What is perhaps even more remarkable is that this history of the shift of corporations from publicly accountable, chartered enterprises to private enterprises is virtually unknown among the general public in the United States. Such accounts seldom, if ever, are taught in American history classes, nor are they taught in colleges of education, in spite of the current view of public schools and the entire public sector as a profit center.

Why should we care whether a corporation is state-controlled or not? This question goes to the heart of the debate about the nature of public institutions and what makes them different from private ones. It also influences the nature of the work of public-sector professionals. Increasingly, corporations are taking over many public functions and heavily impacting public policy. For instance, corporations affect political outcomes with their campaign contributions and lobbyists. Today, of the 100 organizations that spend the most on lobbying, 95 represent businesses. The largest companies have upward of 100 lobbyists representing them (Drutman, 2015). In the following chapter, we will describe how corporations and legislators actually are co-writing policies that serve corporate interests. The American Legislative Exchange Council skips over the lobbying stage to the more direct approach of writing model legislation with corporate CEOs and legislators at the same table (G. L. Anderson & Montoro Donchik, 2016).

We have provided a brief history of how corporations have gained inordinate power and how new managerialism has become the new normal in the corporate world and increasingly in the public sector. This cross-sector transfer of new managerialism to education has created what Gewirtz (2002) called the *managerial school* and what Evetts (2011) called the *new professional.* In the next section, we attempt to explain some of the political and discursive strategies through which this was accomplished.

THE APPEAL OF NEW PUBLIC MANAGEMENT: POLITICAL SPECTACLE, CROSS-SECTOR BORROWING, AND COGNITIVE FRAMING

A common approach that is used by those who seek to impose change is the creation of *political spectacle* (Edelman, 1988). According to Edelman, political spectacle is ultimately media driven, a phenomenon we are witnessing today with talk radio, 24/7 cable "news," and social media. But he also emphasized the importance of language and discourse. Perhaps more than any other political scientist, Edelman (1978) focused on the relationship between language and politics and what he called "the linguistic structuring of social problems" (p. 26), anticipating Lakoff's (2008) later work on cognitive framing, which we will discuss below.

Edelman (1988) was also aware of the importance of defining events as crises. He stated, "A crisis, like all new developments, is a creation of the language used to depict it; the appearance of a crisis is a political act, not a recognition of a fact or a rare situation" (p. 31). Naomi Klein's (2007) writing on disaster capitalism extended this insight to help us understand how this operates globally in the context of dictatorships and natural disasters. In this regard, several educational researchers have documented the post-Katrina privatization of the New Orleans school district (Buras, 2014; Saltman, 2016). But a crisis also can be manufactured and become part of a larger political spectacle, as Berliner and Biddle (1995), Smith, Miller-Kahn, Heinecke, and Jarvis (2004), and others have documented, particularly with reference to *A Nation at Risk* (National Commission on Excellence in Education, 1983), which portrayed public schools as in crisis.

Other scholars have documented how political spectacle is being used to destabilize the public sector and attack public-sector unions, with the goal of privatization. Drawing on Whitfield's (2001) study of the privatization process in Britain, Ball (2007) describes three stages through which the creative destruction of the public sector is accomplished. While this is not a coordinated, linear process, it has the following internal logic. The public sector is *destabilized* through constant ridicule to undermine its credibility. This is accompanied by *disinvestment* from and shifting resources within the public sector. As public institutions like schools and universities become more financially strapped, they need to seek new revenue streams from the private sector, in some cases from venture philanthropic organizations with privatizing agendas.

Ball (2007) quotes a deputy head teacher to illustrate how this occurs under austerity policies: "You can't run on your ordinary budget, everyone knows that, so you have to get involved in various initiatives and cater for that, the initiative's priorities, and bend your curriculum and your priorities in order to get hold of that bit of money" (p. 23). By creating the constant need for additional revenue streams, public–private partnerships help to breach and rework key boundaries between the public and private. Finally, a process of *commodification* "reworks forms of service, social relations and public processes into forms that are measurable and thus contractible or marketable" (Ball, 2007, p. 24).

In this way, new markets are created that attract private providers, creating whole new arenas of commercial activity for corporations and social entrepreneurs. A growing education industry aggressively promotes data management and assessment products, educational software, tutorial services, educational design and management companies, professional development, school construction, surveillance cameras, private security companies, and metal detectors (G.L. Anderson, 2007). These industries have mined NCLB, Race to the Top, and the Common Core to create niche school markets in the interstices of these policies (Burch, 2009). Part of the commercial appeal of the Common Core is its single national set of standards, which obviates the need to design products for each state.

Once the public sector is destabilized and delegitimated, it is only a small step to raising the questions of what should replace it. Early promoters of public–private partnerships, or using charter schools to incubate ideas, did not talk about replacing the public sector, but rather complementing, supplementing, or "modernizing" it. Yet we are seeing some troubling trends that suggest "replacement" may in fact be the agenda of the powerful new networks of policy entrepreneurs that we describe in Chapter 4. Many urban school districts are being restructured as "portfolio" districts with an array of products to choose from (Barnum, 2017). The New Orleans school district is composed almost solely of charter schools today, and charters now represent over 50% of the schools in Washington, DC, Detroit, and Philadelphia.

Transferring ideas, technologies, and even products from the private to the public sector is not inherently problematic. But any time we transfer ideas or technologies from one sector to another, we must look carefully at whether the fit is appropriate and carefully analyze the motivations behind such a transfer. Not only do many attempt to argue that what is good for business is automatically good for education, but there are some who suggest that democratic public institutions are obsolete and need to be replaced by more market-oriented, private ones (Chubb & Moe, 1990; Friedman, 1962). The stakes are therefore high, since our very democracy—imperfect though it is—might be at risk.

Some blurring between sectors is inevitable and may be quite benign and even helpful (Minow, 2002). But the only way to create an authentic public sphere is through political and social processes that treat human beings as a community of shared interests and responsibilities, not atomized individuals seeking the maximization of their own and their family's good at the expense of others.

The application of business-crafted solutions to public schools (better managers, getting the incentives right, choice, market competition, accountability) has become so thoroughly embedded in policymakers' thinking about improving schools, particularly in urban districts, that these policies are taken for granted and often seen as "common sense" rather than as having been borrowed from the corporate closet (Cuban, 2004, p. 13).

Even academics serve as carriers of corporate discourses. Consider the following excerpt from a 2017 article in *Educational Researcher*, a major journal of the American Educational Research Association:

Presumably, thoughtful use of high-quality teacher *effectiveness measures* can improve *talent management* decisions in ways that elevate *teacher quality* and *instructional delivery*. Yet numerous studies have demonstrated that simply collecting measures and making them available to *users* is far from sufficient for ensuring that *data are utilized for decision making*. . . . Failure to understand the institutional and individual obstacles to principals' use of *teacher effectiveness measures*—and thus how school systems can address those obstacles—risks wasting an important source of *leverage* for school improvement. (Grissom et al., 2017, pp. 21–22, emphasis added)

The italicized terms are examples of how corporate managerialist discourse enters the public sector with little acknowledgment of the lifeworld of teachers or principals, who now are "talent" to be managed, expected to "utilize data" instead of engage in inquiry, "deliver" instruction, and "leverage" measures to improve schools. The linking of "quality" to "effectiveness measures" harkens back to Total Quality Management, which was heavily critiqued in the 1990s (Capper & Jamison, 1993). None of this language honors the professional integrity or complexity of teaching and leading, but gains legitimacy and status by transferring language from the corporate institutional field to the education field. It also mimics the positivist language of engineering and measurement as a nod to the higher status hard sciences.

This article is not atypical of the corporate discourse used to gain legitimacy within the academic institutional field (J. W. Meyer & Rowan, 1977). Yet such discourses, perhaps unintentionally, perpetuate NPM policies that can deprofessionalize teachers and principals. Language is used not simply to communicate, but also as part of a larger arena in which power struggles over meaning take place.

Many scholars are attempting to better understand how ideas are borrowed or transferred between sectors and fields (Mautner, 2010; Mazzucato, 2015). When discourses and practices travel across fields, organizations begin to adopt language and behaviors that make them appear legitimate within their institutional field (H. Meyer & Rowan, 2006). The colonization of the education field by the discourse and practices of the business field since the 1970s helps explain why a district superintendent might prefer to be called a CEO, or why we borrow notions of measuring outcomes such as the *statistical control of product quality* and apply them to students, teachers, and schools as if they had the kind of uniformity of hamburgers or jet engines (Cuban, 2004).

Mautner (2010) has developed a model of interdiscursive alignment to document the communicative flows between the business sector and various public sectors. Focusing on the meso level of institutional fields, she asks: "How do individual acts of linguistic accommodation solidify into conventionalized discursive practices which, in turn, are constitutive of social systems?" (p. 22). Addressing this question requires discourse analysis, which can excavate the ideological work that language and texts perform (Fairclough, 1992). By following the discursive chains that flow across institutional fields, we can document the discursive struggles over control that take place within them. Within schools, we can document the principal's role in mediating these discourses, and everyday discourse practices of teachers can be mapped. These chains can provide us with a way to explore the linkages among micro-, meso-, and macropolitics (G. L. Anderson, 2009).

Unfortunately, given the hierarchical nature of organizations and the power relations embedded in them, discourses tend to trickle down more easily than they trickle up. Mautner (2010) provides an example of how intertextual chains are mediated within hierarchies: "If market discourse is embraced by top management, it will cascade down the system. Chains of command thus become chains of intertextual adaptation, with the less powerful actors adapting to the more powerful ones. Over time, individual acts of adaptation solidify into discursive practice, and a new norm emerges" (p. 28). This process highlights the important role of management professionals, such as principals and superintendents, who serve as mediators at different points in the hierarchy. They occupy pivotal discursive spaces through which policies and practices flow, and these can be complied with, modified, superficially performed, accommodated in complex ways, or outright resisted (G. L. Anderson & Cohen, 2015; J. Ryan, 1998; Turner, 2014).

Mautner's (2010) work helps us see how NPM, in spite of its many failures to improve education, retains its appeal not only through the material interests of those who profit from it, but also through subtle and intentional forms of linguistic and ideological colonization of the public sector and the general public.

The example above of academics using corporate discourse in journal articles does not represent an intentional use of corporate discourse. These academics are likely unintentional carriers of NPM through language that has seeped into academic discourse. However, reformers who promote managerialist policies use language and discourse in intentional ways through what Lakoff (2006) calls deceptive frames. For instance, equity language, like "No Child Left Behind" and "closing the achievement gap," is a case of using a social justice discourse to promote high-stakes testing and market-based policies. In fact, although some defended such language for its rhetorical call for social justice, it ended up being a Trojan horse carrying many tenets of NPM that not only diminished an emphasis on resources and public investment, but also narrowed how we approach the complexity of professional activities such as teaching and learning, especially for the low-income students that defenders claimed they wanted to help.

But according to Lakoff (2006), besides engaging in deception, framing is used to tap into deeper and often unconscious systems of belief. He makes a distinction between *surface* frames and *deep* frames.

> Surface frames are associated with phrases like "war on terror" that both activate and depend critically on *deep frames*. These are the most basic frames that constitute a moral worldview or a political philosophy. Deep frames define one's overall "common sense." Without deep frames, there is nothing for surface frames to hang onto. Slogans do not make sense without the appropriate deep frames in place. (p. 29, emphasis in original)

Lakoff explains that after the 9/11 terrorist attacks, the George W. Bush administration's use of the phrase "war on terror" as a surface frame tapped into deep frames of American military might, patriotism, and retributive justice. In treating the terrorist attacks as an act of war, rather than as an international policing issue requiring diplomacy, criminal justice proceedings, and due process, the Bush administration legitimated its use of military power and the accompanying risk of civilian casualties in other sovereign nations.

Cognitive framing reveals why some explanations of complex social phenomena such as poverty tend to prevail over others. Wilson (2009) provides data comparing attitudes among Europeans and Americans that indicate that Americans overwhelmingly explain the existence of poverty as an individual shortcoming, whereas Europeans "focus much more on structural and social inequalities at large, not on individual behavior, to explain the causes of poverty and joblessness" (pp. 45–46). Therefore, surface framing that emphasizes "rags to riches" stories about individual social mobility will resonate with these American deep frames, even in the face of evidence that the United States is an increasingly unequal and downwardly mobile society (Wilkinson & Pickett, 2010).

The political arena of school reform is rife with discourse that resonates with deeper American values. The term "school choice," for example, activates deeper cognitive frames of freedom and consumerism. It also conveniently positions those who question choice policies as opponents of personal liberties—or as proponents of an intrusive and restrictive government. In activating the deeper frames of freedom and consumerism, "school choice" deflects our attention from the unequal distribution of goods within a marketized system. The term "pay-for-performance" activates a deep frame of meritocracy, a purportedly equitable system in which people get what they deserve. For some, it may also activate the American ethos of competition, similar to the title of the Obama administration's signature school reform legislation, "Race to the Top." At the same time, "pay-for-performance" obscures the complex and inherently value-laden nature of defining good "performance" in teaching. Moreover, in delegitimizing traditional salary schedules composed of "steps and lanes," it glosses over the history of collective struggles to achieve equitable pay for women.

Research in cognitive framing helps explain why discourse and ideas from the domains of business and the market can be spontaneously appealing despite their often deceptive character. Lakoff (2008) has demonstrated that our brains use the logic of frames, prototypes, and metaphors, not the logic of rational argument based on factual information, to make sense of the world and that these frames are physiological in the sense that they reinforce neural networks in our brains. This means that the constant repetition of frames quite literally embeds them in our brains. This also suggests that if we are to engage in critical analysis of ideas in the political arena of school reform, we need to bring into view, and question, the deeper cognitive frames that support them.

CONCLUSION

In this chapter, we have provided an all too brief history of how a second wave of business influence began to gain ground in the 1970s and has grown with each decade since then. We also have explored how the transfer of business models into the public sector was facilitated by the growing influence of business schools, venture philanthropy, media and political spectacle, and the mechanisms, such as cognitive framing, used to transfer new discourses and logics of action across institutional fields.

Our concerns with the NPM of the 1990s seem increasingly quaint as NPM 2.0 enters a new phase in which public-sector professionals are viewed largely as obstacles to the corporatization, privatization, and marketization of public institutions. As we have seen, in the United States, school administrators increasingly are trained in business schools. Countries are outsourcing their beleaguered public education systems to for-profit corporations (Riep & Machacek, 2016). Before long, most university graduate programs may be delivered online by for-profit corporations like Hotchalk and 2U.

An entire private parallel system to public education has been created in the United States with its own teachers and leaders (e.g., Teach for America, New Leaders for New Schools), its own charter school franchises (e.g., KIPP, Uncommon Schools, Green Dot), and its own teacher preparation programs (e.g., Relay Graduate School) (Mungal, 2016). NPM 2.0 is no longer only about school reform, but also about the privatization and financialization of the public sector. It is what Harvey (2005) refers to as capital "accumulation by dispossession" in which capital has exhausted its sources of accumulation within the private sector and now seeks to exploit the public commons: public schools, prisons, the military, Social Security, and Medicare/Medicaid.

While our focus in this book is on how NPM and a market ideology have created a "new professional" within education and the public sector in general, a broader understanding is needed of why public-sector professionals have been politically targeted. This is because the Trump administration and the Department of Education, led by Betsy DeVos, will deepen and expand neoliberal policies that the Bush and Obama administrations have laid the groundwork for. The goal of NPM no longer seems to be to restructure the public sector by making it more innovative, efficient, and flexible, but rather to eliminate it as much as possible as part of what Steve Bannon called the "deconstruction of the administrative state." In the following chapter, we will explore who these new political actors are and how they have formed powerful, global policy networks that are transforming national systems of education.

CHAPTER 4

New Policy Actors and Networks Design the New Teacher and Leader

Move fast and break things. Unless you are breaking stuff, you aren't moving fast enough. (Mark Zuckerberg)

Whenever a college student asks me, a veteran high-school English educator, about the prospects of becoming a public-school teacher, I never think it's enough to say that the role is shifting from "content expert" to "curriculum facilitator." Instead, I describe what I think the public-school classroom will look like in 20 years, with a large, fantastic computer screen at the front, streaming one of the nation's most engaging, informative lessons available on a particular topic. The "virtual class" will be introduced, guided, and curated by one of the country's best teachers (a.k.a. a "super-teacher"), and it will include professionally produced footage of current events, relevant excerpts from powerful TedTalks, interactive games students can play against other students nationwide, and a formal assessment that the computer will immediately score and record.

I tell this college student that in each classroom, there will be a local teacher-facilitator (called a "tech") to make sure that the equipment works and the students behave. Since the "tech" won't require the extensive education and training of today's teachers, the teacher's union will fall apart, and that "tech" will earn about $15 an hour to facilitate a class of what could include over 50 students. This new progressive system will be justified and supported by the American public for several reasons: Each lesson will be among the most interesting and efficient lessons in the world; millions of dollars will be saved in reduced teacher salaries; the "techs" can specialize in classroom management; performance data will be standardized and immediately produced (and therefore "individualized"); and the country will finally achieve equity in its public school system. (Godsey, 2015)

If this new professional scenario seems futuristic, it soon may seem outdated, since it retains some role for at least a "super-teacher." Here are some other examples of how teachers are being de-centered: Sugata Mitra was given a $1 million TED

Prize in 2013 in recognition of his work and to help build a School in the Cloud to encourage self-organized learning. In his previous work, he developed the now popular notion of *minimally invasive education* (Mitra, 2003). And Jacque Ranciere's book *The Ignorant Schoolmaster* (1991) makes a compelling argument for more horizontal learning that is essentially teacherless. Virtual schools are another "innovation" that promises to sideline teachers and leaders. Talk to world language teachers in public schools and chances are that some of them are already merely "facilitating" students plugged into Rosetta Stone. As curricular and IT decisions are made in far-off corporate headquarters, educational leaders, too, will become irrelevant (Courtney, 2018).

Examples of the ways technology is marginalizing or replacing teachers could fill this whole book, but there are more optimistic views of how the role of technology in teaching could play out. Shaffer, Nash, and Ruis (2015) argue that while educational technologies will de-center teachers, their new roles of coordinator, mentor, translator, and learner, along with previous roles of counselor and disciplinarian, ultimately will reprofessionalize teaching in new ways and create new skills that will need to be taught in teacher preparation programs. However, the issue is not just technology and its potential to enhance teaching and professionalize teachers. Most would agree that technology can facilitate learning in numerous ways and provide teachers with important instructional resources. For example, the so-called sharing economy has arrived in education, and teachers share and sell their lesson plans and other resources online.

Yet much of the research touting the effectiveness of fully online or blended-learning schools (hybrids of traditional brick-and-mortar schools and online schools) has been conducted or supported by the very organizations that stand to profit from their expansion, and the research has been largely debunked for its poor quality of evidence (Molnar et al., 2017).

Moreover, virtual schools have been as scandalous as predatory, for-profit universities in siphoning off public money (McMillan Cottom, 2017). The largest virtual school in the country, Electronic Classrooms of Tomorrow, was forced to close in 2017. The school, like most other virtual schools, had extremely low graduation rates and academic performance. Yet the state of Ohio allocated more than a billion dollars to the charter school, making its founder a multimillionaire. As with many charter schools, state oversight was extremely lax. Finally, it was shuttered when it became apparent that it had inflated its enrollment numbers, was insolvent, and owed taxpayers $80 million. Twelve thousand students and their families were suddenly without a school midsemester (Pogue, 2018).

Ironically, much of the promotion of technology in education is done using progressive discourses of student-centered learning, project-based learning, and self-organized learning. Unfortunately, as the State disinvests from public education, public-sector professionals increasingly are seeking cost savings, which often require contracting to technology companies that promise economies of scale. As tech companies' shareholders' demands for greater quarterly profits lead to "scaling up" innovations, those progressive discourses too often become mere window dressing. The typical online instructional approach is something we used to call "mastery learning" in the 1970s. If you remember those color-coded SRA kits, you get the idea.

Whether more technology in education is good or bad may be the wrong question to ask. The larger question is who will be in control of education technology and who will decide what impact it should have on professional expertise. Currently, the drivers of these changes are not educational researchers, but venture philanthropists and profit-seeking edubusinesses. The latest project of venture philanthropist Bill Gates is to put a video camera in every classroom. In a recent TED Talk, he proposes to build a $5 billion teacher feedback and improvement system that will place a video camera in every classroom so teachers can have constant feedback on their teaching. Although teachers are not clamoring to have video cameras in their classrooms, few districts can afford to turn down that kind of money. As mostly White, male, wealthy individuals, and the think tanks and foundations they sponsor, increasingly make public policy, the professionals and citizens are sidelined as active democratic participants in how their children should be educated (Scott, 2009).

In the previous chapter, we provided an overview of the second wave of business influence in education and the discursive mechanisms used to transfer a business mindset from the private to the public sector through the tenets of NPM. In this chapter, we discuss the policy actors and networks that are promoting this agenda. If educators are to reclaim and democratize their notion of professionalism, they will need to better understand who the players are behind the powerful policy networks that promote NPM and what the impact is on public-sector professionals.

Evidence of the impact of these new policy actors and networks is everywhere. But these shifts to corporate management did not come about naturally. They were the product of intentional and well-resourced political actors who worked to promote neoliberal social policies and an ideological shift that achieved a new common sense about the role of markets and business in society. In this chapter, we will describe who these new political actors are, the various policy networks they have formed to promote their interests and ideologies, and the sometimes-incongruous social alliances that have come together in the United States to promote NPM reforms. The construction of the new public-sector professional is a complex phenomenon that is promoted by different groups with different interests. We begin with a description of how different social and ideological groups in the United States have achieved a kind of strategic alliance to promote neoliberal and NPM reforms.

STRANGE BEDFELLOWS:
WHO SUPPORTS NEW PUBLIC MANAGEMENT REFORMS?

As markets, metrics, managerialism, technology, and profit have become the hallmarks of education reform globally, it has become apparent that the old interest-group politics of the era of the Keynesian welfare state have shifted as new policy actors and networks have entered the political arena (Ball, 2008, 2012). As Chapter 2 outlined, the business community in the late 19th and early 20th centuries had an inordinate amount of political influence on public-sector organizations and professionals.

However, from the 1930s to late 1970s, U.S. educators, represented by their professional associations and unions, had less competition from other policy actors and therefore a more significant voice in education policy (Debray, 2006). School boards during this period, while highly contentious, were less dominated by business interests. Social policies, often derived from court cases and pressure from social movements, supported funding for greater equity for women and people of color, programs in special and bilingual education, and compensatory spending on schools in low-income communities.

In education, progressive interest groups such as teachers' unions, professional associations, community control activists, and other advocacy organizations also were part of a policy regime based on what Harvey (2005) called "embedded liberalism." This meant that markets, personal freedoms, individual choices, and schools themselves were embedded in regulatory and social welfare policies aimed—in theory, at least—at a common good. The schooling of low-income children was viewed as embedded in out-of-school societal supports. Many of the federal policies of that era, including the passage of the Elementary and Secondary Education Act of 1965, were attempts to provide equal educational opportunity as part of a "war on poverty."

While important advances in social welfare were made, as we noted previously, it is important not to romanticize the post–World War II, Keynesian welfare state years. We did not win the "war on poverty," and Hinton (2016) argues that the seeds of mass incarceration were sown under Johnson's Great Society. The American war in Vietnam also diverted funding away from public investment in human needs. Many federal policies, especially housing policies, discriminated against non-Whites (Rothstein, 2017), and it took a massive civil rights movement to achieve the legal dismantling of gender discrimination and Jim Crow laws in housing and education, although institutional sexism and racism have continued in other forms (Bonilla-Silva, 2014).

As discussed in the previous chapter, a series of events, including an economic downturn that was blamed on public schools, the *Nation at Risk* report commissioned by Ronald Reagan, the influence of the Powell memo on mobilizing the business community, and the prospect of making a profit from public funds, were all influential in bringing the business community back into the education arena in full force. Today the Keynesian welfare state policy regime has been replaced by a neoliberal, market regime promoted by wealthy philanthropists, corporate-funded think tanks, private "edubusinesses" and their lobbyists, and other policy entrepreneurs (Ball, 2009; Scott, 2009). These relatively recent policy players have formed powerful policy networks aimed at disembedding markets and individuals from regulatory policies and social welfare protections. Schooling is viewed as disembedded from out-of-school factors that impact children (Berliner, 2009), as expressed through the school reform slogan, "no excuses." This process of disembedding requires new policies and new ways of thinking about the individual, society, and what it means to be a professional.

By the 1980s, Margaret Thatcher had famously said, "There is no such thing as society. There are individual men and women, and there are families." She was also known for saying that "there is no alternative" to free-market capitalism. This mantra became common sense, and was known as the TINA principle. With the fall of communism, life after what Fukuyama (1992) called the "end of history" was life under unbridled and unopposed capitalism. You could either celebrate it or be resigned to it, but there was no room for imagining another way of organizing society. Along with this new restructuring of society came a restructuring of professional organizations around new managerial principles that have changed professional life dramatically (Locke & Spender, 2011). In order to understand the emergence of the new professional, it is necessary to understand how society is being restructured and in whose interests this is being politically engineered.

Michael Apple (2006) has identified four overlapping groups that have successfully shifted the American discourse to the political Right over the past 40 years: (1) neoliberals and libertarians inspired by Milton Friedman's free-market ideology; (2) economic and cultural conservatives who promote zero tolerance, high standards, discipline, and personal responsibility; (3) a group of "authoritarian populists" associated with the religious right who want prayer and the teaching of creationism in schools, advocate for traditional family values, and, like conservatives and neoliberals, are suspicious of "big government"; and (4) middle-class professionals, often Democrats, "whose own professional interests and advancement depend on the expanded use of accountability, efficiency, and management procedures that are their own cultural capital" (p. 6). Here we will provide a brief description of each. For a more elaborate discussion of each of these, see Apple (2006).

Neoliberals and libertarians who follow Milton Friedman's (1962) call for privatization and smaller government see NPM as part of a project to dismantle the public sector, which they see as big government that "steals" people's income through taxation to give to undeserving others. These groups see educators as agents of the state, with little incentive to improve, protected by their unions, unaccountable to the public, and enjoying "gold-plated" pensions. These groups include mainly Republicans, but also many New or "Clinton" Democrats who may be progressive on social issues, but neoliberal on economic ones. NPM is viewed positively as making public-sector organizations function more like the private sector, which is perceived as more effective and efficient.

Conservatives support exerting more control over educators because they view "government schools" as supporting multiculturalism, a lack of patriotism and family values, and a watered-down curriculum. Some conservatives, who support a rigorous, but traditional, curriculum and teaching methods, are beginning to question the impact that testing and scripted curricula is having on narrowing the curriculum. This was a large part of former conservative Diane Ravitch's (2011) decision to oppose the reform agenda. Conservatives also tend to see the Common Core State Standards as pushed by big government and have joined some progressives in opposing the standards.

The *religious right* share many of the conservatives' ideas, but are more concerned about public schools teaching secular humanism in general, and evolution in particular. Because many of them send their children to private religious schools or home school, they have little investment in funding public education. They also might support New Public Management to the extent that its focus on standardization and the discipline of the market tends to squeeze out any focus on multiculturalism, civics, or the teaching of "values" in general. Moreton (2009) has provided a history of the parallel development of Walmart, modern religious conservatism, and political advocacy for Right-wing politics. Apple (2013) documents Walmart's link to Students in Free Enterprise (SIFE), a student movement on college campuses funded by Walmart, Coors, and other corporations.

Middle- and upper-class professionals share the general principles of NPM. Since many work in the private sector, they have internalized business notions of measuring outcomes or using quasi-markets to allocate values and resources. Their own children also benefit from accountability systems that reward schools that tend to perform well on standardized exams, especially as those children seek admission to elite colleges. More recently, however, many middle-class parents have joined the anti-testing, opt-out movement, since the excessive and high-stakes use of tests can narrow the curriculum and the type of instruction their children receive.

Some of the professional middle class may be less likely to support the privatization of public schooling, since they often live in suburbs where their public schools are well-funded. They may, however, support choice policies since their schools are typically not among the choices open to low-income urban communities. Those middle-class professionals who are gentrifying urban centers also can use choice policies and charter schools to escape their local zoned schools (E. Brown & Makris, 2017; Mann & Bennett, 2016; Posey Maddox, 2014). Here, one can see how a marketized system that includes increased accountability and testing regulations for traditional public schools only strengthens the appeal of charter schools and other alternatives for individual families. In a similar vein, E. Brantlinger (2003) documented how middle-class professional parents justify their self-interested educational choices, while maintaining a liberal or progressive image.

These four social groups make up a powerful support base for NPM policies and help to explain why they have tended to resonate with and be supported by both political parties. We would add two other groups to Apple's (2006) coalition: profit-seekers and many low-income parents and parents of color.

Profit-seekers view public education as a $1.6 trillion market to exploit. According to Vellanki (2015):

There is $1.6 trillion spent annually in the US on education, and $5.5 trillion globally. The government alone spends $1 trillion. The US K-12 market and US post-secondary markets (both public and private funding combined) are $688 billion and $535 billion in size, respectively. To tackle this market, start-ups have also raised a fair amount from venture investors—$320 million in 2009 and approaching $2B in 2015. (para. 3)

While the practice of contracting services to the private sector is not new to school districts, recent policies and new aggressive "edubusinesses" have placed greater pressures on districts to contract out services (Burch, 2009; Scott & DiMartino, 2009). For instance, the vouchers provided by NCLB for supplemental education services, such as tutoring, required districts to hire private companies—not school districts—to provide these services, although many districts were able to subvert the companies or incorporate the tutoring into their curriculum (Koyama, 2011).

The Education Industry Association (EIA), which advocated and lobbied for tutoring companies, was instrumental in getting the vouchers for tutoring services and other supplemental services into NCLB, transforming the tutoring market into a $2 billion a year industry, and lifting Kaplan and Sylvan up from small test prep companies to multinational corporations (Koyama, 2011). More recently, EIA was bought by Education Technology Industry Network, which is the education division of the Software and Information Industry Association, one of many industry associations lobbying Congress. In addition, private education businesses, including testing companies, spend millions of dollars to lobby Washington for policies that favor their industries (G. L. Anderson & Herr, 2011; Drutman, 2015).

Many *low-income parents and parents of color* have never been served well by public schools. Low-income communities of color have long battled teachers and their unions for a greater voice in their schools. The battles for community control in the 1960s in New York City and other urban centers, which we described in Chapter 2, often are cited as examples of the disregard teachers' unions have had for low-income communities of color (Podair, 2002). Black leaders like Howard Fuller of Black Alliance for Education Options have supported Milton Friedman's original voucher proposals, arguing that low-income communities of color are deprived of the choices middle-class parents take for granted (Pedroni, 2007). In the wake of a perceived lack of accountability of police and the criminal justice system, some Black leaders also argue that high-stakes testing, while not perfect, holds teachers accountable in communities where parents may lack the social, cultural, and economic capital to do so themselves. Both the National Association for the Advancement of Colored People (NAACP) and the Mexican-American Legal Defense Fund, as of this writing, still support high-stakes testing. In a speech to the NAACP during his presidential campaign, George W. Bush (2000) tapped into the tensions between communities of color and professional educators, referring to "the soft bigotry of low expectations," a phrase he would use later in his support of NCLB.

At the same time as the new market ideology is couched in a common sense manufactured by think tanks, it also appeals to the "good sense" of many who have been the victims of an economic system that has left them trapped in neighborhoods of concentrated poverty and racial segregation (Apple, 2006). In a context of disinvestment in the public sector, deteriorating public schools, and a surplus of minimum-wage jobs, having any choice at all—even a limited one—may seem hard to pass up.

To parents living in a low-income neighborhood where teen pregnancy and gang violence are common, a "boot camp" charter school, where students wear uniforms and walk the halls in straight lines, might look preferable to a public school. After all, public schools have to take everyone. Charter schools typically are able to prioritize students from families who have the time and knowledge to make school visits and attend open houses and school fairs. These are not the same parents whose children attend public schools, even if their demographics are similar.

On the other hand, there is considerable evidence that poor communities of color also have resisted many aspects of NPM reform. For instance, communities have organized to oppose for-profit charter schools in New York City (Scott & Fruchter, 2009) and they have protested school closings in many other cities (Lipman, 2011). We also are seeing coalitions of teachers' unions and communities of color joining forces to oppose NPM policies. In 2017, after 16 years of state control, the Philadelphia schools took back control and will be governed by a local school board (Sasko, 2017). While teachers and the teachers' union were central figures in the struggle, a much broader coalition formed to elect a progressive mayor of Philadelphia and governor of Pennsylvania. They also elected civil rights lawyer Larry Krasner as district attorney for Philadelphia. So while low-income parents and parents of color do not represent an ideological interest group in the same way the groups discussed above do, there are many within this group who are supportive of some NPM policies and others who oppose them.

There are also groups that are opposed to NPM policies for diverse reasons. Many teachers experience these policies as deprofessionalizing their work (Achinstein & Ogawa, 2006; Wills & Sandholtz, 2009). Teachers' unions have similar concerns but also see privatization as a challenge to unionism and to the material well-being of teachers (Compton & Weiner, 2008; Weiner, 2012). Gallup poll data show that 75% of Americans are happy with their children's public school (Huffington Post, 2012), even if they may have bought the larger ideological critique of public schools in the abstract. A large opt-out movement of parents who opt their children out of high-stakes testing has developed in many states (D. Mitra, Mann, & Hlavacik, 2016). In New York State, 20% of parents opted their children out of testing (Wang, 2017). With the exception of teachers' unions, though, these groups are not as well-funded or generally as well-networked as groups that support NPM and privatization. In the next section, we will describe in more detail who these new non-state actors who support NPM are, who funds them, and how they form and maintain their powerful networks.

NEW POLICY ACTORS: THE EMERGENCE OF ISSUE NETWORKS

The new professional, then, is the creation of a convergence of interests that is bipartisan and supports deregulation of capital in general, high-stakes accountability, markets as a way to discipline professionals, anti-unionism, and the transfer of business principles into the public sector. These interests are represented by dense global *policy networks* that work to promote ideological narratives, policies, and resources that perpetuate their ideological projects (Ball, 2012). By "policy networks" we mean "the properties that characterize the relationships among the particular set of actors that form around an issue of importance to the policy community" (Coleman & Skogstad, 1990, as cited in Collyer, 2003, p. 14). We do not assume that policy networks share a common worldview or "conspiracy"; rather they may have nuanced differences or even work at cross-purposes on some issues. In the aggregate, however, constellations of policy networks ultimately can end up promoting similar ideas and broad agendas (Scott, 2009).

Heclo, as early as 1978, identified what he called "issue networks," drawing attention to what then was viewed as a new phenomenon. Eventually this has led to the finding that shared ideologies have a positive effect on collaborative ties within networks and that actors form networks to translate shared beliefs into policy. Policy networks are not limited to the political Right. There have always been liberal policy networks as well, and more recently new neoliberal policy networks have spawned a series of progressive counter-networks, although these networks seldom have the same number of wealthy individual donors or corporate support (G. L. Anderson & Montoro Donchik, 2016; Kelley & Mead, 2017). Overall, the emergence of dense and well-funded issue networks has been instrumental in promoting a rightward shift in U.S. policy, especially as business organizations and fundamentalist religious organizations, like Focus on the Family and SIFE, have become more politically mobilized (Moreton, 2009).

The notion that a global and national rightward ideological shift has occurred over the past 4 decades is widely accepted and empirically evident, but *how* the shift from Keynesianism to neoclassical economic models has occurred is still being documented by historians and political scientists (Harvey, 2005). In the U.S. context, Burris (2008) has provided a network analysis of shifting power relations during this period. Building on a body of research in business schools on interlocking corporate boards, he has extended this research to the boards of what he calls policy-planning organizations, which include think tanks and advocacy organizations.

Burris (2008) found that moderate conservative big-business associations like the Business Council and the Business Roundtable consistently have remained central nodes of this policy-planning network. However, in the 1970s, they were linked with the corporate liberals (e.g., Brookings Institution, Council on Foreign Relations, etc.), whereas by the 1990s, they became more closely linked to ultra conservatives (e.g., American Enterprise Institute, Heritage Foundation, Hoover Institute, the U.S. Chamber of Commerce, etc.). Based on these findings, he argues that changes in the structure of these policy networks over time help account for the rightward shift in U.S. policy during the 1970s, 1980s, and 1990s. And this tendency has accelerated as new policy entrepreneurs have come online.

But who are these new policy entrepreneurs and their policy networks? Before we focus on some of the most powerful players—venture philanthropists, think tanks, and edubusinesses—we will discuss a unique and powerful organization, the American Legislative Exchange Council (ALEC), which has amassed significant power at the state level and is linked to larger powerful networks. ALEC is worth highlighting because it is a key node within U.S. policy networks. It was incubated by the Heritage Foundation and later developed the State Policy Network and partnered with the Franklin Institute, creating linkages among advocacy think tanks, legislative lobbyists, the corporate sector, and media organizations.

The American Legislative Exchange Council

Beginning in 2011, with the passing of anti-labor laws in Wisconsin, Americans woke up to new state laws attacking public-sector unions and requiring official IDs for voting, and "stand your ground" laws that removed the duty to retreat before using force in self-defense. Trayvon Martin and George Zimmerman became household names, and the voter ID laws in multiple states were viewed as a thinly veiled attempt to take Democratic voters off the rolls. Investigative journalists, especially those working with the Center for Media and Democracy, began connecting the dots and identified a little-known organization, ALEC, as a central culprit in all three new laws.

What was perhaps less evident was that ALEC did not act alone, but rather was part of a large and proliferating network of new policy actors who over the past 4 decades have worked largely behind the scenes to accrue significant policy influence at the state, national, and global levels. For example, when several corporations decided to leave ALEC, and ALEC dissolved its elections and safety task force (chaired by the National Rifle Association) under public pressure, another node in ALEC's policy network, the conservative National Center for Public Policy, formed a voter identification task force to take over ALEC's role in this area.

ALEC was created in 1973 and originally housed at the Heritage Foundation in Washington, DC. It flew largely under the radar until 2011. In 1992, ALEC launched the State Policy Network (SPN). SPN's goal was to build a Heritage-like, Right-wing infrastructure in all the states. SPN later partnered with the Franklin Center to create news websites and train journalists to report "fake news." Today there are 64 state-level SPN think tanks, at least one in every state. They focus on producing reports and placing opinion pieces in local newspapers, as well as helping to politically promote the issues ALEC supports.

ALEC is composed of state legislators and corporate leaders who collaborate to write model or template bills that are introduced or promoted by ALEC members within state legislatures. Corporate CEOs pay $50,000 and legislators pay a mere $50 a year for membership. There are eight task forces: education and workforce development; civil justice; commerce, insurance, and economic development; communications and technology; energy, environment, and agriculture; health and human services; international relations; and tax and fiscal policy. Each task force is co-chaired by a corporate leader and a state legislator.

The for-profit, digital education company K12 Inc. recently has co-chaired the education and workforce development task force. Through its leadership, ALEC has been writing and supporting bills to promote virtual online schools that seek the same state funding allotment as brick-and-mortar schools, in spite of research that shows dismal results for such schools (Miron & Gulosino, 2016). In this way, edubusinesses use taxpayer money to make big profits and pay large executive salaries. The top five executives at K12 Inc. made over $12 million in 2015 (Beilke, 2016). They also use taxpayer money to pay millions for advertisements and lobbying, something public schools are not allowed to do.

The model bills ALEC produces and promotes in education fall under three main categories: (1) the privatization of public assets or the transfer of taxpayer dollars from public schools to the private sector through vouchers, charter schools, and contracting out of services; (2) opposition to teachers' unions, tenure, and certification; and (3) the transfer of business models to the public sector (New Public Management) (G. L. Anderson & Montoro Donchik, 2016). The corporate education industry seeks to deregulate and de-unionize teaching because it is difficult to make a profit in a labor-intensive field like education unless employers have freedom to terminate teachers' positions. The demise of early for-profit education management organizations (EMOs) like the Edison Schools was partly a result of small profit margins (Abrams, 2016), pushing edubusinesses to seek profits in more lucrative areas, such as technology, testing and data warehousing, and curriculum and professional development.

Ultimately the goal of ALEC and its policy networks is to reverse New Deal and Great Society programs that provided a social safety net and redistributed wealth more equitably. As of 2017, with Republicans in control of 32 state legislatures, ALEC has been actively pursuing the idea of a second Constitutional Convention to rewrite the U.S. Constitution. It is only six states short of the 38 needed to call for a convention. It is pushing for an austerity amendment to privatize or cut Social Security, Medicare, and Medicaid. Perhaps most troubling, ALEC has achieved not only the increased privatization of the public sector, but also the privatization of the policymaking process itself, leaving the public in the dark, as it promotes bills written by wealthy individuals and corporations to benefit their own interests.

As ALEC and other members of the network have seen the light of day, counter-networks have formed through the work of investigative journalists. Color of Change, an organization formed in 2005 during the post-Katrina period, was responsible for getting several corporations to withdraw their membership from ALEC. Other organizations that formed part of this counter-network included Common Cause, the NAACP, People for the American Way, Presente!, the National Urban League, Moveon.org, the Center for Media and Democracy, and the Sierra Club.

While the attempts by ALEC and its network allies to shift public opinion and state-level policies toward neoliberal and managerialist policies have been generally successful, the growth of counter-networks has the potential to provide some balance. Although these networks tend to lack sustainability without the kind of support conservative organizations receive from the corporate sector and growing numbers of wealthy philanthropists, this is not exactly a David and Goliath struggle. In spite of the *Citizens United* Supreme Court decision that has flooded corporate money into electoral politics, allowing billionaires and their networks unprecedented influence, other organizations such as teachers' unions, professional associations, progressive think tanks, advocacy organizations, and incipient, but growing, educator-led grassroots movements have been able to hold the line in many cases. In fact, in 2014, a group of political progressives formed an ALEC-like counter-organization called State Innovation Exchange (SIX) (formerly ALICE). SIX currently has a network of 1,500 elected officials in all 50 states. The organization's mission on its website states:

> We support state legislators who seek to strengthen our democracy, fight for working families, defend civil rights and liberties, and protect the environment. We do this through training, emphasizing leadership development, amplifying legislators' voices, and forging strategic alliances between our legislative network and grassroots movements.

One element of the success of neoliberal policy networks and organizations like ALEC is that they are proactive rather than reactive. This is, in part, because they have a strong ideological alliance and a dense, well-funded network, are committed to cross-sector advocacy, and engage effectively in both political and discursive strategies. Progressive networks, on the other hand, seem to lack a strong ideological alliance, have a more precarious policy network, have not engaged in cross-sector advocacy, and have not been very politically or discursively effective (Kovaks & Christie, 2009; Lakoff, 2004). While the development of counter-networks has had some small successes, discursively these counter-networks have yet to articulate a coherent counter-narrative that might reframe the neoliberal narrative of freedom, individualism, and meritocracy versus a rigid, inefficient, monopolistic, and oppressive public sector with its public bureaucracies and obstructionist unions (Lakoff, 2004).

We have described ALEC and the counter-networks it has spawned in some detail, in order to provide an inside look at one node of a much larger global policy network that is transforming the public sector and public-sector professionals. We will take up in more detail in Chapter 5 other ways public-sector professionals are resisting such networks. In the following sections, we provide an overview of other policy actors that constitute these neoliberal policy networks.

The Emergence of Venture Philanthropy

Like their venture capital brethren, venture philanthropists aggressively pursue prospective fundees instead of issuing requests for proposals as traditional philanthropists tended to do, and they seek a return on their investment in the form of measurable social or political outcomes (Scott, 2011). These approaches to philanthropy have become dominant among both progressive (Korten, 2009) and conservative and neoliberal philanthropies. However, because most philanthropies are funded by wealthy individuals who made their money through their success in business, there is a tendency to seek private-sector solutions to public problems (Edwards, 2008, 2010). Convinced that the public sector would benefit from the strategies and tenets that led to their success in the private sector, many tend to promote deregulatory policies in education, such as school choice, charter schools, and privatization (Scott, 2009).

Perhaps the most significant difference between traditional and venture philanthropy is the massive increase in the resources of the wealthy and the inordinate level of influence this funding can have on public policy (Mayer, 2017). For instance, venture philanthropists have had a strong impact on deregulation of teaching and administration, and on the creation of a parallel, deregulated and largely nonunion education market that competes with public schools (Mungal, 2016).

Wealthy venture philanthropists are also overwhelmingly White and male. As noted in Chapter 2, a similar generation of White, male philanthropists designed the education of Black children and youth in the South under Jim Crow laws. These perhaps well-meaning philanthropists did help to build new schools and universities for Black children and youth, but their view of what Black children could aspire to was limited, and the largely vocational curriculum reflected that (Scott, 2009). We see a similar sense of paternalism in current attempts by largely White philanthropists and corporate hedge fund managers to provide an education for children of color in low-income communities that they likely would not want for their own children.

This remaking of public schools requires the remaking of education professionals as well, and this remaking is well underway, led by organizations funded by venture philanthropists.

Think Tanks and the War of Ideas

One of the things that neoliberal venture philanthropists have funded heavily is advocacy think tanks, which have grown exponentially since the 1970s. Think thanks once referred to academic institutes, contract shops like Rand Corporation, or centrist think tanks like Brookings or Russell Sage. These think tanks were largely legitimate producers of research that existed outside universities. Some advocacy think tanks, such as the Heritage Foundation, did exist, but they became major influences only after the 1970s. Today, the term *think tank* tends to be associated with a plethora of ideologically driven organizations.

Advocacy think tanks, particularly those with a neoliberal or conservative bias, have been effective at getting their ideas into the media and often are treated by the media as equivalent to academic think tanks and university-based researchers (Haas, 2007). In reality, though, with few exceptions, they produce ideas, talking points, and policy framings rather than serious research. Unlike university researchers, who are hesitant to enter the political fray, think tanks are adept at moving among the media, corporate, political, and education fields (Anderson, De La Cruz, & Lopez, 2017). Rich (2013) notes that conservative think tanks have an ideology about how to construct a new common sense:

> For conservatives, that ideology is one that values the power of ideas—and positions think tanks to be the infrastructure for advancing ideas, above all else. By contrast, even when they profess to be attracted to think tanks for the same reasons, the leaders of liberal think tanks are often preoccupied by deeply held commitments to producing objective research, on the one hand, and to connecting their work to issue-based grassroots activism, on the other hand. These commitments are compatible with the tenets of liberal ideology, but they are far less helpful to fighting a war of ideas. (p. 74)

Neoliberal and conservative think tanks have been very effective at undermining public schooling and the notion of a democratic public sphere, and replacing it with individualism and market choice.

Think tanks are part of a larger strategy that includes discursive destabilization, disinvestment from the public, and commodification in order to prepare the terrain for standardized technological solutions that can financially exploit the public purse. In addition to think tanks, major industries, such as fossil fuel, fracking, pharmaceuticals, tobacco, and sugar, have produced their own research that serves the interests of those industries. A recent, widely reported study by Kearns, Apollonio, and Glantz (2017) documents how the sugar industry covered up a 1967 research study it conducted that showed sucrose might be associated with heart disease and bladder cancer. The industry terminated the study and did not publish it. Then it funded a study that claimed that reducing cholesterol and saturated fat was the only way to prevent heart disease (Kearns et al., 2017).

This also is occurring in education. The tech industry sees education as a major profit center, aiming to make $21 billion by 2020 on their computer and software market alone. Consequently, the tech industry is engaging in similar strategies, funding university research that promotes technology in schools and engaging in questionable marketing practices in school districts, such as making donations and funding trips and meals for superintendents (N. Singer & Ivory, 2017).

Another way to think about the importance of think tanks is to return to Milton Friedman's (1962) famous statement in *Capitalism and Freedom*, written at a time when his views were on the intellectual fringe:

Only a crisis—actual or perceived—produces real change. When that crisis occurs, the actions that are taken depend on the ideas that are lying around. That, I believe, is our basic function: To develop alternatives to existing policies, to keep them alive and available until the politically impossible becomes politically inevitable. (p. ix)

Think tanks have continued to create an echo chamber, repeating the mantra of the failure of American public schooling. Once public schooling was discursively undermined, disinvestment, marketization, and deprofessionalization eventually followed. The 2018 rolling teacher strikes and walkouts are essentially a reaction to the success of venture philanthropists and ideological think tanks as they protest the degradation of their jobs and their professionalism.

THE GROWING ROLE OF PRIVATIZATION, CONTRACTING, AND "EDUBUSINESSES"

Abramovitz and Zelnik (2015) have identified three historical stages in the development of the privatization of the public sector in the post–World War II years: (1) marketization, (2) managerialism, and (3) financialization. We draw here from research in social work and public services as a reminder that privatization not only affects public education professionals, but is a cross-sector phenomenon.

Forms of privatization as marketization occurred earlier in the social services than in education, which had a strong ethos of public schooling. In education, marketization didn't arrive till the 1990s with the advent of charter schools, vouchers, and public–private partnerships. In public services, it arrived in the early 1960s when the so-called "war on poverty" sought to provide social services to individuals and families in need. According to Abramovitz and Zelnik (2015), "Instead of following the European pattern of creating a national health and social service system, and reflecting the American antipathy to government intervention, the federal government began to contract with private non-profit agencies to provide the needed services" (p. 285).

By 1979, nonprofits were providing a higher percent of social services than all levels of government combined (Abramovitz & Zelnik, 2015). During this time, the government also began contracting to for-profit companies. These *public–private partnerships* (PPP) were not a new phenomenon, as private and religious schools and hospitals had long been part of the mix of delivering public services in the United States (Minow, 2002). However, the extent of contracting to the private sector and entry of the for-profit sector into the mix increasingly have shifted the material conditions and ethos of public services and of those who deliver them.

With the advent of Reaganomics in the 1980s, the economic downturn and high inflation of the 1970s were blamed on the welfare state, public education, and big government. Instead of using the government to create jobs as was done in the 1930s, neoliberals, both Republicans and Democrats, chose a politics of austerity and began to dismantle the New Deal and Great Society programs. Abramovitz & Zelnik (2015) list the now-familiar tactics that were employed:

> (1) tax cuts, (2) retrenchment of social programs, (3) devolution (shifting social welfare responsibility from the federal government to the states), (4) privatization (shifting social welfare responsibility from the public to the private sector), (5) support for traditional "family values" and a color blind social order and (6) reducing the influence of social movements best positioned to resist this austerity program. (p. 285)

These austerity policies ushered in the second stage of privatization, *managerialism* or New Public Management. To achieve this retrenchment, managerialist business principles were transferred into the public sector, and public-sector organizations were treated as if they were competitive businesses. Doing more with less and producing "revenue streams" to replace state funding, the use of markets and outcomes measures to discipline workers, and the sidelining of unions were some of the core principles of NPM. This, in turn, made inevitable the third stage of privatization, *financialization*, or commercialization in which investors sought to profit from a social service sector that they saw as a potential $120 billion market. We have seen similar stages in sectors such as education, criminal justice, health care, public works, and the military.

The new professional lives in a privatized and commercialized world in which knowledge increasingly is commodified and sold; services are contracted to the private sector, typically to for-profit companies; and jobs are less secure. The cafeteria worker and the bus driver no longer are employed full time as state employees with benefits, and teachers are not far behind. The canary in the mine is university faculty, of whom, in 2014, a mere 19.51% were full-time tenured and another 7.37% were full-time tenure track (American Association of University Professors, 2015). The rest either have no job security or are part-time temp workers. DiMartino and Scott (2012) argue that the unprecedented levels of private-sector contracting also have important implications for democratic accountability since the private sector does not have to be responsive to the public nor open its books to public scrutiny.

Globally, we see similar issues with a lack of corporate accountability as the tech industry enjoys massive profits from developing countries that are enticed to purchase its products and services (Bhanji, 2012; Junemann & Ball, 2015). Technology is a massive revenue stream for companies like Microsoft, Google, and Pearson. Bill Gates, co-founder of Microsoft Corporation, provided financial support to promote the passage of Race to the Top, which encouraged using student test scores to evaluate teachers, and $200 million more for the Common Core State Standards (Layton, 2014). In a speech he gave at the 2009 National Conference of State Legislatures, Gates stated, "When the tests are aligned to the common standards, the curriculum will line up as well. . . . For the first time, there will be a large base of customers eager to buy products that can help every kid learn and every teacher get better." The potential conflict of interests should be apparent. It is not far-fetched to interpret Gates's largesse as expecting a return on investment. Typically, the new breed of venture philanthropists expect a political or ideological return on their investments, but increasingly the return is financial as corporations seek to profit from a trillion-dollar market of taxpayer, public education money.

We have only scratched the surface in terms of documenting the many new policy entrepreneurs and networks operating globally. There is a growing body of research that is documenting these networks and the new forms of governance they are creating (Au & Ferrare, 2015; Ball, 2007, 2012; Ball & Junemann, 2012). These networks are creating the NPM policies that are shaping the new professional, but they also are influencing the initial training of teachers and leaders.

TRAINING THE NEW EDUCATION PROFESSIONAL

From policing to teaching to practicing medicine, the shift to New Public Management has reconstituted most occupations and professions. Nearly 25% of teachers no longer are prepared in universities through coursework and student teaching, but rather through alternative pathways, such as Teach for America. These teachers develop very different professional identities, are more scripted in their teaching methods, and tend to be more anti-union; most do not see teaching as a career (M. Thomas & Mockler, 2018). Increasingly, school administrators also are being developed similarly through alternative pathways, such as New Leaders for New Schools, and many are from the Teach for America pipeline (Mungal, 2016). As we noted in the previous chapter, educational leaders increasingly are being trained in business schools. But is this a good idea?

Increasingly, school districts and charter management organizations are run by businesspeople, a trend we are seeing across professions. The corporatization of universities has been widely documented (Ginsberg, 2013; Slaughter & Rhoades, 2009) and actively promoted by business consultants (Beardsley, 2017), but educators may be unaware that the same is happening to hospitals.

> Today, less than 5 percent of America's roughly 6,500 hospitals are run by chief executives with medical training. Most hospital executive suites are disproportionately filled with lawyers or business-people. Indeed, the number of non-medically trained hospital administrators has gone up 30-fold in the past 30 years, while the number of physicians has remained relatively constant. Independent practices are also disappearing, as hospitals buy them up and put doctors on salary. The result for many physicians is the feeling that they are pawns of a big organization that does not want to hear, let alone, act on, their concerns. (Juahar, 2017, p. A23)

Yet, Juahar (2017) goes on to note that the top hospitals in the country are run by physicians (e.g., Mayo Clinic, Cleveland Clinic). He notes that "overall hospital quality scores were about 25 percent higher when physicians, not business managers, were in charge" (p. A23).

Of course, training teachers and administrators outside of universities is not new. The idea of preparing teachers and administrators in universities is fairly recent, and it is only since the 1960s that universities have trained the vast majority of teachers and administrators. Previously teachers were trained in normal schools, teachers institutes, teachers colleges, or even school districts, and administrators often were merely handed the keys to the building with the well wishes of the superintendent. Since the 1990s, there has been an explosion of alternative pathways to teacher and administrator preparation outside of universities, as well as increasing numbers of for-profit and online programs. M. Smith and Pandolfo (2011) report that since 2007, the leading producers of teachers in Texas are two for-profit online programs, A+ Texas Teachers and iTeach Texas.

As noted above, new policy networks have laid the groundwork for this shift, heavily funded by venture philanthropy. For decades, philanthropists such as the Carnegie, Rockefeller, and Ford Foundations have funded initiatives to improve the preparation of teachers and administrators in colleges and universities. However, in the past 2 decades, venture philanthropy has shifted toward supporting alternative pathways outside of universities for the preparation of teachers and administrators (Mungal, 2016; Reckhow, 2013). This support ultimately has resulted in legislation that opens up teacher education to a free market of nonprofit and for-profit operators, and in some states hardly any regulations at all.

Known as the "warm body" law, Arizona Senate Bill 1042 was signed into law in May 2017 by Republican Governor Doug Ducey, permitting "persons" with a college degree to bypass Arizona's regular teacher certification process to obtain grades 6–12 teaching certificates (Strauss, 2017). They should have 5 years of relevant experience, but "relevant experience" was not defined. In Arizona, charter school "teachers" were already exempt from state certification requirements. Since 2009, the Arizona legislature has cut school district capital funding by 85%, while it has increased charter school funds for capital purchases and facilities by 15% (Strauss, 2017).

Many of these alternative pathways, including Teach for America when it was created, were justified at times or in areas where there was a shortage of certified teachers. In the past, in such emergency cases, teachers often were hired on waivers and, like many Teach for America members, took coursework while they were teaching. But what may have started as a response to a teacher shortage, today typically becomes an anti–public school agenda. Teach for America, which has gone global, no longer claims to be addressing a teacher shortage.

In many cases, charter school franchises like KIPP are creating programs to train their own school leaders (Scott & DiMartino, 2009). While many of the alternative pathways initially had to collaborate with universities in order to obtain authority to certify teachers, most of them now can grant certification themselves (Mungal, 2015).

Section 2002(4) of Title II of the 2015 Every Student Succeeds Act (ESSA) encourages states to support independent "teacher preparation academies." The previous version of the law encouraged alternative certification programs within education schools, and in most states alternative teacher education programs were required to partner with a certification-granting institution. The new law also requires states to recognize certificates from these stand-alone academies, "as at least the equivalent of a master's degree in education for the purpose of hiring, retention, compensation, and promotion in the state" (ESSA, 2015, p. 115).

This legislation was strongly supported by, among others, the New Schools Venture Fund (NSVF), founded by social entrepreneur Kim Smith and funded by venture philanthropists John Doerr and Brook Byers (Horn & Libby, 2011). NSVF is a single node of a dense network of venture philanthropists promoting the privatization of teacher and administrator preparation.

While there are many legitimate criticisms of university-based teacher education programs (Friedrich, 2014; Labaree, 2004), Zeichner (2014), while calling for significant reform, defends it on the following grounds:

1. With over 3.6 million teachers, and with between 70 and 80% prepared in university programs, it is doubtful whether a free market of private programs could meet the capacity needs of such a large system. The emphasis of alternative pathways, such as Teach for America or the New Teacher Project, on attracting the "best and brightest" ignores the content of teacher preparation and the fact that we can't recruit all of the teachers we need from the ranks of elite colleges.
2. Shifting the preparation of teachers and administrators to a more school-based, clinical model runs the risk of merely reproducing the status quo. Nor do districts have the capacity to take over the preparation of teachers and administrators without a significant infusion of resources.
3. Countries that lead the world in educational performance have done so in part because of public investment in the preparation of teachers in colleges and universities.

Zeichner (2014) concludes that "the solution to the problems of college and university-based teacher education is to redesign and strengthen the system, not to abandon it" (p. 561). The new public-sector professionals are in part a product of the kind of professional preparation they have received, but, as we have documented throughout, they also are formed by new neoliberal policies and the ways these policies have transformed organizational management culture.

CONCLUSION

This chapter has provided an overview of those political coalitions and policy entrepreneurs, largely noneducators, that have formed dense state, national, and global networks to promote their neoliberal and NPM policies and practices. Not only do these networks have the goal of privatizing public education for either ideological or profit-driven reasons, but they also have privatized the public policy process itself. While ALEC is perhaps the most extreme example, the considerable policy influence of unelected wealthy individuals does not bode well for democratic governance. However, there is a growing movement to defend public education, which, while not as well funded as those funding privatization, has widespread grassroots support. In the next chapter we will focus on how education professionals are resisting NPM individually and collectively.

CHAPTER 5

Responding to NPM and New Professionalism

In 2014, the administration of Sacred Heart Medical Center in Springfield, Oregon, announced plans to outsource its doctors. Instead of maintaining hospitalists (doctors who work exclusively for the hospital and provide inpatient care), Sacred Heart would pay a physician services firm to staff the hospital. Outsourcing would be an opportunity to enhance productivity and efficiency, allowing the hospital to farm out a number of onerous responsibilities such as human resource management and the tracking of data related to physician performance and patient health outcomes (Scheiber, 2016).

Staffing companies tend to pay higher salaries and bonuses for hitting performance metrics, so outsourcing can be a boon for doctors' paychecks. But the doctors at Sacred Heart didn't respond the way hospital administrators had hoped. Bucking trends not only in medicine, but more generally in labor–management relations throughout the United States, the doctors announced plans to organize a union.

A union would enable the doctors, collectively, to negotiate for better terms on a number of critical issues pertaining to their work. Shift schedules and vacation allotments, for example, could be structured so as to ensure that doctors had sufficient rest and alertness for treating patients. Performance metrics could focus on the quality of patient care rather than incentivize doctors to see more patients each day. Additional doctors could be hired when staffing levels proved insufficient. Burdensome administrative tasks could be handled by non-medical staff. With more time to dedicate to individual patients, doctors could listen carefully to patients' narratives, build trusting relationships with them, and make informed diagnoses and treatment decisions.

Like the vast majority of doctors in the United States who report that their job satisfaction derives not from high salaries but from working conditions that are conducive to providing high-quality medical care (Brook, Friedberg, Chen, Tutty, & Crosson, 2013), the doctors at Sacred Heart bristled at the idea of management schemes that ran counter to their sense of professionalism. For many physicians, incentive payments, which have become increasingly prevalent under recent health care reforms in the United States, constitute a basic misunderstanding of physician professionalism (Herzer & Pronovost, 2014).

Physicians who oppose incentive structures often note that their medical decisions should be based on expert judgment and a set of ethics specific to their profession, not on the prospect of bonuses or profit-sharing agreements (Jain & Cassel, 2010). For the doctors at Sacred Heart, unionization would protect them against what they understood as a series of assaults on their professionalism.

Ultimately, the collective response of the doctors at Sacred Heart caused the administrators to back down; they would not outsource their hospitalists—at least for the time being. As of the beginning of 2018, the doctors are still organized and continue to fight for conditions that protect not simply their professional autonomy, but also the well-being of their patients—values they see as intimately connected.

Although the plight of doctors and that of teachers are by no means equivalent—substantial differences in compensation and the public's perception of their expertise are obvious—we share this story as an example of the way professional identity is being contested in other occupations serving the public good. As we have shown throughout this book, productivity, cost-cutting, efficiency, and accountability for quantifiable outcomes are among the most important virtues of the new professional under NPM, but not all public service professionals have accepted these uncritically. Many are pushing back, arguing that new professionalism and managerialism, left unchecked, pose significant threats to their occupational ethics and mission.

As we will demonstrate in this chapter, teachers and school leaders increasingly are engaging in forms of resistance. Beyond documenting the ways in which teachers and leaders are responding to assaults on their professionalism, we take a critical stance and consider the merits of various strategies in the context of the political and economic circumstances of our time. As we have shown in previous chapters, powerful new market- and audit-based forms of public management have influenced the emergence of a new professional. Therefore, resistance for teachers and leaders cannot look the same as it did under previous public bureaucracies.

A contemporary theory of resistance would have to consider the way education professionals make sense of, and negotiate, a complex ecosystem of federal and state policy, district mandates, venture philanthropy, policy networks, local advocacy groups, and market competition (Koyama, 2014). It would have to be clear about not only *what* and *who* are being resisted, but also *toward what end*. In fact, for some professionals, the term *resistance* might connote being "unprofessional" or uncooperative in their workplace, perhaps pointing to the need for new language (Gunzenhauser, 2007). With this in mind, we propose a new framework for resistance, one that may generate a new model of educator professionalism, capable of defending the democratic mission of a public education—a mission that has been more an ideal than a reality in the history of American public schools.

HOW NEW PUBLIC MANAGEMENT AND NEW PROFESSIONALISM BECAME THE NEW NORMAL

In Chapter 4, we noted one of the most insidious aspects of neoliberal reforms and New Public Management: their tendency to seep into our ways of thinking and doing things in such a way that we may not recognize how we are being normalized into a new "common sense." In other words, neoliberal ideology is "out there" in the sense that it is promoted by new policy entrepreneurs who are changing laws and economic policy, but it also is "in here" in the sense that it changes our relationship to ourselves and others: how we think about ourselves and others, what we believe, what we value and what we don't value (Peck, 2010). Building on this point, Stephen Ball (2012) argues that "neoliberalism gets into our minds and our souls, into the ways in which we think about what we do, and into our social relations with others" (p. 18). Ward (2011) makes a similar claim about managerialism, arguing that it is not simply a set of practices, but an accepted way of thinking: It is "the widely-held belief that all organizations can only work properly if decision-making is centralized in some manner in the hands of professionally trained and 'objective' managers" (pp. 205–206).

NPM is difficult to resist particularly because it appears in the guise of common sense, or in some cases, scientifically proven ways to govern and carry out the functions of an organization. In some instances, the evangelists of NPM characterize their reforms as attempts to modernize public organizations (Gunter, 2012), as if the reforms did little more than ensure that organizations adapted to our changing times. The problem with such views, however, is that the circumstances of the present—what we may consider "commonsense" realities—are themselves contingent products of political decisions and competing ideas and discourses about how society should be organized; they are far from a natural state of affairs (Howarth, 2010). Thus, any well-conceived effort to push back against NPM will require an exploration of how NPM becomes our new normal, how it taps into our deep frames (Lakoff, 2008), and how it informs our understanding not only of our institutions, but also of our *selves* within those institutions. For this purpose, we introduce a concept of power developed by Michel Foucault, the late-20th-century French philosopher whose studies of social institutions have influenced decades of research and critique in the humanities and social sciences, including the sociology of education (Ball, 2017).

Power and Norms

Foucault's concept of power is one of his most important contributions to postmodern philosophy and critique. Developed in his extensive historical studies of modern social institutions such as schools, factories, hospitals, and prisons, and of disciplines such as psychiatry, human sexuality, and political economy, Foucault's (1975/1995, 1976/1990, 1980) concept of power overturned conventional ideas of power as a top-down, repressive force that dominant individuals or groups possess and use to keep others in subjection. According to Foucault, the conventional understanding of power failed to account for the complex ways it functions in our everyday lives. Of course, sometimes power does appear as an expression of top-down force—for example, when a governing body enacts new legislation, or when police officers enforce a law on the street—but for power to be as efficient as it is today, Foucault argued, it has to function almost invisibly throughout the social body.

According to Foucault (1975/1995), this subtle form of power, which he called "disciplinary power" in his earlier work, operates in the social norms that guide people's behaviors; in the knowledge or truths they possess, seek, produce, or profess; and in the discourses they hear and recirculate. In his later work, as his concept of power evolved and he began to take on the study of global neoliberalism, Foucault would coin the term "governmentality" to signify the broad array of techniques through which societies and individuals are made controllable or governable—not only by the state, but also by markets and other institutions.

One of Foucault's central points about power is that we enforce it upon ourselves in the course of our everyday lives. Power does not require that a dominant person or group aggressively subdue others or place explicit demands on them; it is much subtler and more efficient than that. The structures and practices of our social institutions and the norms that guide people's production of knowledge (e.g., the scientific method) create a rather unassuming, relatively anonymous, nonviolent, and yet no less effective system of control. Within this system, people keep *themselves* in subjection, acting according to the demands of their roles and basic norms of conduct. In the context of an organization, for example, a supervisor need not look over an employee's shoulder all day to make sure the employee is doing what is expected. The employee has already been socialized into the norms of the organization and of the wider society, and also is aware that at any point in time someone *may* be observing and evaluating him or her (Foucault, 1975/1995)—whether directly through a security camera or indirectly through data analytics.

Some examples of disciplinary power and governmentality in education can be found in teacher evaluation systems and observation rubrics, school performance frameworks and ranking systems, and state-mandated curriculum standards. Each of these examples codifies a set of performance expectations for educators and their students, and while the expectations may raise questions and controversies when they first appear—for instance, when state officials announce that a new school performance framework will be mandated—over time they become part of our everyday understanding of the world, regulating our conduct and the way we think about problems in the field of education.

School leaders and other educators may argue about the fairness of specific elements of a school performance framework—for example, how some components are weighted in relation to others—and at times they may even be successful in convincing policymakers to make revisions, but often there are deeper norms undergirding these policies, norms that may remain unquestioned in the public discourse and taken for granted by individuals on both sides of the debate. In the case of school performance frameworks, one of the deeper norms operating in the debate is the idea that outcomes-based accountability (of the quantifiable sort) should be the chief mechanism of school improvement. Over time, it may become difficult even to imagine ways of improving schools that aren't centered on outcomes-based accountability techniques.

More recently, scholars in other fields have made similar claims about the power of norms. Political scientists who study the role of ideas in policy sometimes refer to these deeper norms as paradigms, demonstrating how they structure our thinking about public issues by defining the problems in advance and setting the parameters for what can be considered legitimate points of view (Mehta, 2010; Schmidt, 2008). Behavioral economists such as Daniel Kahneman (2011), and cognitive linguists such as George Lakoff (2008), use the term "frame" to describe the effects of ideas, and the language tapping into those ideas, on our perceptions. Some social psychologists studying political views have demonstrated that ideologies can function in a similar way to cognitive schema in that they can structure and bias our interpretations of what we observe and experience, usually without our conscious awareness (Jost, Federico, & Napier, 2009). This research helps to explain why, instead of revising our political beliefs according to available evidence, we often rationalize discrepancies between our ideological values and the circumstances we observe or experience in everyday life.

The following story may help to illustrate the normalizing power of ideas in public education. After 2009, the year in which the Obama administration introduced Race to the Top, standardized testing in K–12 schools was gaining unprecedented importance. Although central to the accountability reforms of NCLB, the role of testing was expanding from holding schools accountable to holding individual teachers accountable for their students' achievement growth from year to year. Increasingly, test scores would be used in teachers' annual evaluations and in decisions related to their compensation—highly controversial moves, but supported by enough policy entrepreneurs and policymakers at all levels of government to make them a reality. However, even the most ardent supporters of high-stakes testing had to acknowledge a seemingly insurmountable policy obstacle on the ground: test scores accounted for student performance in only literacy and math, and typically only 25% of the teachers in a given school district—elementary teachers and secondary math and English teachers—taught these subjects, leaving the vast majority of teachers unaccountable.

This policy environment offered mixed blessings to those who taught subjects like fine and performing arts. Many were seeing their programs reduced or even completely cut, especially after the financial crisis of 2008 and the budget cuts that followed. Yet many art and music teachers who still had their jobs felt shielded from the worst excesses of the accountability reforms since there was no way, short of tying their evaluations to math and literacy scores, to hold them accountable for students' test performance (although some school districts did end up tying all teachers' evaluations, regardless of subject, to math and literacy scores).

Between 2009 and 2015, I (Michael Cohen) worked in two school districts in two different states, New Jersey and Colorado. In each place, I saw curriculum leaders in the arts beginning to develop districtwide assessments for their subjects, based on an argument that had become common among them: It could be seen as an opportunity to "legitimize" their subjects, especially at a time when so many programs were being reduced or completely cut. It also was seen as a time to be "proactive." Rather than wait for the state to fill the gaps in the new testing policies, leaders and the teachers who joined them could be in the "driver's seat," creating portions of their own accountability system.

Accountability and testing would raise the importance of their subjects, some leaders and teachers claimed, both in the eyes of the public and within the schools themselves. As several teachers noted, it would be hard for math teachers to pull students out of their art classes to make up a math test (a common practice in many schools), since the art teachers would now be just as accountable for measurable student growth as the math teachers. Perhaps students also would begin to see the arts as having equal importance to math and literacy; it no longer would be a question of "non-core" versus "core" subjects, an old and disparaging binary that seemed to have made a comeback with the adoption of the Common Core.

To be fair, not all teachers of the arts felt this way, but these were commonly expressed sentiments among those who sat at the planning tables in both states where I worked. In this case, power operated implicitly as well as explicitly. Accountability mandates placed explicit demands on educators, but an equally strong, if not stronger, form of power operated on an implicit level. This was the subtle power of norms and discourse that caused educators to associate legitimacy and importance with test-based accountability.

Moreover, we can see the power of normative ideas at work in the tendency of the educators to see these moments as opportunities to be "proactive"—a commonly stated value in school leadership discourse—or in the "driver's seat," as some of them said. One needs to ask, was the test development initiative in the arts really a "proactive" decision, or was it merely a reactive decision in response to long-established institutional ideas and norms, such as the value of formal assessment, or the idea that leaders could defend the arts only if their classrooms and rituals looked more like those in math, English, or social studies? Could it be said that being "proactive" amounted to little more than being "reactive" to anticipated future policies? Considering the enormous expense, in time and money, that the arts-testing initiative required, were these leaders really in the "driver's seat," as some of them claimed? It seemed to me that if they were in the driver's seat, they were chauffeuring someone else around town.

Power, Identity, and Agency

The story above is but one illustration of the way power operates subtly in the institutions where we do our work. According to Foucault, however, power does even more than direct the behavior of individuals. In a sense—and this brings us back to an earlier point we made about NPM influencing our thinking—power *produces* certain kinds of individuals. Foucault (1980) argued that because of power, "certain gestures, certain discourses, certain desires, come to be identified and constituted as individuals" (p. 98). This is to say that power shapes our identities, the way we understand ourselves, our roles, and our relationships with others.

For example, in a public school district with open enrollment policies and an accountability system based primarily on test scores, the principal of a low-performing school may feel pressured to recruit high-performing students to attend her school. This principal will need to market the school toward parents whose children can help raise the school's test scores. In this situation, a certain type of school principal identity emerges: the principal as vendor. To a certain extent, she will have to think and act like a marketer, and some of her decisions will be based not only on what is educationally sound, but also on what will make the school appeal to families of prospective students.

Of course, educational soundness and marketing appeal will not always be compatible. Furthermore, parents develop new identities in this situation, increasingly seeing themselves as consumers of their children's education, shopping around the city for what they perceive to be the best product on the market. This may not be all bad, since parents can choose from options beyond their neighborhood school, and as consumers, if they are unhappy with a vendor, they are empowered to take their business (their per-pupil funding) elsewhere. On the other hand, consumerism does not always entail equity: Not all consumers have access to the best products, or even to high-quality information, disposable time, and other resources with which to shop around for the best schools.

And, of course, in a marketized system with accountability policies that value short-term results, principals will have more incentive to recruit the best teachers than to spend time developing the teachers who are already in their buildings. In the neediest districts, principals often are competing with other principals in the same district to attract the best teachers to their schools (Mongeau, 2015). A principal's recruitment of a good teacher from another low-income school may make her school better and help raise her school's test scores, but it merely moves a valuable resource from one classroom of low-income children to another. It does nothing to increase the capacity of the overall system. So the professional goal of improving education for all underprivileged children is converted into an individual concern for "my" or "our" school, and "my" or "our" test scores—often within the same city.

Over time, the marketized system we just described becomes an everyday reality, and as a result, its discourses and practices become taken for granted as norms or truths regarding what it means to be a school leader, a teacher, a student, a parent, and so on. With practice, the principal's identity as vendor and recruiter and competitive actor in a marketplace becomes the new normal (some may say it already is). Thus, it will not feel like an identity imposed by someone else or adopted under the coercion of a powerful system of policies; it will feel simply like the duty one must carry out in order to be a good school leader (and perhaps get promoted). As graduate degree programs in school leadership increasingly are offered in business schools, the coursework is beginning to include school marketing. This will further institutionalize the new normal and new professional identities.

But Foucault makes an important point about the role of individuals in creating the new normal. In saying that power produces individual identities, Foucault (1980) does not mean we are merely dupes of the system or automatons following someone else's orders, incapable of resistance in thought or action.

> The individual is an effect of power, and at the same time, or precisely to the extent to which it is that effect, it is the element of its articulation. The individual which power has constituted is at the same time its vehicle. (Foucault, 1980, p. 98)

In this view, individuals are not simply shaped by power and its normalizing effects; they also are responsible for the functioning of power. For example, the norms of leadership (being proactive, embracing change) or of educational testing ("if it really matters, we should be able to measure it") cannot function and circulate on their own; they do so only as people enact them. For Foucault, there is a positive implication here: If we are the vehicles of power, then we have agency to resist the norms, ways of speaking and writing, modes of thinking, and desires that make us up as individuals.

Although power produces new identities—of professionals, of parents, of students—and a new common sense, it cannot completely *determine* people's actions. According to Foucault (1987), all parties in a relation of power must possess agency, which includes the power to say no; otherwise, the relation is merely one of domination—like that of a master over a slave—and not of power. Hence Foucault's (1976/1990) oft-quoted words, "Where there is power, there is resistance" (p. 95).

To be sure, the doctors in Springfield, Oregon, whom we described in the opening of this chapter, engaged in a type of resistance, setting some clear limits on external attempts to control their professionalism. In organizing and questioning incentive policies, outsourcing, and other trends in the management of medical care, the doctors raised some public discussion about the ethics of the new normal, keeping it at bay for the time being. What would it look like for educators to claim more agency and begin shifting the power dynamics in their profession?

RESISTING NEW PUBLIC MANAGEMENT AND NEW PROFESSIONALISM

In the remainder of this book, we will explore how educators might address the challenges of NPM and create a new model of professionalism. The creation of a new model is a key point here. Teachers and school leaders who seek to defend their professionalism certainly need resistance strategies, each of which must be tailored to the circumstances at hand. Strategies of resistance that enable educators merely to work *around* NPM, however, will have a very limited and short-term impact. Resistance needs to be more than a refusal; it must be productive—that is, it must generate an understanding of public education that transcends market ideology and the audit culture. The resistance we have in mind would generate a *democratic professionalism.*[‡]

As we have demonstrated in previous chapters, the professionalism of educators has been under assault for several decades. However, many educators have not been willing to accept the new normal. There is an expanding body of evidence in the research literature and in the news documenting strategies of resistance that educators have used in response to NPM. Before we put forth our own theory of *productive* resistance, leading to a more democratic professionalism, we will examine the strategies of resistance that have been reported thus far, highlighting their strengths and limitations (G. L. Anderson & Cohen, 2015). We will show how these strategies, notwithstanding their real limitations, lay the foundation for a more comprehensive education movement, one based on new alliances of educators, students, parents, and communities (J. Anyon, 2014). Finally, we will show how such a movement, and the alliances it entails, would mark the most significant step toward forging the democratic professional in public education.

Teacher and principal resistance to NPM has taken a variety of forms, ranging from strategies that individuals use to cope with NPM and maintain the integrity of their professional mission, to more collective actions, like those of the physicians at Sacred Heart, in which groups of educators openly challenge the current state of affairs, or even work subversively toward progressive ends. The following three categories of resistance strategies constitute an attempt to identify the major forms of resistance and place them along a continuum from individual to collective acts (G. L. Anderson & Cohen, 2015). Artificial as categories tend to be, we find them helpful in conceptualizing the current state of educator resistance.

1. *Critical vigilance:* individuals' ongoing questioning, introspection, and critical awareness of competing interests that pose a threat to their professional identities
2. *Counter-discourses:* development of new ways of speaking and writing about public education, attempting to shift its narrative on a large scale
3. *Counter-conduct:* working subversively within the constraints of current policy and political culture

While critical vigilance tends to be a strategy that individuals use, it lays a foundation for the more collective strategies of counter-discourses and counter-conduct. We will discuss each of these in turn.

---

‡ Alfred W. Dzur also uses this term in his 2008 book, *Democratic Professionalism: Citizen Participation and the Reconstruction of Professional Ethics, Identity, and Practice*, which focuses primarily on professions in medicine, law, and journalism.

Critical Vigilance

Some have argued that developing and maintaining a critical stance, in and of itself, can be a form of resistance to NPM (Ball & Olmedo, 2013; M. Cohen, 2013; Herr, 2015; Leask, 2012). As we noted earlier in this chapter, power is not merely a prohibitive force; it is *productive* in the sense that it creates new identities that come to accept certain norms and their discourses with little, if any, critical questioning. Increasingly, for many new teachers and school leaders, NPM is all they have ever known, so as the years go by, it stands to reason that fewer educators will readily question its norms. Even those of us who began our careers prior to NPM, or those of us who have experienced the onslaught of market-driven reforms over the past 15 years, can become "disciplined" individuals. As such, not only do we begin to treat some norms as common sense or objective facts, but we also recirculate them, concealing over time the very power dynamics that produced them in the first place. In this sense, we are not simply the passive targets of power; rather, in policing and governing ourselves, we solidify the norms we live by. When individuals adopt a critical stance toward these norms, however, they are taking a necessary first step toward more active and even collective forms of resistance.

Critically vigilant professionals might question norms such as the following: that quantitative measures of student performance are inherently superior to other ways of determining the quality of educators; that market-driven competition logically will result in the improvement of individual schools and the overall system; that the chief function of schools is to produce human capital to ensure our nation's global economic competitiveness; that "good" schools or universities are the ones that outrank others in the local newspapers and other publications; that a principal's major responsibility with respect to curriculum is to find the best pre-packaged products on the market for instruction and assessment; that randomized controlled experiments are the most legitimate source of knowledge about education practices and their efficacy; and that public schools can reduce our society's income and wealth inequality, even in the absence of a robust series of social programs and policies. A careful critique would recognize these norms as culturally and politically constructed, inextricable from relations of power—not as natural or commonsense truths. It would recognize how these norms function as paradigmatic ideas (Mehta, 2010) that determine what is and isn't a legitimate claim about education.

Critically vigilant professionals also detect the political implications of policies. One of the achievements of NPM and of the broader system of neoliberal ideology is that they often appear apolitical. Whereas some debates about education are clearly political—for example, debates about the way a social studies curriculum addresses topics like American exceptionalism or the heroism of certain historical figures (Tumulty & Layton, 2014)—the basic principles of governance in NPM, such as the norms we listed above, often are depoliticized and closed to debate (Clarke, 2012; Fitzgerald & Savage, 2013).

Market-driven reform policies in education, however, are based on specific perspectives of the role of government in the provision of public goods—an inherently ideological or political question. Bates (2008) notes that under Thatcher in the UK, educators who questioned the new market-oriented policies, audit culture, and centralized curricula often were "characterized as subversive of the economy and driven by self-interest" (p. 197). It is as if the economy were something other than a human and political creation, driven by a set of natural laws that humans simply need to respect. An alternative vision of educators' resistance under Thatcher might argue that their own professional "good sense" (Gitlin & Margonis, 1995) made some of them question the "commonsense" truth that the purpose of public schools is to carry out the needs of the economy.

Because the policies of NPM often are depoliticized and presented as common sense, resistance needs to begin with educators' own critical thinking about NPM, especially in its everyday forms. This critical thinking renders explicit the methods through which NPM, or neoliberalism in general, has become embedded and normalized within our thinking. Resistance, then, means inaugurating a process of questioning the obvious (Ball & Olmedo, 2013), of recognizing the way educators' professional identities—including the very meanings of teaching and leading—have been redesigned within NPM. In this view, resistance begins at the level of the critical, reflective individual who is willing to engage in day-to-day micro-political struggles, always interrogating the relationship between oneself and one's organization (Thomas & Davies, 2005).

Ball and Olmedo (2013) refer to this critical stance as a "constant vigilance" (p. 94). Through an analysis of particular cases in which educators have resisted dominant discourses, they claim that at the moment when the teacher questions norms that seem binding,

> the power relations in which the teacher is imbricated come to the fore. It is then that he or she can begin to take an active role in their own self-definition as a "teaching subject", to think in terms of what they do not want to be, and do not want to *become*, or, in other words, begin to *care for themselves*. Such care also rests upon and is realized through practices, practices of critique, vigilance, reflexivity, and of writing. (p. 86, emphasis in original)

If, as Foucault claims, our identities are products of power relations, then resistance must involve questioning ourselves, questioning what NPM demands us to be. For the principal who is pressured to recruit high-performing students to her school, as discussed earlier, a critical vigilance would involve recognizing the way NPM constructs her as a vendor, and parents and students as consumers. It would involve questioning the educational and democratic implications of these role constructions, perhaps even considering alternative ways of relating to parents and students.

However, we need to acknowledge the risks that individuals take when they begin to question NPM and organizational identity construction, particularly when they voice their concerns publicly or shift their behaviors in unsanctioned ways. Such behaviors are viewed as "irresponsible" and identify those who refuse to conform to the expectations of NPM (Gillies, 2011). Ball and Olmedo (2013) recognize this as well, noting that "there are *costs* to be considered" (p. 94, emphasis in original). Such costs can include the stress and time it takes to maintain a critical perspective in the face of a constant barrage of demands in an audit culture. For example, teachers who recognize a conflict of values between the test-oriented curriculum required by their district and their own goals of promoting democratic citizenship and critical analysis may attempt to fulfill both district mandates and their individual sense of what counts as good teaching. In effect, they may find themselves teaching a "double curriculum" (Sondel, 2015, p. 301), which can be exhausting and unsustainable. And for some teachers, years of critical vigilance ultimately can lead to resignation from the profession—a category of resistant educators that Santoro and Morehouse (2011) call "principled leavers." At some point, these teachers see that their core beliefs about education and the ethics of caring for their students are simply incompatible with new policy programs and organizational expectations.

Furthermore, individuals can do only so much on their own. While some individual educators may feel greater security within their schools and districts—perhaps due to their longer tenure, the respect they enjoy within the community, or high performance on state tests (Thomson, 2008)—this kind of security among educators is an exception to the norm, and it is becoming even more rare as states repeal tenure laws or roll back the due process procedures for dismissal. Precarious and short-term employment, typical in private-sector organizations in neoliberal societies (Lazzarato, 2009; Sennett, 2006), has found its way to the public schools, especially among charter schools where teachers often lack union protections.

In addition to the dangers of speaking out on one's own, we also should consider whether the new professional has had sufficient opportunity to develop the tools of critique. A number of scholars have noted that teacher and principal education programs need to provide meaningful opportunities for preservice educators to take risks and question neoliberal assumptions (Costigan, 2013; Poole, 2008; Samier, 2013). Providing opportunities to question NPM, however, may be increasingly unlikely as non-university programs—sometimes located within school districts—funded by venture philanthropists offer alternative routes into teaching and leadership positions (Zeichner, 2014). These programs frequently recruit candidates with little or no professional experience in education, candidates who may bring a business orientation into the classroom or administrator's office.

There also may be an opening and closing of windows of opportunity to recognize that a process of normalization is occurring. For instance, there is a growing concern about a hyper-Taylorist use of metrics to control workers in a variety of occupations (Muller, 2018). Employers can now monitor every aspect of a worker's life and use these metrics to make decisions about hiring and firing. They monitor Internet use and emails and track employees' mouse navigation.

Telematics, a combination of telecommunications and informatics, monitors the behaviors and locations of UPS truck drivers every second of their day (Kaplan, 2015). Cashiers at supermarkets are being timed as they scan groceries and bag them for customers. And while such tracking may seem more apparent in nonprofessional occupations, teachers and other professionals are starting to experience these regimes of control. In some corporate settings (including central offices of some large school districts), employees get weekly reports detailing a variety of metrics culled from their computer and mobile device use, like the following ones I (Michael Cohen) was once surprised to receive:

> During work hours, you read 177 emails within 30 minutes of receiving them last week. That's 73.4% of emails read during work hours.
> You had the most focus time on Tuesday, December 1.
> You emailed in more than 74% of your meeting hours.
> Goals keep you motivated. Set them to track your progress.

While this level of surveillance and control is disturbing to many, at some point it may not be, especially when these practices appear relatively benign. For example, the tracking of employees' mouse navigation can help IT departments determine the best way to organize tools on a user's interface. Online curriculum mapping and lesson-planning software, which can open teachers' daily plans to an entire faculty and administration, also can make it easy for teachers to share materials and ideas. At some point, the surveillance will be viewed simply as the way things are and the way they just have to be.

There may be two points at which critical vigilance can lead to resistance. One is at the liquid transition point before normalization solidifies. The other may be at the extreme end of normalization, when the accumulation of techniques of control has become so thorough that behaving "irresponsibly" becomes the only ethical alternative (Ball & Olmedo, 2013).

If, as Foucault (1980) theorizes, individuals are the vehicles of power, then they are invested with power—not simply repressed by it. This investment makes resistance possible, and those individuals who are ready to question the very assumptions of NPM and examine their own subjectivities in relation to those assumptions (Ball, 2015) are indispensable to the project of resistance and of transforming the profession. J. Ryan (1998) discusses the need for school leaders to engage in a constant struggle against structures of domination, but he emphasizes that leaders also need to create the conditions for communal action. The key for leaders, J. Ryan (1998) argues, is to provide a space for the marginalized to have a voice, thereby causing others to question their own assumptions and actions, and to recognize that their assumptions are shaped by power. This is a far cry from a management culture that seems increasingly bent on silencing those who disagree with the leader's vision (Courtney & Gunter, 2015). Such dissenting voices, however, can play a key role in more collective forms of resistance, which we explore next.

Counter-Discourses

Those who through critical vigilance are able to penetrate the disciplinary practices of NPM are engaging in a kind of policy literacy by deconstructing discourses and practices. This is a remarkable feat, since the daily practice and the reinforcement of most professional training tend to discourage such literacy when one is trapped *within* both practice and discourse. Gee, Hull, and Lankshear (1996) state that

> immersion in such practices—learning inside the procedures, rather than overtly about them—ensures that a learner takes on perspectives, adopts a world view, accepts a set of core values, and masters an identity without a great deal of critical and reflective awareness of these matters or indeed about the Discourse itself. (p. 13)

For example, Lipman (2009) points out that even when some groups protest against neoliberal reforms such as school closings, they can reinforce a discourse of high-stakes testing by using the tests scores' upward trajectory to defend keeping the schools open. This is an understandable strategy, given the practical necessity of crafting a message that the intended audience will perceive as legitimate. Nevertheless, such a defense can have the unintended effect of further legitimating the prevailing ideas and discourse, which tend to define the problems of public schools as substandard achievement on tests and insufficient accountability. When the problem is defined in this way, the solutions tend to be limited to an array of efforts to raise test scores and dole out consequences. An alternative problem definition might call attention to a crisis of opportunity for low-income children and children of color, or of democratic voice and public deliberation in school governance and major policy decisions like school closings.

According to Luke (2003), "Educational policies are bids to centrally regulate and govern flows of discourse, fiscal capital, and physical and human resources across the time and space boundaries of educational systems" (p. 132). While the importance of fiscal, physical, and human resources is the bread and butter of policy analysis, until recently, less attention had been paid to the role of discourse. Controlling discourse may not directly determine events on the ground, but discourses often provide insight into the limits of what is deemed legitimate for discussion, or even doable, at a particular historical moment. Those who control discourses exercise a considerable amount of influence over social policies and the practices that flow from them.

Poole (2008) argues that teacher and leader preparation programs and professional development ought to engage participants in the development of authentic professional identities, separate from the discourse of managerialism that often is privileged within the institutions where they work. If school leaders are prepared to engage in discourse critique, they can become leaders of resistance and transformation at their sites. Ylimaki (2012), for example, studied school leaders who engaged teachers in close readings, or discourse analysis, of policy texts, encouraging them to formulate their own questions about the underlying assumptions of those texts. The participating principals and teachers noted that they developed "counternarratives" (p. 336) in response to policy texts that threatened their own work toward social justice. In these activities, some of the participants recognized for the first time that working toward equity for their students required them to be thoughtful readers of policy—indeed, modeling the critical thinking they wanted to foster in their students. Studies like Ylimaki's (2012) suggest that a bold leader can empower the resistance of others who may have lacked the necessary tools (or boldness) to question dominant narratives (Thomson, Hall, & Jones, 2013).

Up to now we have treated discourse as the equivalent of broad normalizing narratives, or what Gee (2005) calls discourse with a capital D. But counter-discourses that produce new narratives can be aided by changes to everyday language. While changing "Mrs." to "Ms.," or using hyphenated last names, did not eliminate patriarchy (and many women have reverted to using "Mrs." and taking their husband's name for pragmatic reasons), these changes at the level of language represented a challenge at the cultural level to patriarchal structures. And it is at the level of culture and consciousness that change must begin (Freire, 1970).

Mautner (2010), for instance, describes the many ways that the language of business has colonized the public and personal spheres, influencing the discursive practices of the latter. Between 2002 and 2013, the Bloomberg administration in New York City intentionally privatized many aspects of the public school system (Scott & DiMartino, 2009) and imported business language and practices in the process. Bloomberg created a "market maker" that turned the district into a series of networks and "vendors" to provide choices among a diverse array of "products" to "entrepreneurial" teachers and principals.

Elected largely by New York's low-income communities of color in 2013, the Bill de Blasio administration entered with a new counter-discourse, eliminating as much of the business language as possible and replacing it with the language of education and community: "community schools," "universal pre-K," "a tale of two cities," "inequality," and so on. At the same time, he started replacing with experienced educators most of the "boundary workers" with MBAs whom the Bloomberg administration appointed at all levels of the system. de Blasio also has been less inclined to create markets, support charter schools, or contract out services to the same extent.

While it often appears that discourse and ideas are controlled by elites such as politicians, corporate executives, and mass media outlets, political scientists note that large-scale changes in the way we think, speak, and write about public issues do not always follow a top-down process (Schmidt, 2008). Social movements, for example, are notable for bringing about shifts in ideas and discourses—and therefore institutions themselves—from the bottom up, although such shifts depend on a variety of factors: the effectiveness of the activists' rhetorical strategies, their timing, and the practical viability of the policies they propose, to name just a few. Change is possible because, while prevailing ideas and discourses certainly constrain us, they cannot determine all of our thoughts and behaviors. The very fact that people engage in critique of their institutions in their day-to-day lives is evidence that they are able to think outside of prevailing discourses. These discursive abilities enable people "to communicate and deliberate about taking action collectively to change their institutions" (Carstensen & Schmidt, 2016, p. 325).

According to Carstensen and Schmidt (2016), people can change their institutions when they combine collective critique with "strategic agency" (p. 323). Merely presenting empirical evidence of a policy's failure, no matter how extensive, usually proves insufficient in efforts to shift the ideas, discourses, and practices of an institution (Blyth, 2013; Carstensen & Schmidt, 2016; Lakoff, 2008; Schmidt, 2017). Witness the resilience of neoliberal ideas among people with diverse economic interests and racial/ethnic backgrounds (as we discussed in Chapter 4), even as empirical evidence paints a clear picture of the role these ideas have played in creating economic crises and wealth and income inequality (Schmidt & Thatcher, 2014). Witness also the persistence of accountability regimes and market-based school reform policies, despite mounting empirical evidence of their failure to bring about equal opportunity and close achievement gaps (Adamson et al., 2016; Lubienski & Lubienski, 2014). Evidence plays a key role for actors who want to disrupt the status quo, but as Blyth (2013) points out while describing the failure of the 2008 global financial meltdown to discredit neoliberal economics, facts alone cannot overturn ideology. When it comes to shifting ideas at the level of paradigms or deeper public philosophies, what often matters more than the facts is how the facts are interpreted, how meaning is constructed (Blyth, 2013). This is where counter-discourses play a role.

Resistance to discourses that have become ingrained, or that tap into our deep frames (Lakoff, 2008), requires sophisticated theoretical tools to disrupt what is taken for granted about public education or about what it means to be a good teacher or leader. Political actors who aim to discredit and replace prevailing discourses will need to convince others that they have the authority to do so (Blyth, 2013)—a steep challenge, given the way educators' authority on public education matters has given way in recent decades to think tanks, venture philanthropists, and corporations that stand to profit from school reform. Furthermore, counter-discourses and their strategic employment are a necessary but insufficient condition for the kind of collective action capable of reversing the worst excesses of NPM. In the following section, we discuss the way counter-discourses can lead to collective acts of counter-conduct.

Counter-Conduct

Critical vigilance and the creation of counter-discourses may set the stage for forms of counter-conduct, actions that either challenge or reappropriate neoliberal policies and practices toward progressive ends. There is a growing number of cases in which individual and collective efforts of teachers or principals have managed to do this (Costigan, 2013; Malsbary, 2016; Niesche, 2010; Palmer & Rangel,

2011; Picower, 2011; Sondel, 2017; Wood, 2011). Gleeson and Knights (2006) wonder whether, paradoxically, the excesses of NPM might have the unintended consequence of restoring professional power.

Sometimes, counter-conduct involves pushing back on, rather than reappropriating, NPM reforms. For example, university faculty have engaged in pushing back on narrow, quantitative evaluation schemes. Faculty at the University of Texas at Austin followed Georgetown and Rutgers in challenging contracts their administrations signed with a faculty-productivity company named Academic Analytics. Faculty members cited concerns "about the accuracy of Academic Analytics' data, the lack of opportunities for professors to correct errors, and the inappropriateness of numerical rankings for making complex decisions about people and education" (Basken, 2018, para. 3). The UT–Austin faculty council approved a resolution that the university make no use of Academic Analytics for tenure, promotion, salaries, curriculum, or other faculty issues.

But in public schools such pushback frequently can be risky, and too often teachers' unions, where one would expect to find pushback, have made accommodations with the administration or, as discussed in Chapter 2, have adopted an industrial unionism model limited to bread-and-butter issues. Sometimes reappropriation of reforms is more strategic.

Wood (2011), for example, describes how groups of teachers and a principal reappropriated a mandated collaboration model, a professional learning community (PLC), to develop their values of teacher-led inquiry and professional judgment in the face of policies that valued technical solutions to predefined problems. The teachers in this situation found a way to use their PLC for the dual purpose of improving test scores (as mandated by the state and district) and using inquiry-based data analysis to improve their instructional decisionmaking overall, beyond test preparation. The managerialist version of PLCs, which the teachers reappropriated, touted teachers' capacity for distributed leadership even as it had already defined the parameters of collaboration and the necessary outcomes. Such approaches often render teachers' inquiry into little more than a task of addressing a predefined problem (Herr & Anderson, 2008), but in this case, the teachers and their principal used the official discourse of forming a PLC to engage in authentic inquiry. In her discussion of the teachers' efforts, Wood (2011) noted that "although the PLCs described here were often constrained by test scores, they fought to teach for meaning rather than to teach to tests. Interestingly, their test scores went up anyway" (p. 495).

Notably, this work required a supportive principal who respected teachers as professionals, one who could withstand constant pressures from the district to implement PLCs in a scripted manner (Wood, 2011). Furthermore, the teachers and principal had to be willing to engage in a constant "uphill battle" (Wood, 2011, p. 494)—a potentially unsustainable state of affairs—as evidenced by the district's ultimate delivery of a set of basal readers, designed specifically for test preparation, that the teachers would be required to use. Thus, the principal and teachers would be in the position of developing yet another set of creative workarounds. We should question how long educators can reappropriate policies that increasingly run counter to their professional identities and missions. And we also should question how long educators can maintain professional identities and missions that are antithetical to prevailing ideas and policies.

Some research has explored the phenomenon of "third spaces" or independent communities of teachers from different schools who meet regularly to discuss and plan social justice curricula for their classrooms, develop their professional agency, and create strategies to challenge policies at the school, district, and even national levels (Picower, 2011; Quinn & Carl, 2015; Sondel, 2017). Although the teachers in these studies were expected to teach highly scripted, test-driven curricula, meeting outside their schools and districts gave them a chance not only to develop instructional plans collectively, but also to support one another in coping with unsympathetic colleagues at their schools and administrators who demanded compliance.

Sondel (2017) describes the way members of a democratically organized group of teachers can foster one another's critical vigilance, which can evolve into forms of counter-conduct and collective action involving community members as well as teachers. Her study focuses on the New Teachers' Roundtable in New Orleans, which provides a forum where teachers can examine issues of racial and economic justice in the public schools and "are inspired to take action with their students' communities to build a more liberatory education system" (New Teachers' Roundtable, 2015, as cited in Sondel, 2017, p. 2). Sondel notes that the members of this group, primarily White charter school teachers who were trained in non-university pathways such as Teach for America, intuitively sensed that something was wrong in their schools, where mandated practices promoted a deficit perspective of students and workloads were so overwhelming that there wasn't even time to reflect on their practice, much less voice concerns or pose critical questions about pedagogy to colleagues and administrators. And yet, Sondel (2017) writes, "[the teachers] were too exhausted or unsure of themselves to trust their intuition" (p. 8).

In the context of the New Teachers' Roundtable, however, the teachers began "cultivating the self-confidence, vocabulary, and analytic tools they needed to openly articulate their critique and condemn their experiences" (Sondel, 2017, p. 9). They also formed alliances with local activists, built relationships with community organizations, and deepened their understanding of the neighborhoods where they taught. These connections helped the teachers more readily recognize systemic racism and White privilege, develop a critical stance toward the messages of NPM, and plan strategies to integrate culturally responsive, student-centered, and socially just practices within their classrooms.

In Picower's (2011) study of an independent community of novice teachers working on social justice pedagogy, the teachers found that in the trusting environment of the group, they were able to share lesson plans and exchange the kind of professional feedback and critique that were missing from their schools, focused as they were on implementing mandated curricula. Taking a broader notion of critique, Quinn and Carl (2015) found that members of the Teacher Activist Group in Philadelphia developed their professional agency through "(1) facilitating efforts to alter classroom instruction, (2) creating opportunities for teachers to challenge educational structures, and (3) fostering a shared belief in the collective power of teachers" (p. 754). In groups such as these, teachers are engaging in counter-conduct that can extend beyond their individual classrooms and schools; they also are advocating for large-scale institutional change.

Often, however, counter-conduct may seem impossible in the context of data-driven, compliance-oriented schools, leading many educators to resort to performance. As Ball (2001) points out, in heightening our visibility, a culture of accountability tends to become a performance culture, one in which professionals use fabrication and gaming of the system to ensure that their work aligns with external accountability criteria. In a similar vein, Niesz (2010) describes a principal who seemed to do little more than promote the positive image of her school, hoping to prevent sanctions or closure due to declining test scores. There are real dangers in this kind of fabrication, including a counterproductive and time-consuming focus on managing images or impressions (Niesz, 2010), which can result in the psychic costs of living personally and professionally inauthentic lives (Ball, 2001).

One of my (Michael Cohen's) former colleagues, a charter school principal in a Colorado city, based his decision to become a school leader on the premise that, in such a position, he could find creative ways to work around the long list of unreasonable bureaucratic policies that plagued teachers and principals in traditional public schools. Essentially, he and his leadership team would reappropriate the policies of a market-based school choice system that, for the most part, had made him skeptical over the years. Although the pressure to post high test scores would be the same as in noncharter schools, he believed the autonomy afforded to charter school leaders would enable him to fulfill the school's mission of ensuring that students from the most blighted neighborhoods in the city would be ready for college—not just as test-takers, but as critical thinkers. He supported a teacher-developed curriculum that encouraged students to question prevailing ideas. He painted the words "Question Authority" on the walls of the main hallway—a clear distinction from the rather militant, corporate-run charter schools that had become prominent in the city. He created a school leadership team composed entirely of teachers, and following a head teacher model, he continued to teach a partial load of classes every year.

My colleague shared with me, however, that as the pressure to meet an unrealistic set of enrollment targets increased, he found himself spending much of his time boosting the image of his school to attract new students. Fearing financial insolvency, and worried that his school's image had been suffering for about a year, he felt pressured to budget $85,000 for a professional website for the school and additional funds for billboard marketing—money that could have been used for instructional materials. He claimed that these were "necessary evils" to keep the school open and carry out its real mission. At a certain point, a few months before he resigned, he questioned whether the "necessary evils" had themselves become the mission.

Constructing a positive image and reappropriating market-based policies become increasingly difficult in an audit culture that focuses more on student outcomes such as test scores than on inputs such as developing a relevant and motivating curriculum. And over the course of the past 15 years in the United States, austerity policies have caused states and their school districts to rely increasingly on private funders such as philanthropists and on federal grant programs such as Race to the Top and the Teacher Incentive Fund (TIF), which place their own demands on how schools should operate and how professionals should do their work. Grants from these sources include burdensome requirements for participating states and districts, essentially coercing them to adopt reforms that were designed from a distance in return for basic levels of funding.

The TIF program, for example, mandates that teacher compensation systems be based partly on quantifiable student growth measures such as test scores. These kinds of requirements not only increase the pressure on teachers and principals to meet performance targets, but also create additional financial obligations, as districts often need to purchase new data management systems and software packages to collect and calculate student growth scores and attribute them to teachers. Furthermore, although accountability structures like these focus chiefly on outcomes rather than requiring schools to adopt specific instructional or curricular programs, they necessarily limit the curricular choices educators can make, as not every approach to teaching and learning will yield the type and amount of data that the accountability system demands. As school districts throughout the United States see their budget deficits rise, they must seek these alternative sources of revenue, each of which has its own set of mandates and can place serious limits on forms of counter-conduct.

Furthermore, time spent creating strategies that appease policymakers can foreclose opportunities for educators to develop and maintain their critical identities. As we described above, the culture of NPM constitutes a complex system of power; the new professionals it creates and who serve as its agents are easily drawn into its tacit and self-sustaining claim that it is apolitical, common sense, and consequently outside the parameters of debate. We contend, therefore, that reappropriation may be a productive form of resistance in the short term, particularly in places where openings for such action still exist, but we need a more deliberate and collective strategy, one that digs deeper into our collective understanding of what it means to be an educator.

FROM RESISTANCE TO DEMOCRATIC PROFESSIONALISM

Each of the three major strategies we have discussed contributes an important vision of resistance, and, taken together, they lay a foundation for an evolved strategy of resistance to NPM. The continued reports of resistance strategies also should give us cause for optimism, as they demonstrate that many educators—principals as well as teachers—are not allowing their professional identities and missions to pass away quietly. Indeed, as Foucault has shown, norms and discourses are powerful, but so are the individuals who uphold and use them. Given the tools, conditions, and opportunities for critical thought and collective action, these very individuals are capable of creating new norms and discourses. In order to make this ambitious goal a reality, we need an overarching strategy of resistance. As we noted earlier in this chapter, such a resistance would have to be more than a refusal; it would have to be a *productive* resistance, productive in the sense that it would generate a new model of educator professionalism, one based on the democratic values of public education.

Specifically, we see a need—and a developing opportunity—to build a larger education movement, one based on new alliances of educators, students, parents, and communities (J. Anyon, 2014). Those involved in this movement—what N. Fraser (1990) has called counter-publics—would need to find a common interest in order to harness their diverse concerns regarding the high-stakes testing regime, school closings, mayoral control, the privatization of public services, and many other issues. A professionalism that promotes democratic values, that places the public good at its center, cannot be created in isolation from communities.

Figure 5.1 illustrates how a movement for public education would incorporate and build upon the other forms of resistance and advocacy, from the micro-level of individuals' critical vigilance and forms of coping with NPM, to more collective kinds of action that include explicit attempts to build counter-discourses and deliberate acts of counter-conduct. As we have seen, teachers and principals are beginning to challenge the various manifestations of NPM discussed in this book. When teachers, principals, parents, and students form a movement to defend the democratic mission of public education, policymakers may begin to act in accordance with their constituents' advocacy.

To be sure, NPM is not monolithic, and neither are professionals and communities. Some communities may support particular aspects of NPM based on histories of oppression under the old regime. For example, one can see why some parents in a low-income community might prefer charter school options—even the for-profit variety—in cases in which their zoned school is under-resourced and perceived as failing and unsafe. In such situations, a "boot camp" charter school where students wear uniforms and walk in straight lines could be attractive.

The fact remains that while public schooling for all and occupational professionalism may be considered ideals, they have not served all equally. This is why a new model of professionalism cannot harken nostalgically to the past. We propose instead a democratic professionalism—one that entails some elements of the old professionalism along with an activist orientation and a strong connection to the communities that professionals serve.

Figure 5.1. A New Framework for Resistance

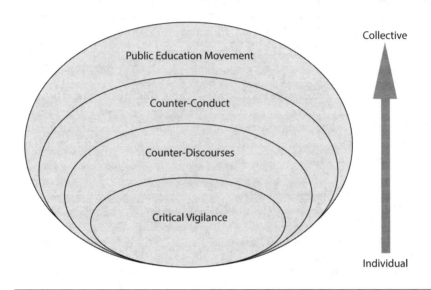

A framework for forms of resistance, illustrating the way a public education movement would incorporate a series of other forms, from the critical vigilance of individuals to increasingly collective actions.

CONCLUSION

In this chapter we have discussed the various strategies of resistance that teachers and leaders are using, from individuals maintaining a critical vigilance to collective efforts to shift the discourse of public education, reappropriate the policies of NPM for progressive ends, and advocate for broader, systemic change. While an ever-growing audit culture and marketized system can place severe limitations on resistance, the strategies we described in this chapter lay the foundation for a larger education movement, one that places the public good at its center. We contend that educators' role in such a movement will need to involve the forging of a more democratic model of professionalism. In the final chapter, we develop this concept of professionalism and show how it can build on some innovative practices that are already gaining momentum.

CHAPTER 6

The New Democratic Professional
Building New Alliances for Change

> It is . . . advisable that the teacher should understand, and even be able to
> criticize, the general principles upon which the whole educational system
> is formed and administered. He [sic] is not like a private soldier in an army,
> expected merely to obey, or like a cog in a wheel, expected to respond to
> and transmit external energy; he must be an intelligent medium of action.
> (Dewey, 1895)

This book has focused mainly on the "new professional" and the historical and political forces that are leading to the construction of a new entrepreneurial disposition. And yet, while we have seen the emergence of this new entrepreneurial teacher and leader over the past 30 years, we also have seen the emergence of a new democratic professional, one that is refusing to be deprofessionalized and depoliticized and is challenging the neoliberal and NPM forces we have described. As explored in Chapter 5, these teachers and leaders are busy creating "workarounds" to many NPM practices; forming study and activist groups; lobbying Congress; working through, and sometimes against, their unions and professional organizations for changes in district, state, and federal education policies; and building a broad social movement to change inequitable social policies.

Meanwhile, corporate reformers cast those who work in public schools as rigid "educrats" and hail markets and the private sector as more effective, efficient, and innovative than public institutions. Michael Bloomberg, the former mayor of New York City, who brought a corporate education model to City Hall, referred to 110 Livingston Street, notorious for its longtime bureaucratic governance of the district (Rogers, 1968/2006), as "the Kremlin." In Chapters 2 and 3, we attempted to debunk this notion that public schooling in the United States was designed by a cabal of socialist apparatchiks. Rather, as we documented, it was the brainchild of the same corporate sector that brought the corporate model to New York City under former Mayor Bloomberg.

This chapter will provide a discussion of the characteristics of a democratic professionalism in education as it is developing in real time in schools, districts, and communities. While we will present a vision of a new kind of democratic professionalism, we are not simply theorizing it or offering vague prescriptions. We will provide existing cases of this type of professionalism, drawing on existing examples of what classrooms, schools, districts, and unions can look like when teachers and leaders rethink what it means to be a professional educator. As the 2015 Every Student Succeeds Act rolls back some testing requirements, it may enable us to promote a professionalism more grounded in communities of practice, as well as advocacy for and input from school communities. On the other hand, greater state and local control can also lead to vast differences in how states approach school reform and curriculum, and in levels of investment in teachers and schools.

There is a growing number of accounts of school districts that have made impressive progress without adopting NPM, and these can serve as exemplars. For example, David Kirp, in *Improbable Scholars* (2013), describes a district (Union City, NJ) with a large immigrant population that largely rejected an NPM approach. The district patiently implemented strong internal accountability, investment in professional development and strong supports for teachers, and smaller class sizes, along with a deep understanding of the community, made possible in part because many of the teachers were from the area and had been educated at local universities.

Cuban picks up this theme in his book, *As Good as It Gets* (2010), which repeats his past critiques (Cuban, 1990) of the constant churn of reforms and consultants over decades and their failure to "trickle" into teaching in classrooms or create more equitable outcomes. Describing a decade of school reform in Austin, Texas, he contrasts the "effective schools and districts crowd" with the "improved schools and communities crowd" and argues that the Austin district represents what linking schools and communities can accomplish. However, he acknowledges that structurally little has changed in a decade. Post-*Brown* segregation has not budged, and students continue to attend schools tracked largely by class and race.

While Kirp is more optimistic, Cuban is wary, implying that unless we move beyond short-term, school and district improvement reforms, we will see at best small incremental, but unstable, changes at the classroom, school, and district levels. While hard to accept, the jury is in. Neither the corporate reforms that shaped the factory-model school, nor the idealistic and well-paid reformers of the charter management organizations, nor the cynical reforms of the profiteers will address the intractable inequities of our public school system.

The question we must ask now is, why has this decades-old endless cycle of restructuring, redesign, reculturing, privatizing, and profit-seeking resulted in, at best, negligible improvements and failed to address schools segregated by class and race? In fact, in the wake of gentrification and school choice, many urban schools are more segregated than the neighborhoods they are located in (Hemphil & Mader, 2015). As we noted in the previous chapter, a growing number of activist teachers and leaders are organizing for deeper, structural reforms both in schools and outside schools. Scholars are beginning to study the education industry infrastructure that is behind this churn of NPM reforms. Many of these scholars have been cited throughout this book. As autocratic "democracies" proliferate across the globe, social inequalities and anti-immigrant animosities soar, and citizens are retooled as passive consumers, professionals across all sectors will be called upon to stand up for basic democratic principles. What those principles are today in education in the context of NPM is the subject of this chapter.

Table 6.1 delineates the central characteristics of previous occupational professionalism (1950–1990), current organizational or "new" professionalism (1990–present), and a vision of democratic professionalism, which exists in embryonic form in many districts.

As noted in Chapter 1, we are not proposing a return to occupational professionalism or "taking back" the profession. The professionalizing of teaching was important, moving teacher preparation from normal schools, to teachers colleges, to universities. This trajectory moved teaching from being a "calling" for young unmarried women to a university-based profession. But the problem with nostalgically looking to the past is that the pre-NPM world of occupational professionalism in public education gets mixed reviews by most historians of teaching.

With notable exceptions, too many education professionals from the 1950s to today supported or tolerated the myth of meritocracy, institutionalized individualism, curricula and a teaching force that failed to reflect racial diversity, and, in low-income neighborhoods, schools tracked by social class, segregated by race, and under-resourced. In addition, teachers and principals, who were disproportionately White, were not immune from society's prejudices and often had lower expectations for low-income children and children of color than they did for middle-class, White children—an issue that continues to be a problem in too many schools (Howard, 2016; Rist, 1973; Valencia, 2010).

Neither a return to some golden age of old professionalism nor the new professional that is managed from above through NPM policies is a viable model for the kind of education that can promote the creativity and commitment required to help build a just and sustainable society. Both our former and current systems of education have provided a lower level education for those whom the economy views as surplus populations, destined to work in the low-wage service sector (J. Anyon, 1980; Labaree, 2012; Wacquant, 2016). The difference is that in the era of the post–World War II welfare state, there were more high-paying, unionized, manufacturing jobs for those who did not go on to higher education. In the face of increasing inequality and NPM policies and practices destined to normalize it, new democratic professionals will have to be responsible (although it may appear "irresponsible" to NPM reformers) on multiple tracks. They will need to be responsible professionals in their classrooms, schools, and districts, but also in their advocacy for social and education policies and practices that might produce, for the first time, a public education system designed by educators and the people it is intended to serve.

Table 6.1. Characteristics of Three Models of Professionalism

Dimension	MODEL		
	Professionalism (Occupational)	New Professionalism (Organizational)	Democratic Professionalism (Community-Based)
Professionals as workers	unionized (limited to "bread-and-butter" issues)	anti-union	social movement unionism
Principals' role	managerial, professional development	entrepreneurial, marketer	advocate, professional development
Professional regulation	regulated by the state	deregulated	regulated, but shared responsibility for standards
Professional assessment	by principal supervision	primarily by student test scores	peer assistance and review; more authentic assessments
Participation in governance	little shared governance	"distributed leadership" to build capacity	participatory governance
Professionals' demographics	largely White and middle class	largely White and middle class	should reflect communities in which they teach
Equity stance	color-blind as ideal	color-blind, paternalistic view of poor communities	advocate for racially diverse, equitable, and culturally responsive schools

Source: Adapted from G. L. Anderson and Cohen, 2015, p. 17.

CHARACTERISTICS OF A NEW DEMOCRATIC PROFESSIONAL

In this section, we describe a set of characteristics that provide a vision for a new democratic professional, a vision grounded in actually existing practices and policies that can be built on. While we use the term "democratic" professional, others have suggested other terms, such as "activist" (Marshall & Anderson, 2009; Sachs, 2000), "advocacy" (G. L. Anderson, 2009), "responsible" (Fenwick, 2016; Gunzenhauser, 2012), "dreamkeeper" (Ladson-Billings, 1994), "transformative" (Sachs, 2003), and "community/culturally responsive" (Gay, 2010; Green, 2017; Khalifa,

2012). While each of these terms contains an element of the kind of professional we propose, following Dzur (2008), Keith (2015), and Woods (2005), we use the term *democratic* because, more than anything else, we see NPM and market-based reforms as threatening the very public sphere that is necessary for democracy to be meaningfully exercised.

There are at least three dimensions to a democratic professionalism: inclusion, responsibility, and advocacy. Inclusion is perhaps the most obvious dimension of democracy, since it has taken us well over 200 years to provide Americans who were not propertied, White males with the right to vote. Even today, we find ourselves struggling to defend the Voting Rights Act from those who seek to once again restrict inclusion in our democracy (C. Anderson, 2018).

The Inclusive Democratic Professional

In education, inclusion can be viewed in at least three ways: inclusion in governance, opportunity, and the public sphere.

Inclusion in governance. First, inclusion refers to *inclusion in governance* and decisionmaking. The democratic professional must struggle with how to empower those who are not teachers or leaders with knowledge and a voice in decisionmaking. This is easier said than done as we have not figured out how to effectively create mechanisms for widespread participation by multiple constituencies. As Malen and Ogawa's (1988) study and subsequent studies have shown, school-based participation is difficult to achieve and sustain. School boards represent a democratic space, but have tended historically to be controlled by business elites, a trend that continues with heavy corporate funding of school board elections (Blume & Poston, 2017).

The notion of "distributed leadership" in schools has become popular, but while it has some promise for building organizational capacity, it is grounded not in democratic theory, but rather in social–psychological notions of distributed cognition. The idea is that information, tasks, and leadership should be distributed across a school. But while workplaces are being redesigned to expand teacher *work* and distribute it horizontally, *power* is being distributed *upward* by centralizing policy over curriculum and instruction through high-stakes testing, market discipline, and mayoral control.

As Evetts (2009) argues, the new teacher and administrator are put in a position in which they must look to market- and test-based forms of accountability for direction rather than their colleagues, professional training, associations, or unions. The ability of new digital technologies to integrate management information systems and standardize the labor process promises to intensify this tendency (Burch & Good, 2014; Selwyn, 2011). As we illustrated with our example in Chapter 1 of the inquiry group members who were encouraged to "utilize data" rather than engage with students, conception and execution have been successfully separated, leading to a proletarization of teaching (Apple & Jungck, 1992; Ellis, McNicholl, Blake, & McNally, 2014; Lawn & Ozga, 1987).

Given that teachers as professionals have a long history of being in conflict with their communities (Driscoll, 1998; Podair, 2002), advocating for a more participatory notion of professionalism in education may seem unrealistic. However, there is a growing body of research that has described how school leaders are taking a less school-centric approach to seeking authentic community relations by incorporating some of the research on community organizing (T. Green, 2017; Ishimaru, 2014; P.M. Miller, 2008; Shutz, 2006). Studies of leadership in social change organizations could contribute to this line of work (Ospina & Foldy, 2010).

While this literature attempts to expand leadership horizontally outside the school and into the community, some argue that this fails to address the ways more vertical, macro-level forces, as well as institutional discourses, negatively impact both schools and communities (Carpenter, 2015). This is why educators will have to work both horizontally for broader inclusion, and also vertically to advocate for social and educational policies, such as universal preschool, after-school and summer programs, and health and housing services that address the needs of low-income communities. Professionalization should not be in competition with community empowerment. Only a democratic professionalism can restore the agency of educators while also enabling communities to engage in collective deliberation—including debate and contestation—about what their schools should look like.

Inclusion in opportunity. Second, inclusion refers to *inclusion in opportunity*, which means moving beyond the right to mere access to education to being included in receiving an equitable, appropriate, and quality education. This sense of democracy links it to human and civil rights and *equal educational opportunity*. American public schools have long been viewed as a means toward individual social upward mobility, and yet schools also have provided members of the dominant classes with a variety of means to ensure they stayed ahead of everyone else. In the early decades of the 20th century, for example, while expanded access to comprehensive high schools provided new opportunities to the working class, members of the middle class who already enjoyed access lobbied for tracking within the high school in order to maintain their own advantage (Labaree, 2010).

In Chapter 2 we discussed the way White northern philanthropists designed a strictly vocational education for Black students in the segregated South—providing just enough education to ensure that Black students would support the nation's growing economy, but too little for them to compete with White workers for higher paying jobs (Watkins, 2001). More recently, between the 1990s and 2010, as the State of California implemented an algebra-for-all initiative for its 8th-graders, economically advantaged parents were able to convince leaders in a number of schools to establish new advanced opportunities in geometry for their own children (Domina, Hanselman, Hwang, & McEachin, 2016). This combination of detracking and tracking up illustrates a phenomenon known as "effectively maintained inequality," whereby initiatives to expand opportunities often will be followed by efforts of some to "maintain their advantage by creating new meaningful distinctions" (Domina et al., 2016, p. 1236). Reeves (2017) refers to this broader social tendency as *opportunity hoarding*.

How do we ensure that in our public schools, opportunities are distributed equitably among all members of the public? Professionals who foster inclusion in opportunity, who are aware of the persisting and sometimes increasing inequities in public schools, work to change these conditions. They are aware of disparities in the way children of different races and genders are suspended from school for the same infractions; of the prevalence of zero-tolerance policies and greater police presence, rather than restorative justice practices, to manage student behavior in schools that serve predominantly children of color; of the lack of adequate services and bilingual and dual-language programs for English language learners; and of the use of test-driven, unengaging, and narrow curricula, often stripped of art, music, physical education, and whole-child instruction, in schools in low-income communities. Democratic professionals support the redress of these and other disparities, and they work to implement a culturally responsive curriculum and pedagogy, one that sees students, their families, and their communities from an asset-based perspective.

Inclusion in opportunity requires that education professionals ask questions like: To what extent is our school racially and socioeconomically segregated? Are some groups of students over-represented in special education? Are some groups under-represented in gifted and talented programs or in honors, advanced placement, and International Baccalaureate classes? Are some students getting suspended more than others? Are the students in advanced classes reaping an exorbitant share of benefits, such as weighted grade point averages? Are some groups of students taught predominantly by the least experienced teachers? Are all students receiving adequate support and guidance in the college application and financial aid processes? Are some families being pushed out of the neighborhood by gentrification? Do all families feel welcome in the school? How might economic, social, and cultural capital be more evenly distributed in schools and in society? In collecting the data to answer these kinds of questions about their schools, democratic professionals have a heightened sensitivity to problematic correlations between demographics and performance indicators. For these professionals, such correlations prompt further investigations of the distribution of opportunity in their schools and districts.

Equitable distribution of opportunity also would involve efforts to diversify the teaching force. When a teaching position opened in their school, democratic professionals would focus their recruitment in places where they were likely to expand the diversity of their applicant pool. If there is a local university with a teacher education program that prepares a diverse pool of candidates, school and district leaders might forge partnerships with the university to develop pipelines for candidates of color from college through student teaching and employment. Democratic school leaders would prevent the use of unnecessary and artificial constraints in hiring processes—constraints that may filter out minoritized candidates, whether intentionally or not. To the extent possible, such leaders would ensure that interview committees were composed of diverse teachers and other stakeholders, recognizing that our implicit biases often cloud our evaluations of job candidates who look and sound different from ourselves.

Democratic professionals also would recognize that efforts to recruit and select teachers of color can take us only so far; we also need to retain such teachers. This means our schools must be hospitable places for diverse backgrounds and perspectives. District leaders who acknowledge this need are aware that teachers of color in a predominantly White teaching force may face additional challenges in their induction and might benefit from support systems to ensure their success. And these supports would be combined with redoubled efforts to improve the inclusiveness of the school community.

Inclusion in the public sphere. Third, inclusion refers to *inclusion in the public sphere*, leading to the question of what it means for a school to be "public." A school is "public" not merely because it receives public funds, but rather because it is responsible and responsive to the public and works to foster a democratic public sphere in which an educated polis can deliberate on the issues of the day. It means that democratic professionals have a strong public ethos and a commitment to a social common good. If we are part of the "public," then we relate to public schools as citizens, not as consumers. This confusion is endemic in our society, as markets and choice are being presented as replacements for political democracy (Chubb & Moe, 1990). It is only through the fostering of democratic citizenship and a democratic, public sphere that we, as citizens, can hold both the state and the market accountable (Westheimer, 2015).

As we have documented in earlier chapters, in materially and discursively undermining public schooling and teachers in the United States, corporate leaders and the think tanks they fund have diminished our trust in public institutions (Wilkinson & Pickett, 2010).

It is also true that in a country that was founded by propertied, White men who disenfranchised women, non-Whites, and the poor, we sometimes have given our public institutions far more trust than they deserve (see Rothstein, 2017). And yet, over time and through democratic social movements, we have struggled to expand social justice. While our public schools are segregated by race and class, they are also the spaces in which, at least at the discursive level, children are exposed to ideals of gender and racial equality, discourses they may be less likely to encounter at home, in their religious organizations, or in the media.

Public schooling is the one institution that represents a collective, social, human project in a sea of individualism and self-interest. In this age of Match.com, home schooling, and gated communities, many public schools are "contact zones" in which students are thrown together who otherwise would not come into contact. While too many schools are stratified and segregated by class and race, we have policy mechanisms that could make them less so. Although imperfect, experiments with magnet schools and controlled choice have helped to better integrate schools in some districts, such as Cambridge, Massachusetts, and Wake County,

North Carolina (Willie, Edwards, & Alves, 2002). Integration of students from diverse backgrounds in public schools, when it has been accomplished, may very well be the greatest achievement of public schooling in the United States; it is also, in part, what common schools originally were designed to do (Labaree, 2010). As many give up on integration and return to aspirations of separate but equal, we are likely to end up merely separate and unequal.

The defense of public schooling is even more important in the context of the digitalization of education, which has the potential to further isolate students, while depersonalizing interactions and relations, increasing the pressures for individual accountability and performativity, and reinforcing managerialist reforms. Selwyn, Nemorin, Bulfin, and Johnson's (2017) ethnography of technology use in three high schools confirmed many of these fears, yet they believe that technology can be integrated more effectively into brick-and-mortar schools, rather than abandoning them for virtual schools. This would require that schools lead with progressive values rather than managerial ones.

> So if we are at odds with the conditions to be found in the contemporary "digital school" then what alternatives might there be? How could digital technologies be used to counter rather than compound dominant cultures of inequality, competitive individualism, performativity and/or exploitation? What would meaningful, respectful and/or pleasurable forms of digital schooling look like? What forms of digital tools, techniques and practices would be required to empower otherwise subordinated groups? These are all questions that need to be acknowledged and addressed as the digitalization of schools and schooling continues. (p. 174)

While we call for defending the concept of the "public," we can't expect those whose children languish in mediocre and segregated schools to defend an ideal, while their children suffer. In such cases, a single mother seeking the limited options of private and charter choices provided to her might make good individual sense (Pedroni, 2007). But market systems in the aggregate will always favor the economic, cultural, and social capital of the privileged. It was through strong public investment in public schools and higher education, strong unions, and progressive public policies that working-class Americans were lifted into the middle class under the welfare state of the post–World War II years. While these policies disproportionately favored White Americans, this strong public sector, coupled with the civil rights movement, also led to the emergence of a significant Black middle class, a process that stalled with the neoliberal policies of the 1980s (Wilson, 1997).

Responsibility and the Democratic Professional

While inclusion is a key dimension of the democratic professional, a second dimension, which is often confused with accountability, is responsibility. Professions originated as a contract of trust between society and occupational groups—what sociologists have called the "social trustee" model of professionalism (Dzur,

2008). In this model, professionals enjoyed autonomy, status, and self-regulation in exchange for upholding professional integrity and responsibility that included an ethos of service to the public, ethical and moral rectitude, and rigorous and high-quality professional practice (Sullivan, 2004). As productivity, cost-cutting, efficiency, and accountability for quantifiable outcomes have become the most important virtues of the new professional under NPM, public-sector professionals are beginning to experience more acutely the ethical and moral dilemmas inherent to professional life.

Teachers and leaders who view themselves as democratic professionals consistently ask questions like: *To whom* am I responsible? *For whom* am I responsible? What are the democratic implications of my actions? What is the professionally responsible thing to do in this situation? Such questions proceed from a responsibility ethic rather than a purely outcomes-based accountability orientation.

Principals who see themselves as accountable mainly for achieving high test scores will feel pressured to find the most efficient means toward this end, even if it means scheduling less time for untested subjects, being concerned less about the quality of students' social interactions than about their latest interim scores, grouping students by perceived ability, and generally "gaming" the system. In a system that fosters a democratically responsible orientation, principals would first consider the needs of students, their families, teachers, and the community, without subordinating these needs to the achievement of a set of numeric targets. Such principals would not determine these needs on their own, but would work with stakeholders to identify and understand them.

The current system of outcomes-based accountability often prevents educators from taking responsible action. Biesta (2004) points out the irony of outcomes-based accountability systems:

> At first glance, there seem to be opportunities for a more democratic "face" of accountability, based as it is in the relationship between parents and students as "consumers" of education and schools as "providers." I contend, however, that such opportunities are foreclosed by the fact that there is no direct relationship of accountability between these parties, but only an indirect one. (p. 240)

Accountability, Biesta (2004) argues, is direct only between the school and the state and abstract market forces, and it focuses primarily on the extent to which the school is meeting performance targets and attracting and retaining students. Parents, students, and communities are left out of this direct relationship of accountability, functioning only as consumers who make choices among an array of available products, "but who do not have a democratic say in the overall direction or content of what is being delivered (if delivery is an appropriate concept in the first place)" (Biesta, 2004, p. 239).

In a system that fosters professional responsibility toward the public—as citizens, not as consumers—parents, students, and communities would be engaged in the normative questions of what the curriculum should include, what the budget ought to prioritize, what public schools should set out to accomplish, and the like. In the current system of outcomes-based accountability, these questions have already been decided without democratic input from the very people whom the public schools are intended to serve.

Feeling responsible *for* and responsible *to* others also entails the ability to see people as ends in themselves. Although a professional who sees other people as means toward ends may still seek their input and participation, the motivation for including them will often be limited to getting their "buy in," securing their commitment to implement a predetermined plan, and sometimes boosting their morale. A professional who feels responsible *for* and *to* others will be motivated to include others simply because they matter. As Keith (1996) has put it, "Participation is an ethical imperative, rooted in the fundamental human right of agency—the power to work collectively and interdependently with others to co-construct our world" (p. 50). In this sense, responsibility *for* and *to* others implies an authentic sharing of power and authority.

But as noted in the previous chapter, it is hard to be responsible if we are engaging in what Foucault (1975/1995) called "disciplinary practices" that, in the aggregate, become governmentalities (G. L. Anderson & Grinberg, 1998; Fournier, 1999). In other words, professionals' "mentalities" are governed or disciplined by deeply embedded norms that minimize their resistance or dissent. Dissent, for the disciplined professional, is considered "unprofessional." And it is even harder to be responsible when we are disciplined by things like tests instead of human supervisors. Fenwick (2016), using a sociomaterial approach, examines nonhuman elements, such as standardized tests or software algorithms, as social actors that are intimately tied up with the ways professionals make decisions and are governed.

As we increasingly live in "code space" and algorithms make decisions that professionals used to make, professionals are struggling to retain a sense of professional responsibility and ethics. We saw this in Chapter 3 with the disembodied algorithms that spun out of control on Wall Street, contributing to its implosion. Big data and digital education require that democratic professionals take control of these governing technologies and insist that they serve the interests of citizens and professionals, not those of the profit-seeking corporations that produce them. This need for professionals to push back against policies and practices that do not promote the interests of students, leads us to the third dimension of the democratic professional: advocacy.

The Democratic Professional as Advocate and Activist

As we noted in Chapter 1, historically, there have always been teachers and principals who have seen themselves as part of larger social justice movements (Johanek & Puckett, 2007; L. Johnson, 2017; Siddle Walker, 1996). Today, education professionals confront many of the same social problems of poverty, gender and racial discrimination, segregation, anti-immigrant sentiments, and homophobia. But they have the added concerns of the ways privatization and NPM undermine their professional judgment. Reversing this trend and forging a new, more democratic professionalism will require that teachers and leaders be part of a network of public-sector democratic professionals struggling to form a social movement locally, nationally, and globally.

This may seem daunting, but there is already a proliferation of teacher, parent, student, union, and principal movements against high-stakes testing, school closings, gentrification and displacement, racism, deportations, fiscal inequities, disinvestment, large class sizes, zero-tolerance discipline, Islamophobia, bullying, sexual harassment, privatization, corporate influence, for-profit education, militarization of schools, vouchers, charter co-location, and much more. There are many examples of teachers, principals, and superintendents who are leading these movements. They currently include educators such as Mike Matsuda, John Kuhn, Jamaal Bowman, Carol Burris, Karen Lewis, Anthony Cody, Natalia Ortiz, Rosie Franscella, and Jose Vilson, and tens of thousands more whose names have not appeared in the media.

Education activist organizations, such as the Badass Teachers Association, Teachers for Social Justice in Chicago, The Network for Public Education, and the New York Collective of Radical Educators, have been building national as well as local coalitions among school professionals, families, students, and community groups, often using social media to expand their reach, exchange ideas, and organize campaigns with allies. They are raising awareness about the perverse effects of privatization, profit-driven schooling, and school reform policies that are focused myopically on punitive accountability and marketization. They are also developing social justice and anti-racist curricula, sharing resources to help educators create more inclusive school communities, and pressuring policymakers to fund public education adequately and equitably.

Sachs (2000, 2003) has studied the effects of NPM in Australia and found that professionals are faced with two possible responses to what she calls the "audit society": "to act as an entrepreneurial professional, placing one's career goals at the center, or as an activist professional, promoting the welfare of children at both the individual and collective levels" (Sachs, 2000, p. 77). She provides a strong argument for rethinking professionalism as moving beyond the individual and seeing it as a bottom-up struggle against reforms that deprofessionalize.

As new education professionals who are committed to advocacy both within and beyond the school attempt to bring about progressive change, they can expect to encounter resistance from those who see their privileges threatened (Hynds, 2010; Star, 2011; Theoharris, 2007). They also will encounter a micro-politics of self-interested resistance from some teachers who will not be willing or able to push beyond their professional comfort zone (Payne, 2008). After all, teaching traditionally has been characterized as a conservative and apolitical profession (Lortie, 1977). But through growing principled acts of "irresponsibility," "infidelity," and collective counter-conduct, more teachers and principals are rejecting the tenets of NPM and the new professionalism that it has produced (Achinstein & Ogawa, 2006).

The good news is that activist professionals don't have to reinvent the wheel. There are many current practices and policies that hold promise for reworking school reform around policies that reprofessionalize teachers and leaders, while empowering communities. In the following section, we will provide an overview of those policies and practices that in the aggregate might allow the new democratic professional to thrive.

BUILDING ON EXISTING DEMOCRATIC PRACTICES AND POLICIES

With a businessman in the White House, an anti–public education advocate heading the Department of Education, and daily attacks in the media on public-sector professionals, including teachers, there are many calls to action, but few concrete proposals that have gotten much traction. However, since the passage of the No Child Left Behind Act of 2001, some efforts have been made to reframe NPM discourse. For instance, in 2008, the Forum for Education and Democracy released a report, *Democracy at Risk: The Need for a New Federal Policy in Education*, written by prominent educators and policy experts. The report not only documented the ongoing deterioration of America's schools on the 25th anniversary of the 1983 *A Nation at Risk* report, but suggested that we are on the wrong road to improving them. "While other countries are making strategic investments that have transformed schooling and produced results, we have demanded results without transforming schooling" (Darling-Hammond & Wood, 2008, p. 2).

Another attempt to provide a vision for the future is Hargreaves and Shirley's (2009) advocacy for a "fourth way." They describe aspects of Finland's successful reforms and promote an approach that retains some current aspects of reform while promoting a more democratic professionalism. G. L. Anderson's (2009) book, *Advocacy Leadership*, also presents the elements of what he calls a post-reform agenda. Many of the attempts to move beyond critique to a new vision or agenda were based on the assumption that the current reforms were not succeeding and that the opportunity to change the reform paradigm was imminent. Ten years later, while there has been some small pullback on excessive high-stakes testing, market reforms and privatization actually have grown.

While the paradigm of NPM has shown little empirical evidence of success, even on its own terms, it has been propped up by the powerful and well-funded policy networks we described in Chapter 4. Neoliberalism and NPM are resilient and have shown an incredible ability to absorb resistance and new practices and policies into their framework (Mirowski, 2013). Once a promising and potentially progressive practice (formative assessments, professional learning communities, culturally responsive teaching, common core, etc.) gains some traction, an army of consultants and companies descend on school districts to sell their increasingly digital wares. Some of these may be worth purchasing, but education practitioners are accosted almost daily by a dizzying array of individual and corporate profit-seekers. The challenge then goes beyond merely *adopting* the democratic practices that we propose below to the problem of *enacting* them in a way that provides agency for teachers and leaders to do so authentically (Braun, Ball, & Maguire, 2011).

It is also true that new democratic practices can open up authentic spaces and develop even in the context of dominant NPM policies. Change is often messy and uneven, and sometimes a paradigm shift is the result of a tipping point being reached or interest convergence. For instance, the ongoing work of activists and authors such as Angela Davis and Michelle Alexander has helped to change public opinion about U.S. incarceration rates, while at the same time, states are strapped for funds and no longer able to sustain the high costs of incarceration. Kingdon's (1984) notion of policymaking as the confluence of multiple streams of actors, policy, politics, and windows opening and closing remains a powerful description of how policy change often occurs as interests converge. As Bell (2005) warns, however, in the context of African Americans, the interests of the less privileged are typically sacrificed to the interests of the more privileged.

So while the policies and practices we recommend here are still not dominant and could be commodified and stripped of their democratic potential, they could become part of a new paradigm that is emerging in a the shadow of NPM. Sachs (2003) made this case a decade and a half ago as she saw both an old professionalism and an emerging new one existing side by side. The extreme levels of degradation of teachers' salaries and labor since 2008 may be creating conditions in which teacher activism is reaching new levels.

The list of promising policies and practices we describe below is not exhaustive, but we have tried to address those areas in which alternatives already exist. If space permitted, we could also discuss progressive reforms like controlled choice (Willie et al., 2002), critical civics education (Biesta, De Bie, & Wildemeersch, 2012; Westheimer, 2015), teacher-led cooperative schools (McGhan, 2002), dual-language schools (Steele et al., 2017), AVID programs (Mehan, Hubbard, & Villanueva, 1994), and several more. Internationally, the citizens' schools and the Landless Workers' schools in Brazil (Gandin & Apple, 2012; Tarlau, 2013) and the bachilleratos populares (people's high schools) in taken-over factories in Argentina (Mendez, 2003) represent education movements from below that have opened up "third spaces" where a different kind of education can take place.

We will begin with the community schools movement, which seems to have galvanized some education and community activists, as it has the potential to shift the dominant cognitive frame from choice and testing to resourcing and valuing communities and addressing those out-of-school factors that result in poor achievement for low-income children (Berliner, 2009).

Community Schools

The concept of community schools is not new; it can be traced back to early 20th-century notions of American public schools as community centers and social welfare agencies, ranging from the largely paternalistic efforts of White philanthropists seeking to socialize immigrants in poor urban neighborhoods to the development of schools as vibrant community hubs integral to daily life in segregated African American neighborhoods, where community members struggled for local control and collaborated to provide high-quality education and other social services to residents (J. D. Anderson, 1988; S. Cohen, 1964). Advocates of community schools today see the public school as a full-service agency that not only provides a high-quality education for students, but also supports the well-being of families and their neighborhoods. Although community schools have principals, they typically are governed collaboratively by a site leadership team that includes teachers, coordinators of services, and representatives of families and community-based organizations.

There has been a recent resurgence of interest in community schools among advocates for an equitable and socially just public education. The model of a community school is rather flexible and is meant to adjust according to the needs of particular communities, but researchers have identified "four pillars," or common components, of such schools. In a review of 143 empirical studies of community schools' outcomes, Maier, Daniel, Oakes, and Lam (2017) note that such schools tend to have the following four features:

1. Integrated student supports (e.g., physical and mental health services, housing specialists, legal services)
2. Expanded learning time and opportunities (e.g., year-round schooling, after-school care and enrichment, preschool programs)
3. Family and community engagement (e.g., partnerships with families and community-based organizations to support students' learning, collaboration with community organizers, parent leadership development, adult literacy, and English language classes)
4. Collaborative leadership and practice (e.g., site leadership teams composed of multiple stakeholders, teacher learning communities, union–management partnerships)

While it takes several years to develop each of these four pillars, Maier et al. (2017) present a strong body of quasi-experimental and qualitative evidence that community schools can achieve impressive outcomes in academics, social and emotional well-being, student attendance and engagement, and overall school climate. Maier et al. (2017) also note that some community school programs are making progress in closing racial and socioeconomic achievement gaps. Addressing the barriers to learning that children in low-income neighborhoods and communities of color face, community schools offer a model of school improvement and public accountability that is strikingly different from managerialist practices such as top-down, punitive forms of accountability, use of prescriptive standards-based curricula, and market-based competition.

As we have shown throughout this book, managerialist reforms often take as a given that certain principles of management can be applied to any organization, public or private, to make it more efficient and effective. Such reformers often imply that school-based factors can compensate for, or even neutralize, the effects of poverty and other out-of-school barriers to learning. Some managerialist reformers go as far as to say that to evoke external factors such as poverty is to make excuses for poor academic performance.

Community schools, on the other hand, suggest that the dichotomy of school-based versus out-of-school factors is a false one. They suggest that education professionals *can* make a measurable and positive difference, but only when working in concert with families, communities, and other public service professionals. Crucially, as Maier et al. (2017) note, family and community engagement (pillar 3) extends well beyond keeping families informed and inviting them in for parent conferences and other school-based events. In community schools, parents and other family members have a seat at the leadership table and are involved in decisions concerning important matters such as the budget and school improvement plans. Some research has demonstrated that meaningful involvement of families and community-based organizations, while initially challenging to implement, can help "repair long-standing distrust" among education professionals, community-based organizations, and families (Maier et al., 2017, p. 59).

The community schools model offers a promising vision of reform in part because it pushes the boundaries of current concepts of public educator professionalism. It is clear that a school that focuses on the four pillars identified above must demand a certain kind of teacher and school leader, one who builds and maintains alliances with multiple stakeholders—most important, with the very people who are supposed to benefit from public schooling. What would such a professional look like?

The Coalition for Community Schools, a prominent network of advocates for the model, offers a variety of toolkits for education professionals and policymakers on its website. Several videos on the Coalition's website feature education professionals discussing what it means to work in a community school. Their comments demonstrate an inclusive and collaborative orientation toward families, a variety of community organizations, and noneducation professionals who support student success. Amy Ritchell, a teacher of ethnic studies and modern world history at Mission High School in San Francisco, for example, discusses the way she has partnered with a local ranch to co-produce a food justice curriculum, how she works with local activists to "bring the curriculum alive" when teaching about social issues, and how she engages in ongoing dialogue with the wellness staff in the building to address issues that can impede students' learning (Coalition for Community Schools, n.d.). Ms. Ritchell says she "wish[es] more teachers would advocate for the freedom and the powerful aspect that community schools . . . offer us as professionals" (Coalition for Community Schools, n.d.). And yet, when referring to her "freedom," Ms. Ritchell is not talking about an unaccountable discretion; rather, it is a freedom from the constraints of prepackaged and scripted curricula, and being afforded the autonomy and the time to collaborate with professionals and others in the service of student learning.

Nick Faber, a K–6 science specialist at John A. Johnson Elementary School in St. Paul, Minnesota, describes how his community school prioritizes engagement with families. When he and his colleagues found that it was difficult to get parents to come into the building for conferences and meetings about curriculum, they started a home visit program that allowed teachers and parents to build trust and begin forging what he calls "academic partnerships" (Coalition for Community Schools, n.d.). Mr. Faber and his colleagues interpreted parents' low attendance at school-based functions not as a sign of their lack of interest or misplaced values—all too often the deficit view of families in economically disadvantaged communities—but as a sign that the current strategy of inviting parents to the school building wasn't working. In this version of professional responsibility, educators held themselves accountable for finding a way to connect with families, even if this meant visiting them in their homes. In a very real way, then, the notion of school is extended outside the physical building and into the community.

Mr. Faber also describes what it's like to work as a teacher alongside professionals from other fields, noting that the school's "wraparound services," which include optometry and dental clinics, mental health services, and housing specialists, have helped mitigate some of the typical barriers to learning that children from poverty experience. For example, Mr. Faber notes that if a student

> comes to school and says, "we're not going to be at school tomorrow because we have to move," we can get the housing specialist on that right away to try to keep that kid in the home and keep the kid here at school. . . . Those things that often will distract kids from learning, we can take care of, so that when they're in the classroom they're able to concentrate better and we can do our job better. (Coalition for Community Schools, n.d.)

These services enable students to concentrate on learning and Mr. Faber to concentrate on the core functions of his profession, but his notion of professionalism also suggests that teachers in schools like his are part of an *integrated* system of student supports, Maier et al.'s (2017) first pillar of community schools.

In order for such integrated services to function well, the professionals managing them cannot work in isolation from one another; they need to coordinate their efforts, often across traditional professional boundaries. For this reason, many community schools employ a full-time director to coordinate the work of school professionals, community-based organizations, and families—a point that seems to acknowledge the complexity of school leadership and the need for shared authority, putting the lie to any lingering myths of the heroic do-it-yourself principal.

We are not suggesting that Amy Ritchell and Nick Faber represent the perspectives of community school teachers overall. Rather, we share their comments because they open a window into new forms of professionalism in public schools—alternatives to the entrepreneurial, data-driven model. They help us not only to imagine such new forms, but also to see that they already exist. Ms. Ritchell and Mr. Faber's picture of professionalism can be considered democratic in the sense that they view communities and families not simply as recipients of services, but as "funds of knowledge," to use a term from Moll and Gonzalez's (1994) work on linguistic-minority students—participants who are indispensable to high-quality schooling.

Alternative Systems of Accountability/Responsibility

As we noted in Chapter 1, and discussed in the section above on responsibility, "accountability" used to refer only to financial documentation. But as the managerial meaning was transferred to the public sector, it was expanded to mean the demand for quantitative, auditable accounts of all of an organization's activities. Being responsible or answerable and being accountable (i.e., auditable) are not the same thing (Biesta, 2004). So while we use the term *accountability* here, we use it more in the sense of being *responsible* or answerable to.

A democratic professional cannot emerge out of a *test and punish* framework; it requires a holistic *support and improve* framework. In spite of the hegemony of high-stakes standardized tests, many districts are experimenting with this more holistic framework through authentic assessments. For instance, New York City has a consortium of 36 schools, the New York Performance Standards Consortium, that have a waiver to do alternative assessment for Regents exams. Instead of taking the exams, students must demonstrate mastery of skills in all subjects by designing experiments, making presentations, writing reports, and defending their work to outside experts (Robinson, 2015). Consortium schools report much higher college attendance rates than regular high schools.

These alternative assessments are not new. They have been used in hundreds of schools in Ted Sizer's (1984) Coalition of Essential Schools for well over 20 years. More authentic forms of accountability not only empower teachers professionally in the sense that teachers receive more helpful data for improving instruction, but also can stimulate different conversations among teachers, ones that are less focused on gaming the system and more focused on getting to know their students academically and socially.

Good schools and good teaching are a product of joint labor, not the work of individual teachers. Good teaching is the result of a shared collective effort of a staff and the ways they create environments for collegiality and learning at the school, classroom, and community levels. It is not possible to measure the individual contribution of a teacher. Furthermore, teaching is far too complex to evaluate with quantitative outcomes, such as test scores. Other experienced professionals are in a better position to evaluate the complex decisions that teachers make in classrooms.

In U.S. cities like San Francisco, Minneapolis, Rochester, and Toledo, districts have used a more democratic way of holding teachers accountable, called Peer Assistance and Review (PAR). PAR, or teachers evaluating one another with union and administrative input, is a natural extension of this type of capacity-building accountability. J. Goldstein (2010) describes how PAR works:

With PAR, designated "consulting teachers" provide support to new teachers and struggling veteran teachers (collectively called "participating teachers"), and also conduct the summative personnel evaluations of the teachers they support. The consulting teachers report to an oversight panel composed of teachers and administrators from across the district, co-chaired by the teacher union president and a high-ranking district office administrator. The panel holds hearings several times a year, at which consulting teachers provide reports about participating teacher progress and ultimately make recommendations about the continued employment of each participating teacher. (p. 54)

J. Goldstein (2010) acknowledges that combining support with evaluation is tricky and that veteran teachers may resist being evaluated by peers who are often younger than they are. The success of PAR also requires sufficient trust among the union leaders, the rank and file members, and the district leadership, something that is in very short supply in most districts. Otherwise, teachers may feel that the union is becoming part of management. But the model is a promising step in the direction of providing teachers with greater control over professional decisions and brings the union into the process as well.

Reform Unionism

The endgame for those who promote New Public Management is the demise of teachers' unions, which are seen as an obstacle to NPM reforms. Those reformers who are profit-driven have the same endgame, but for the same profit-driven reasons that unions were busted in the private sector. The subtext of much criticism of public education is that unionized adults are looking out for themselves at the expense of our children. They also are viewed as having "gold-plated" pensions that are bankrupting district and state budgets. (See Ayers, Laura, and Ayers [2018] for a response to the many negative myths about teachers and teachers' unions.)

In some ways, though, teachers' unions deserve this criticism, as they historically have adopted an industrial model with a sole focus on bread-and-butter issues and a business model of collective bargaining. Many have been slow to oppose NPM reforms, and few have built alliances with communities of color. There is, however, some evidence that unions in the United States and globally are moving beyond bread-and-butter issues to attempt to return to their social movement origins (Compton & Weiner, 2008; M. Johnson, 2017; Nunez, Michie, & Konkol, 2015; Stevenson & Gilliland, 2016; Uetricht, 2014). Shirley (2016) sees some hope that unions and community organizers can find common ground, and some private-sector unions, such as the Service Employees International Union (SEIU), have begun organizing to improve the low-income schools their members' children often attend (Rogers & Terriquez, 2009). Some, such as the global union umbrella, Education International, are becoming outspoken advocates for reforms that challenge privatization and NPM policies (Education International, 2017). In many countries and in U.S. school districts, teachers' unions are promoting a more democratic discourse of teacher professionalism (Mausethagen & Granlund, 2012) and are becoming more involved in offering progressive professional development (Naylor, 2015).

The teachers' strike in Chicago during the summer of 2012 demonstrated how a union that views itself as a social movement allied with low-income communities of color can go on strike and have the support of its local communities (Ashby & Bruno, 2016). Teachers in Chicago transcended bread-and-butter issues to frame themselves as a social movement union, spending years building alliances with community organizations. While they focused on specific reforms, they framed their opposition more broadly as resistance to managerial and neoliberal reforms that were deprofessionalizing teachers and closing public schools in low-income communities of color (Nunez et al., 2015; Uetricht, 2014). If more grassroots caucuses like the Caucus of Rank and File Educators in Chicago can win union elections, reformed teachers' unions might be able to support a democratic professionalism. This will depend, however, on whether unions can overcome the legacy of racism described in Chapter 2. The 2018 wave of teacher strikes and walkouts are encouraging, but it will take several years and a strong political will for these teacher activists to build alliances with communities, especially low-income communities of color.

A Participatory Action Research Approach to Professional Learning

Sachs (2016) argues that teacher professionalism requires teachers to engage in collaborative professional knowledge building so they can challenge reforms and policies that deprofessionalize. This will require changes in how we think about preservice education and ongoing professional development. The preparation and ongoing professional development of teachers and leaders should be based on ongoing inquiry and learning not only from one another, but also from students and their communities. If university-based teacher and leader education programs continue to emphasize discrete coursework and a transmission model of teaching, they will continue to hemorrhage students to alternative pathways. More than content, prospective teachers and leaders need to learn how to engage in participatory critical inquiry in schools and classrooms. A participatory approach is grounded in Paulo Freire's (1970) concept of a pedagogy of questions, not answers, which requires a focus on the generative themes of students and communities, not merely a syllabus of course readings.

To return to our example of the teachers in New York City who wanted to better understand what was causing their 9th-graders to drop out of school, we can see that these teachers were seeking the generative themes of their students, that is, those themes in their lives that were central to their survival and success in school. A participatory approach would involve inquiry not merely *on* students, or *for* them, but *with* them. In working *with* their students, teachers might better understand the students' needs as learners, enabling them to provide more relevant and appropriate instruction. If the core of the preparation of teachers and leaders is centered on participatory inquiry, the result will be more horizontal relationships among professionals, colleges of education, public schools, and low-income communities. A participatory stance is capable of both creating professional capacity through organizational learning and also democratizing the organization.

One of the limitations of college of education faculty is that they are trained in a doctoral culture that devalues professional knowledge. The culture of academic faculty (even in applied fields) and the culture of school professionals are at loggerheads (Ginsberg & Gorostiaga, 2001). School professionals see little value in the knowledge produced in the academy, and academics do not take seriously the knowledge that school professionals bring to the table (G. L. Anderson, 2017).

The traditional framework of knowledge production in which knowledge is created in universities, published in journals, and then "utilized" by practitioners has been ineffective for decades and often pathologizes school professionals as "resistant" to academic research and theory. What participatory action research provides is an *emancipatory knowledge framework* that problematizes a linear, top-down reform "delivery" system. It also promotes a more simultaneous, dialogical process in which the creation of knowledge is done in multiple sites and with a participatory stance with multiple parties. Participatory action research can create the kinds of "third spaces" we described in Chapter 5 in which teachers create spaces for forms of counter-conduct that challenge NPM (see also Cammarota & Fine, 2008; Drame & Irby, 2015; Miller, 1990; Wright, 2015).

Culturally Responsive Instruction and Curriculum

Although NPM has intensified educators' focus on the academic outcomes of specific racial and ethnic groups in comparison with their White peers, opportunity and achievement gaps have stubbornly persisted. Furthermore, in the push for more testing and a prescriptive, context-indifferent curriculum, teachers have had less time to deepen their knowledge of individual students' backgrounds and experiences, and less freedom to adapt curriculum appropriately to the students in their classrooms (Crocco & Costigan, 2007). In this context, culturally responsive pedagogy, despite several decades of gaining traction in schools serving culturally and linguistically diverse populations, has been pushed to the margins (Sleeter, 2012).

Geneva Gay (2010) defines culturally responsive teaching as "using the cultural knowledge, prior experiences, frames of reference, and performance styles of ethnically diverse students to make learning encounters more relevant to and effective for them" (p. 31). Responsiveness involves more than multicultural curricula; it also means fostering an environment of connectedness in the classroom. For example, culturally responsive professionals continuously build their understanding and appreciation of the various culturally encoded ways their students—and they themselves—express thoughts and feelings about a topic, and they draw from a wide range of instructional modalities to build upon the learning behaviors of diverse groups (Gay, 2002; Gonzalez, Moll, & Amanti, 2005). Furthermore, taking a critical stance toward knowledge production, they foster their students' ability to challenge prevailing ideas (Ladson-Billings, 1995).

While cultural responsiveness has met barriers in the context of NPM, there is growing evidence that education professionals across the nation are recognizing that equal opportunity is impossible unless they treat ethnic, racial, and linguistic diversity as assets in the learning process and develop their capacity to work across difference. Since 2015, for example, the National Education Policy Center's "Schools of Opportunity" awards have highlighted schools that meet several criteria of equity, including the use of culturally relevant curricula, programs that build on the strengths of English language learners, sustaining a healthy school culture, and engaging meaningfully and equitably with parents and communities.

Culturally responsive classrooms and schools can create a third space in which children and youth develop academic identities. In a cultural sense, third spaces represent hybrid spaces in which students are developing identities relating to their socio-historical location in society. From a post-colonial perspective, first space represents the original culture of home and community (Bhabha, 1994). However, students from nondominant cultures, which can include working-class cultures, must interact with second space, which is the space of the dominant middle-class culture that schools reflect. Many anthropologists and sociologists of education have documented over several decades the dilemmas of identity this interaction presents for students. Some succeed in developing dual identities, but too many have internalized the negative messages of "second space" dominant culture (Mehan, Hubbard, & Villanueva, 1994; Nasir, McLaughlin, & Jones, 2009).

The Mexican-American Studies program in the Tucson Unified School District in Arizona represented an attempt to create a third space to engage in culturally responsive pedagogy. The program began in 1998 as a few courses and grew to 43 classes serving 1,500 students in elementary, middle, and high school in Tucson. The purpose of the program was to create a community centered around culturally relevant learning with Mexican-American history as a central theme. Another goal was to develop critical consciousness and critical thinking to empower students by helping them develop positive identities leading to better academic results (Cabrera, Milem, Jaquette & Marx, 2014).

This program represented a form of student achievement and empowerment that does not rely on paternalistic, boot camp models that teach students obedience and provide a test-driven education. While this humanistic "third" space was created within a public school district, the conservative Arizona context and its focus on Mexican-American history ultimately led to its being closed down in 2012. However, community protests and a lawsuit brought by students and parents resulted in federal Judge A. Wallace Tashima declaring that the ban was motivated by racial discrimination and violated students' constitutional rights (Strauss, December 28, 2017).

Leaders in some state departments of education also are beginning to support the increased use of culturally responsive teaching and programming. Since 2011, for example, the Oregon Department of Education has provided additional funding to districts making targeted efforts to increase opportunities for under-served racial and ethnic groups (Oregon Education Investment Board, 2011). The department has supported local districts in establishing K–12 dual-language pro-grams, developing teachers' capacity in culturally responsive instruction, collab-orating with representatives of Native American tribes in decisions about school policies and the planning of culturally relevant professional development, and cre-ating pipelines between universities and districts to increase the diversity of the teaching force—to name just a few examples (Superville, 2016).

Notably, in stark contrast to the policy language of NCLB, the official guiding document of Oregon's equity initiative communicates boldly and directly about injustice, making explicit references to "white privilege" and to "institutional and systemic barriers and discriminatory practices that have limited access for many students in the Oregon education system" (Oregon Education Investment Board, 2011, pp. 4–6). Indeed, we should not mistake words for action, but the policymakers' professed commitments to equal opportunity, when combined with substantial allocation of resources, practitioners' on-the-ground efforts in their districts and schools, and a recognition that the markets and outcomes-based ac-countability will not bring about equal opportunity, are steps toward democratiz-ing professionalism and our public schools.

Restorative Justice Practices

Student discipline represents another key area for addressing discriminatory prac-tices that impede students' success in schools. Research on the distribution of sus-pensions and other exclusionary discipline practices in schools is clear: Students of color are significantly more likely than White students to receive these severe consequences for the same or similar infractions (Skiba et al., 2011; E. J. Smith & Harper, 2015). Furthermore, students of color frequently are losing classroom time for mild offenses or highly subjective categories of behavior such as "willful defiance" (Gregory, Bell, & Pollock, 2014), calling attention to implicit bias in pro-fessionals' responses to student behavior. Given these disparities, democratically minded professionals have turned to positive discipline practices, such as restor-ative justice, as a more equitable approach to student discipline.

Like a number of other practices we have discussed in this chapter, restor-ative justice is not a new concept; it has historical roots in Native American approaches to justice and more recently in U.S. cities where reformers of the le-gal system have searched for alternatives to incarceration for nonviolent crimes (Dzur, 2008). A restorative approach in schools, in addition to holding individ-uals accountable for violating norms or rules, aims to repair harm done to the community and its members. Common practices such as conflict mediation by trained facilitators, open dialogues in discussion circles, and collective problem solving focus on the importance of learning, understanding root causes of be-haviors, preventing future violations, and developing a safe and inclusive com-munity (Y. Anyon et al., 2016).

In school districts such as Denver, Colorado, and Los Angeles, California, restorative practices have contributed to overall reductions in suspensions and office discipline referrals as well as some narrowing of racial discipline gaps (González, 2015; Hashim, Strunk, & Dhaliwal, 2018). But it is still too soon to conclude that districtwide efforts such as these are resulting in more equitable and inclusive school communities. Furthermore, notwithstanding this progress, racial disparities in discipline persist, and researchers note the need for more empirical studies of outcomes and implementation processes (Y. Anyon et al., 2016; Hashim et al., 2018).

Understanding how leaders in schools and districts implement restorative justice is crucial, particularly as states hold them accountable for reducing suspension and expulsion rates. After almost 2 decades of experience with high-stakes accountability for achievement, we know that governing by numbers has a poor track record in producing equity. It is, of course, possible to reduce suspensions—or even adopt restorative justice practices—without developing more inclusive and just communities.

Lustick (2017) notes the danger of establishing the structures of restorative justice without a critical examination of power relations and institutional racism in schools, and she calls for restorative justice training that includes explicit connections to culturally responsive pedagogy and discipline. Otherwise, Lustick (2017) writes, "restorative practices could recapitulate the same racially disproportionate results they are intended to mitigate" (p. 308). If, however, restorative practices are implemented alongside a cultural shift among educators and students—involving a recognition of implicit bias and a commitment to inclusiveness in their schools—this approach to student discipline may support a more democratic public school and a professionalism that empowers students as well as teachers and leaders.

Return to a Strategy of Public Investment in Education

Warren Buffett begins his 2017 annual report to shareholders of Berkshire Hathaway, Inc. with this introduction: "Berkshire's gain in net worth during 2017 was $65.3 billion, which increased the per-share book value of both our class A and class B stock by 23%." He goes on to say that what was unusual about 2017 was that "a large portion of our gain did *not* come from anything we accomplished at Berkshire. The $65 billion gain is nonetheless real—rest assured of that. But only $36 billion came from Berkshire's operations. The remaining $29 billion was delivered to us in December when Congress rewrote the U.S. Tax Code."

Meanwhile in 2018, President Trump signed the $1.3 trillion omnibus spending bill, approving one of the largest military budgets in history. The U.S. military budget is not only the largest in the world, but larger than that of the next eight countries combined. It is so full of unneeded weapons systems that even the conservative Heritage Foundation claimed it was full of political pork for special interests (Riedl, 2018).

Meanwhile, corporations are given more tax breaks at the state level as they play states off one another for corporate-friendly legislation, and the 2008 recession has drained state and local budgets dry. The problem isn't a lack of money, but where our national wealth is being spent. All of this is occurring at the same time that the public sector (except for the military) is diminished in the name of NPM's austerity discourse and politics.

To some extent, educators have been complicit in the current overemphasis solely on the role of public education in creating human capital for business and the U.S. economy. While public schools historically have served diverse goals, from teaching citizenship to inculcating an appreciation for the arts, when public investment has been sought, the human capital argument for growing education systems has been the most effective. Now rationales for funding public education are almost exclusively economic ones (Labaree, 1997). Strategically, educators will have to continue to use this argument as it is the only one managerialist reformers might support.

Nevertheless, some countries do follow a strategy of public investment and have succeeded in creating education systems that pursue multiple goals, including democratic citizenship, personal and aesthetic development, equitable outcomes, as well as the development of human capital. Global comparisons of countries that have adopted a public investment strategy in education with those that have chosen markets and metrics demonstrate that a public investment strategy achieves higher overall achievement and greater equity of outcomes. Finland, which chose public investment, saw its achievement rates soar, while just next door, Sweden chose a voucher system and high-stakes testing and saw its rates plummet (Astrand, 2016). Canada (especially Ontario) chose public investment over markets and has outperformed the United States (Fullan & Rincon-Gallardo, 2016). And socialist Cuba's academic achievement leaves the rest of Latin America in the dust (Carnoy, 2016).

But one needn't look only to other countries for comparisons. U.S. states that have followed a public investment strategy consistently outperform states that have not. While most states have decreased funding since the 2008 recession (Leachman, Masterson, & Figueroa, 2017), several states in the northeast, such as Massachusetts, Vermont, and Connecticut, have increased and attempted to equalize funding; invested in high-quality standards, assessments, and professional development; reduced class sizes; and supported early childhood education and child health and welfare. These are also states with high levels of unionized teachers.

The pro-charter Center for Education Reform and the corporate-funded, neoliberal American Legislative Exchange Council both give these states Ds and Cs on their annual report cards. ALEC's highest rankings go to states that are largely non-union and deregulated, allowing for-profit charter schools and vouchers. States like Arizona, Florida, Indiana, and Betsy DeVos's Michigan, along with Washington, DC, received the highest ratings. None of these states outperform states that have followed a public investment and teacher professionalization strategy.

Another side-by-side state comparison is revealing. Wisconsin and Minnesota have followed very different paths. In 2010, Wisconsin elected conservative governor Scott Walker and Minnesota elected progressive governor Mark Dayton. Walker, with the support of ALEC and other corporate-led organizations, attacked his state's workers, particularly in the public sector, stripping them of collective bargaining rights. He cut taxes by more than $4.7 billion and deregulated industry. Dayton, on the other hand, raised the minimum wage and increased the income tax on the top 2% of earners to invest in infrastructure and education. From 2010–2016, Minnesota had stronger population, wage, and overall economic growth. It also has reduced poverty and the gender wage gap (Ratliff, 2016).

We also can look to the past for an example of U.S. public investment. Although marred by racist education and housing policies (Rothstein, 2017), and a state finance system based on property taxes, the United States had a strategy of public investment during the years of the Great Society in the 1960s, when the Elementary and Secondary Education Act was passed.

Opportunities were expanding in higher education through state investment that produced low state tuition, increased financial aid, and affirmative action programs. During this period, the City University of New York (CUNY) system had free tuition and open admissions. The civil rights movement also had removed many legal barriers to education for African Americans and women. It should not be surprising that the achievement gap between Black and White students and between income levels saw the largest reductions during the 1970s and 1980s (Barton & Coley, 2010). The gap in higher education enrollments was nearly eliminated during this period. City College (historically referred to as the working class' Harvard) and other CUNY campuses, for instance, between the 1950s and the 1970s went from being overwhelmingly White to being among the most racially diverse campuses in the nation. Since the advent of NPM in the 1990s, the achievement gap has remained largely the same, college tuition has soared, and student debt threatens the future of a generation of students.

As public investment in education decreases, teachers' salaries have fallen dramatically. Not surprisingly, teachers participating in the 2018 strikes and walkouts live in states with some of the largest pay gaps between teachers and other college graduates. In 2018, according to Allegretto (2018):

> In Arizona, teachers earn just 63 cents on the dollar compared with other college graduates. That gap is 79 cents in Kentucky, 67 cents in Oklahoma, and 75 cents in West Virginia. These gaps amount to vast differences in earning over a career. It is not surprising that there are teacher shortages across the United States as college students, especially women, choose other professions . . . . There is no state where teacher wages are equal to or better than those of other college graduates. (Para 4)

Just as policies of public investment were the result of social movements of labor and civil rights, current austerity policies were achieved through a well-funded campaign to dismantle the welfare state and replace it with an ideology of disinvestment from the public sector (Phillips-Fein, 2009). This was accompanied by the idea, promoted by Nobel prize–winning economists like James Buchanan and Milton Friedman, that redistributive economic policies that addressed the opportunity gap were a kind of Robin Hood mentality that stole from the more deserving affluent members of society to give to the undeserving poor (McLean, 2017). The fact that the poor in the United States were disproportionately made up of racial minorities was seldom acknowledged openly by these economists, but a kind of "dog whistle" politics made it clear to those who were listening in a racist frequency that they saw these redistributive policies as taking money from White people and giving it to people of color (Lopez, 2014). In the current climate created by President Donald Trump, the dog whistle has been replaced by a racist and xenophobic megaphone.

BUILDING COUNTER-NETWORKS: NEW ALLIANCES FOR CHANGE

We have documented a daunting and well-funded network of venture philanthropists, think tanks, and wealthy individuals who are using their power and money to influence public education policy. They have even formed fake grassroots groups (referred to as "astro turf," "grasstops," or "tree tops" groups), with names like Families for Excellent Schools, Students First, Educators4Excellence, or Students for Education Reform, all of which are corporate-funded. But there is also a growing network of real grassroots groups that are run by educators, parents, or students that are pushing back on NPM reforms and promoting some of the policies and practices we have discussed above. One successful example was the lawsuit filed by the Campaign for Fiscal Equity in New York that resulted in the state of New York being ordered to equalize public investment in education across the state. When the 2008 recession hit, the state pulled back on its commitment, and a grassroots organization, the Alliance for Quality Education, was formed, now led by parent advocate Zakiyah Ansari. This organization has continued to pressure the legislature and has become a powerful statewide presence.

While it did not have corporate sponsors, the Campaign for Fiscal Equity was funded partially by social justice philanthropists, such as the Schott Foundation for Public Education (Korten, 2009). Similar campaigns are occurring in other states, such as the Campaign for Quality Education in California. Other grassroots organizations challenging NPM are Fair Test, Network for Public Education, Center for Popular Democracy, Class Size Matters, Opt Out, Coalition for Educational Justice, Teachers for Social Justice (Chicago), New York Collective of Radical Educators, Grassroots Education Movement (New York), Teachers Unite!, Badass Teachers Association (Naison, 2014), Save our Schools, and many more.

By building relationships with their communities, better framing issues around democratic principles, and building cross-sector alliances, democratic professionals are less likely to be isolated in their struggles and more able to produce counter-networks to challenge the complex network of policies and practices that make up NPM. A new democratic professional values the ethos of the profession, but embeds it in real communities of difference and an ability to deconstruct dominant discourses by connecting the ideological dots across various policies and practices.

In this chapter we have attempted to describe characteristics of the new democratic professional that is slowly emerging alongside the new professional that NPM is shaping and the old professional that is increasingly a nostalgic and idealistic discourse. We also have provided a brief description of some of the policies and practices that could form the foundation for building an organizational and institutional context for the democratic professional to thrive in. However, these practices will face the challenge of effective dissemination and enactment on a large scale, without replication or "scaling up." They will have to be authentic and have broad participation to avoid cooptation or superficial implementation. They also will have to challenge the nearly 150-year fascination with corporate models and reassert the importance of professional and community knowledge across the public sector.

CONCLUSION

We opened this book with a description of the way New Public Management has been reshaping the professional identities of teachers and leaders over the past 4 decades, pulling them further away from the democratic ideals of a public education. For readers who teach and lead in schools today, whether in K–12 systems or in colleges and universities, our descriptions of the market and efficiency logic that governs public education may have sounded all too familiar, and perhaps all too bleak. And yet, we also have tried to place these shifts within a broader context of changes, both ideological and material, in our increasingly marketized and financialized world—changes that have affected workers in the private sector as well as the public. In doing so, we hope to have demonstrated that educators are not alone in their struggle for meaningful work, just conditions for the people they serve as well as themselves, and freedom and agency to fulfill what they perceive as the ethical mission of their profession.

Those who teach and lead within NPM know well that the forces pushing for more marketization, more privatization, and fewer opportunities for those at the social margins are formidable. At times it may seem impossible to stem the tide of school reforms that have been eroding our democracy. As we have shown in this book, market-driven reforms often have a commonsense—and even "good sense"—appeal, and a resilience that withstands empirical evidence of their failure to make our schools better or more equitable. Those who push for market-driven reforms also have adopted the discourse of equity and civil rights, positioning their democratically minded opponents as enemies of equal opportunity. This is precisely why teachers and leaders cannot look back, nostalgically, to an older model of occupational and bureaucratic professionalism. While the older model promoted democracy at the discursive level, in reality, it excluded and marginalized many communities.

We close this book with an optimistic look toward the future of professionalism in public education—optimistic because so many teachers and leaders are actively working for change. From making their classrooms culturally responsive to engaging meaningfully with families and communities, integrating systems of student supports within their schools, and advocating collectively for a dignified income and policy changes at all levels of government, these professionals are not allowing the democratic ideals of public education to pass away quietly. They also are pushing the boundaries of professionalism, choosing inclusivity, responsibility, and activism over markets, metrics, and managerialism. Forging a democratic professionalism means that the change also must be in us, in the ways we relate to one another and to the communities we serve, in our understanding of what it means to be a teacher or a leader in a public school.

References

Abramovitz, M., & Zelnick, J. (2015). Privatization in the human services: Implications for direct practice. *Clinical Social Work, 43,* 283–293.

Abrams, S. (2016). *Education and the commercial mindset.* Cambridge, MA: Harvard University Press.

Achinstein, B., & Ogawa, R. (2006). (In)fidelity: What the resistance of new teachers reveals about professional principles and prescriptive educational policies. *Harvard Educational Review, 76*(1), 30–63.

Achinstein, B., & Ogawa, R. (2012). New teachers of color and culturally responsive teaching in an era of educational accountability: Caught in a double bind. *Journal of Educational Change, 13,* 1–39.

Achinstein, B., Ogawa, R., & Speiglman, A. (2004). Are we creating separate and unequal tracks of teachers? The effects of state policy, local conditions, and teacher characteristics on new teacher socialization. *American Educational Research Journal, 41*(3), 557–603.

Adamson, F., Astrand, B., & Darling-Hammond, L. (Eds.). (2016). *Global education reform: How privatization and public investment influence education outcomes.* New York, NY: Routledge.

Adamson, F., & Darling-Hammond, L. (2016). The critical choice in American education: Privatization or public investment? In F. Adamson, B. Astrand, & L. Darling-Hammond (Eds.), *Global education reform: How privatization and public investment influence education outcomes* (pp. 131–168). New York, NY: Routledge.

Addison, J. (2009). *The economics of codetermination: Lessons from the German experience.* New York, NY: Palgrave Macmillan.

Allegretto, S. (2018). *Teachers across the country have finally had enough of the teacher pay penalty.* Washington, DC: Economic Policy Institute.

American Association of University Professors. (2015). *Busting the myths: The annual report on the economic status of the profession, 2014–15.* Retrieved from www.aaup.org/reports-publications/2014-15salarysurvey

Amrein-Beardsley, A., Berliner, D. C., & Rideau, S. (2010). Cheating in the first, second, and third degree: Educators' responses to high-stakes testing. *Educational Policy Analysis Archives, 18*(14). Retrieved from epaa.asu.edu/ojs/article/view/714

Anderson, C. (2018). *One person, no vote: How voter suppression is destroying our democracy.* London, UK: Bloomsbury.

Anderson, G.L. (2007). Media's impact on educational policies and practices: Political spectacle and social control. *The Peabody Journal of Education, 82*(1), pp. 103–120.

Anderson, G. L. (2009). *Advocacy leadership: Toward a post-reform agenda.* New York, NY: Routledge.

Anderson, G. L. (2017). Participatory action research as democratic disruption: New public management and educational research in schools and universities. *International Journal of Qualitative Studies in Education,30*(5), 432–449.

Anderson, G. L., & Cohen, M. (2015). Redesigning the identities of teachers and leaders: A framework for studying new professionalism and educator resistance. *Education Policy Analysis Archives, 23*(91), 1–23.

Anderson, G. L., De La Cruz, P., & Lopez, A. (2017). New governance and new knowledge brokers: Think tanks and universities as boundary organizations. *Peabody Journal of Education, 92*, 4–15.

Anderson, G. L., & Grinberg, J. (1998). Educational administration as a disciplinary practice: Appropriating Foucault's view of power, discourse, and method. *Educational Administration Quarterly, 34*(3), 329–353.

Anderson, G. L., & Herr, K. (2011). Scaling up "evidence-based" practices for teachers is a profitable but discredited paradigm. *Educational Researcher, 40*, 287–289.

Anderson, G. L., & Montoro Donchik, L. (2016). The privatization of education and policy-making: The American Legislative Exchange Council (ALEC) and network governance in the United States. *Educational Policy, 30*(2), 322–364.

Anderson, J. D. (1988). *The education of blacks in the south, 1860–1935.* Chapel Hill: University of North Carolina Press.

Anyon, J. (1980). Social class and the hidden curriculum of work. *Journal of Education, 162*, 67–92.

Anyon, J. (2014). *Radical possibilities: Public policy, urban education, and a new social movement.* New York, NY: Routledge.

Anyon, Y., Gregory, A., Stone, S., Farrar, J., Jenson, J. M., Mcqueen, J., . . . Simmons, J. (2016). Restorative interventions and school discipline sanctions in a large urban school district. *American Educational Research Journal, 53*(6), 1663–1697.

AP-NORC (April, 2018). *American attitudes toward teacher pay and protests.* The Associated Press-NORC Center for Public Affairs Research. Retrieved from apnorc.org/projects/Pages/American-Attitudes-toward-Teacher-Pay-and-Protests.aspx

Apple, M. (2004). Schooling, markets, and an audit culture. *Educational Policy, 18*(4), 614–621.

Apple, M. (2006). *Educating the "right" way: Markets, standards, God, and inequality.* New York, NY: Routledge.

Apple, M. (2013). *Can education change society?* New York, NY: Routledge.

Apple, M. W., & Jungck, S. (1992). You don't have to be a teacher to teach this unit: Teaching, technology and control in the classroom. In A. Hargreaves & M. Fullan (Eds.), *Understanding teacher development* (pp. 20–42). New York, NY: Teachers College Press.

Ashby, S., & Bruno, R. (2016). *A fight for the soul of public education: The story of the Chicago teachers strike.* Cornell, NY: ILR Press.

Astrand, B. (2016). From citizens into consumers: The transformation of democratic ideals into school markets in Sweden. In F. Adamson, B. Astrand, & L. Darling-Hammond (Eds.), *Global education reform: How privatization and public investment influence education outcomes* (pp. 73–109). New York, NY: Routledge.

Au, W. (2011). Teaching under the new Taylorism: High-stakes testing and the standardization of the 21st century curriculum. *Journal of Curriculum Studies, 43*(1), 25–45.

Au, W. (2016). Meritocracy 2.0: High-stakes, standardized testing as a racial project of neoliberal multiculturalism. *Educational Policy, 30*(1), 39-62.

Au, W., & Ferrare, J. (2015). Sponsors of policy: A network analysis of wealthy elites, their affiliated philanthropies, and charter school reform in Washington state. *Teachers College Record, 116*(8), 1–9.

Ayers, W., Laura, C., & Ayers, R. (2018). *"You can't fire the bad ones": And 18 other myths about teachers, teachers' unions, and public education.* Boston, MA: Beacon Press.

Baker, B., & Miron, G. (2015). *The business of charter schools: Understanding the policies that charter operators use for financial benefit.* Boulder, CO: National Education Policy Center.

Baldridge, B. (2014). Relocating the deficit: Reimagining black youth in neoliberal times. *American Educational Research Journal, 51*, 440–472.

Ball, S. (2001). Performativities and fabrications in the education economy: Towards the performative society. In D. Gleason & C. Husbands (Eds.), *The performing school: Managing, teaching and learning in a performance culture* (pp. 210–226). London, UK: Routledge/ Falmer.

Ball, S. (2003). The teacher's soul and the terrors of performativity. *Journal of Education Policy, 18*(2), 215–228.

Ball, S. (2007). *Education plc. Understanding private sector participation in public sector education.* London, UK: Routledge.

Ball, S. (2008). *The education debate.* Bristol, UK: The Policy Press.

Ball, S. (2009). Global Education, Inc.: New policy networks and the neo-liberal imaginary. New York: Routledge.

Ball, S. (2012). *Global education inc.: New policy networks and the neo-liberal imaginary.* London, UK: Routledge.

Ball, S. (2015). Subjectivity as a site of struggle: Refusing neoliberalism? *British Journal of Sociology of Education, 37*(8), 1129–1146.

Ball, S. (2017). *Foucault as educator.* London, UK: Springer.

Ball, S., & Junemann, C. (2012). *Networks, new governance and education.* Chicago, IL: Policy Press.

Ball, S., & Olmedo, A. (2013). Care of the self, resistance and subjectivity under neoliberal governmentalities. *Critical Studies in Education, 54*(1), 85–96.

Bancroft, K. (2009). To have or have not: The socioeconomics of charter schools. *Education and Urban Society, 41*(2), 248–279.

Barnum, M. (2017). A 'portfolio' of schools? How a nationwide effort to disrupt urban school districts is gaining traction. *Chalkbeat.* Retrieved from www.chalkbeat.org/posts/us/ 2017/12/06/a-portfolio-of-schools-how-a-nationwide-effort-to-disrupt-urban-school-districts-is-gaining-traction/

Barrow, C.W. (2018). *The entrepreneurial intellectual in the corporate university.* New York, NY: Palgrave McMillan.

Barton, P. E., & Coley, R. J. (2010). *The black-white achievement gap: When progress stopped* (Policy Information Report). Educational Testing Service.

Basken, P. (2018, January 24). UT-Austin professors join campaign against faculty-productivity company. Retrieved from www.chronicle.com/article/UT-Austin-Professors-Join/242332

Bates, R. (2008). States, markets and communities: Is there room for educational leadership? *Journal of Educational Administration and History, 40*(3), 195–208.

Beardsley, S. (2017). *Higher calling: The rise of non-traditional leaders in academia.* Charlottesville: University of Virginia Press.

Beck, U. (1992). *Risk society: Toward a new modernity.* Thousand Oaks, CA: Sage.

Beilke, D. (2016). *K12 Inc. tries to pivot from virtual school failures to profit from "non-managed" schools.* Madison, WI: Center for Media and Democracy.

Bell, D. (2005). *Silent covenants: Brown v. Board of Education and the unfulfilled hopes of racial reform.* Oxford, UK: Oxford University Press.

Berliner, D. (2009). *Poverty and potential: Out-of-school factors and school success.* Boulder, CO, & Tempe, AZ: Education and the Public Interest Center & Education Policy Research Unit. Retrieved from nepc.colorado.edu/publication/poverty-and-potential

Berliner, D., & Biddle, B. (1995). *The manufactured crisis: Myths, fraud, and the attack on America's public schools.* Reading, MA: Addison-Wesley.

Bhabha, H. (1994). *The location of culture.* New York, NY: Routledge.

Bhanji, Z. (2012). Microsoft corporation: A case study of corporate-led PPPs in education. In S.

Robertson, K. Mundy, A. Verger, & F. Menashy (Eds.), *Public private partnerships in education: New actors and modes of governance in the globalizing world* (pp. 182–200). Northampton, MA: Edward Elgar.

Biesta, G. J. (2004). Education, accountability, and the ethical demand: Can the democratic potential of accountability be regained? *Educational Theory, 54*(3), 233–250.

Biesta, G., De Bie, M., & Wildemeersch, D. (Eds.). (2012). *Civic learning, Democratic citizenship and the public sphere.* New York, NY: Springer.

Blanco Bosco, E. (2009). Efficacia escolar y desigualdad: Aportes para la politica educative. *Perfiles Latinoamericanos, 3/4,* 51–85.

Blount, J. M. (1998). *Destined to rule the schools: Women and the superintendency, 1873–1995.* Albany, NY: State University of New York Press.

Blowfield, M., & Murray, A. (2014). *Corporate responsibility.* Oxford, UK: Oxford University Press.

Blume, H., & Poston, B. (2017, May 21). How L.A.'s school board election became the most expensive in U.S. history. *Los Angeles Times.* Retrieved from www.latimes.com/local/la-me-edu-school-election-money-20170521-htmlstory.html

Blyth, M. (2013). Paradigms and paradox: The politics of economic ideas in two moments of crisis. *Governance, 26*(2), 197–215.

Boggs, C. (2000). *The end of politics.* New York, NY: Guilford Press.

Bonilla-Silva, E. (2014). Racism without racists: Color-blind racism and the persistence of racial inequality in America. Lanham, MD: Rowman & Littlefield.

Bottery, M. (1996). The challenge to professionals from the New Public Management: Implications for the teaching profession. *Oxford Review of Education, 22*(2), 179–197.

Bowles, S., & Gintis, H. (1976). Schooling in capitalist America: Educational reforms and the contradictions of American life. New York, NY: Basic Books.

Brantlinger, A., & Smith, B. (2013). Alternative teacher certification and the new professional: The pre-service preparation of mathematics teachers in the New York City teaching fellows program. *Teachers College Record, 115,* 1–44.

Brantlinger, E. (2003). Dividing classes: How the middle class negotiates and rationalizes school advantage. New York, NY: Routledge.

Braun, A., Ball, S., & Maguire, M. (2011). Policy enactments in schools: Towards a toolbox for theory and research. *Discourse: Studies in the Cultural Politics of Education, 32*(4), 581–583.

Breneman, D., Pusser, B., & Turner, S. (Eds.). (2006). *Earning from learning: The rise of for-profit universities.* Albany: State University of New York Press.

Bronfenbrenner, U. (1979). *The ecology of human development.* Cambridge, MA: Harvard University Press.

Brook, R. H., Friedberg, M. W., Chen, P. G., Tutty, M., & Crosson, F. J. (2013). *Factors affecting physician professional satisfaction and their implications for patient care, health systems, and health policy.* Santa Monica: CA: Rand Corporation.

Brown, E., & Makris, M. V. (2017). A different type of charter school: In prestige charters, a rise in cachet equals a decline in access. *Journal of Education* Policy, *33*(1), 85–117.

Brown, J. (1992). *The definition of a profession: The authority of metaphor in the history of intelligence testing, 1890–1930.* Princeton, NJ: Princeton University Press.

Buffett, W. (2018). *Berkshire Hathaway, Inc. 2017 annual report.* Omaha, NE: Berkshire Hathaway, Inc.

Buras, K. (2014). *Charter schools, race, and urban space: Where the market meets grassroots resistance.* New York, NY: Routledge.

Burch, P. (2009). *Hidden markets: The new education privatization.* New York, NY: Routledge.

Burch, P., & Good, A. (2014). *Equal scrutiny: Privatization and accountability in digital education.* Cambridge, MA: Harvard Education Press.

Burris, V. (2008). The interlock structure of the policy-planning network and the right turn in U.S. state policy. *Research in Political Sociology, 17,* 1–35.

Bush, G. W. (2000, July 10). *George W. Bush's speech to the NAACP.* Speech presented at NAACP 91st Annual Convention, Baltimore. Retrieved from www.washingtonpost.com/wp-srv/onpolitics/elections/bushtext071000.htm

Butler, J. S. (1974). Black educators in Louisiana—A question of survival. *The Journal of Negro Education, 43*(1), 9–24.

Cabrera, N., Milem, J., Jaquette, O., & Marx, R. (2014). Missing the (student achievement) forest for all the (political trees): Empiricism and the Mexican-American Studies controversy in Tucson. *American Educational Research Journal, 51*(1), 1084–1117.

Callahan, R. (1962). *Education and the cult of efficiency.* Chicago, IL: University of Chicago Press.

Cammarota, J., & Fine, M. (Eds.). (2008). *Revolutionizing education: Youth participatory action research in motion.* New York, NY: Routledge.

Campbell, D. (1976). Assessing the impact of planned social change. *Evaluation and Program Planning, 2*(1), 67–90.

Capper, C., & Jamison, M. (1993). Let the buyer beware: Total Quality Management and educational research and practice. *Educational Researcher, 22*(8), 25–30.

Carnoy, M. (2016). Four keys to Cuba's provision of high quality public education. In F. Adamson, B. Astrand, & L. Darling-Hammond (Eds.), *Global education reform: How privatization and public investment influence education outcomes* (pp. 50–72). New York, NY: Routledge.

Carnoy, M., Elmore, R., & Siskin, L. (2003). *The new accountability: High schools and high stakes testing.* New York, NY: RoutledgeFalmer.

Carpenter, S. (2015). The "local" fetish as reproductive praxis in democratic learning. *Discourse: Studies in the Cultural Politics of Education, 36*(1), 133–143.

Carstensen, M. B., & Schmidt, V. A. (2016). Power through, over and in ideas: Conceptualizing ideational power in discursive institutionalism. *Journal of European Public Policy, 23*(3), 318–337.

Center for Research on Education Outcomes. (2009). *Multiple choice: Charter school performance in 16 states.* Stanford, CA: Author. Retrieved from credo.stanford.edu/reports/MULTIPLE_CHOICE_CREDO.pdf

Center for Research on Education Outcomes. (2015). *Online charter school study.* Stanford, CA: Author. Retrieved from credo.stanford.edu/pdfs/OnlineCharterStudyFinal2015.pdf

Chubb, J., & Moe, T. (1990). *Politics, markets, and America's schools.* Washington, DC: Brookings Institution.

Clarke, M. (2012). The (absent) politics of neo-liberal education policy. *Critical Studies in Education, 53*(3), 297–310.

Coalition for Community Schools. (n.d.). Teacher. Retrieved from www.communityschools.org/leadership/teacher.aspx

Cochran-Smith, M., & Lytle, S. (2009). *Inquiry as stance: Practitioner research for the next generation.* New York, NY: Teachers College Press.

Codd, J. (2005). Teachers as "managed professionals" in the global education industry: The New Zealand experience. *Educational Review, 57*(2), 193–206.

Cohen, M. (2013). 'In the back of our minds always': Reflexivity as resistance for the performing principal. *International Journal of Leadership in Education,* pp. 1–22.

Cohen, S. (1964). *Progressives and urban school reform: The Public Education Association, of New York City, 1895–1954.* New York, NY: Bureau of Publications, Teachers College, Columbia University.

Collyer, F. M. (2003). Theorizing privatisation: Policy, network analysis, and class. *Electronic Journal of Sociology.* Retrieved from www.sociology.org/ejs-archives/vol7.3/01_collyer.html

Compton, M., & Weiner, L. (Eds.). (2008). *The global assault on teaching, teachers, and their unions: Stories for resistance.* New York, NY: Palgrave Macmillan.

Connell, K. W. (2016). *Degrees of deception: America's for-profit higher education fraud.* Lanham, MD: Rowman & Littlefield.

Corcoran, S., & Stoddard, C. (2011). Local demand for a school choice policy: Evidence from the Washington charter school referenda. *Education Finance and Policy Quarterly, 6*(3), 323–353.

Costigan, A. (2013). New urban teachers transcending neoliberal educational reforms: Embracing aesthetic education as a curriculum of political action. *Urban Education, 48*(1), 116–148.

Courtney, S. (2018). Privatizing educational leadership through technology in the Trumpian era. *Journal of Educational Administration and History, 50*(1), 23–31.

Courtney, S. J., & Gunter, H. M. (2015). Get off my bus! School leaders, vision work and the elimination of teachers. *International Journal of Leadership in Education,* pp. 1–23.

Crary, J. (2014). *24/7: Late capitalism and the ends of sleep.* Brooklyn, NY: Verso Books.

Cremin, L. A. (1961). *Transformation of the school: Progressivism in American education, 1876–1957.* New York, NY: Knopf.

Crocco, M. S., & Costigan, A. T. (2007). The narrowing of curriculum and pedagogy in the age of accountability: Urban educators speak out. *Urban Education, 42*(6), 512–535.

Cuban, L. (1990). Reforming again, again, and again. *Educational Researcher, 19*(1), 3–13.

Cuban, L. (1993). *How teachers taught: Constancy and change in American classrooms, 1890–1990.* New York, NY: Teachers College Press.

Cuban, L. (2004). *The blackboard and the bottom line: Why schools can't be businesses.* Cambridge, MA: Harvard University Press.

Cuban, L. (2010). *As good as it gets: What school reform brought to Austin.* Cambridge, MA: Harvard University Press.

Cuban, L. (2013). *Inside the black box of classroom practice: Change without reform in American education.* Cambridge, MA: Harvard Education Press.

Cubberley, E. P. (1923). The principal and the principalship. *The Elementary School Journal, 23*(5), 342–352.

Darling-Hammond, L., & Wood, G. (2008). *Democracy at risk: The need for a new federal policy in education.* Washington, DC: Forum for Education and Democracy.

Datnow, A. (2011). Collaboration and contrived collegiality: Revisiting Hargreaves in the age of accountability. *Journal of Educational Change, 12*(2), 147–158.

Davis, G. F. (2011). *Managed by the markets: How finance reshaped America.* Oxford, UK: Oxford University Press.

DeBray, E. (2006). *Politics, ideology, and education: Federal policy during the Clinton and Bush administrations.* New York, NY: Teachers College Press.

Denhardt, J., & Denhardt, R. (2011). *The new public service: Serving, not steering.* Armonk, NY: M.E. Sharpe.

Derber, C. (1998). *Corporation nation.* New York, NY: St. Martin's Press.

DiMartino, C., & Jessen, S. B. (2016). School brand management: The policies, practices, and perceptions of branding and marketing in New York City's public high schools. *Urban Education, 51*(5), 447–475.

DiMartino, C., & Scott, J. (2012). Private sector contracting and democratic accountability. *Educational Policy, 27*(2), 307–333.

Domina, T., Hanselman, P., Hwang, N., & McEachin, A. (2016). Detracking and tracking up: Mathematics course placements in California middle schools, 2003–2013. *American Educational Research Journal, 53*(4), 1229–1266.

Drame, E., & Irby, D. (2015). *Black participatory research: Power, identity, and the struggle for justice in education.* New York, NY: Palgrave Macmillan.

Driscoll, M. E. (1998). Professionalism versus community: Is the conflict between school and community about to be resolved? *Peabody Journal of Education, 73*(1), 89–127.

Drutman, L. (2015). *The business of America is lobbying: How corporations became politicized and politics became more corporate.* Oxford, UK: Oxford University Press.

Dunleavy, P., Margetts, H., Bastow, S., & Tinkler, J. (2005). New Public Management is dead—long live digital-era governance. *Journal of Public Administration and Theory, 16*, 467–494.

Dzur, A. (2008). *Democratic professionalism: Citizen participation and the reconstruction of professional ethics, identity, and practice.* University Park: Pennsylvania State University Press.

Edelman, M. (1978). *Political language: Words that succeed and policies that fail.* New York, NY: Academic Press.

Edelman, M. (1988). *Constructing the political spectacle.* Chicago, IL: University of Chicago Press.

Edmonds, R. (1979). Some schools work and more can. *Social Policy, 9*, 28–32.

Education International (2017). *EI research reinforces advocacy against growing privatization of public education.* Retrieved from ei-ie.org/en/detail/15075/ei-research-reinforces-advocacy-against-growing-privatisation-of-public-education

Edwards, M. (2008). *Just another emperor? The myths and realities of philanthrocapitalism.* London, UK: Demos.

Edwards, M. (2010). *Small change: Why business won't save the world.* Oakland, CA: Berrett-Koehler.

Ellis, V., McNicholl, J., Blake, A., & McNally, J. (2014). Academic work and proletarianisation: A study of higher education-based teacher educators. *Teaching and Teacher Education, 40*, 33–43.

Every Student Succeeds Act, 115 § II-2002(4) (Government Publishing Office 2015).

Evetts, J. (2009). New professionalism and New Public Management: Changes, continuities, and consequences. *Comparative Sociology, 8*, 247–266.

Evetts, J. (2011). A new professionalism? Challenges and opportunities. *Current Sociology, 59*(4), 406–422.

Exworthy, M., & Halford, S. (1999). *Professionals and the new managerialism in the public sector.* Buckingham, UK: Open University Press.

Fairclough, N. (1992). *Discourse and social change.* Cambridge, UK: Polity Press.

Fenwick, T. (2016). *Professional responsibility and professionalism: A sociomaterial examination.* London, UK: Routledge.

Ferguson, K. (2013). *Top down: The Ford Foundation, black power, and the reinvention of racial liberalism.* Philadelphia: University of Pennsylvania Press.

Fitzgerald, T., & Savage, J. (2013). Scripting, ritualising and performing leadership: Interrogating recent policy developments in Australia. *Journal of Educational Administration and History, 45*(2), 126–143.

Foroohar, R. (2016). *Makers and takers: The rise of finance and the fall of American business.* New York, NY: Crown Business.

Forsey, M. (2009). The problem with autonomy: An ethnographic study of neoliberalism in practice at an Australian high school. *Discourse: Studies in the Cultural Politics of Education, 30*(4), 457–469.

Foucault, M. (1980). *Power/knowledge: Selected interviews and other writings, 1972–1977* (C. Gordon, Ed.). New York, NY: Pantheon Books.

Foucault, M. (1987). The ethic of care for the self as a practice of freedom: An interview with Michel Foucault on January 20, 1984 (R. Fornet-Betancourt, H. Becker, A. Gomez-Muller, & J. D. Gauthier, Eds.). *Philosophy & Social Criticism, 12*(2–3), 112–131.

Foucault, M. (1990). *The history of sexuality.* New York, NY: Vintage Books. (Original work published 1976)

Foucault, M. (1995). *Discipline and punish: The birth of the prison.* New York, NY: Vintage Books. (Original work published 1975)

Fournier, V. (1999). The appeal to "professionalism" as a disciplinary mechanism. *The Sociological Review, 47*(2), 280–307.

Frankenberg, E., Siegel-Hawley, G., & Wang, J. (2011). Choice without equity: Charter school segregation. *Education Policy Analysis Archives, 19*(1). Retrieved from epaa.asu.edu/ojs/article/view/779

Fraser, J. A. (2002). *White collar sweatshops: The deterioration of work and its rewards in corporate America.* New York, NY: Norton.

Fraser, J. W. (1997). *Reading, writing, and justice: School reform as if democracy matters.* Albany: State University of New York Press.

Fraser, N. (1990). Rethinking the public sphere: A contribution to the critique of actually existing democracy. *Social Text,* (25/26), 56.

Frederickson, H. G. (2010). Searching for virtue in the public life. *Public Integrity, 12*(3), 239–246.

Freire, P. (1970). *Pedagogy of the oppressed.* New York, NY: Continuum.

Friedman, M. (1962). *Capitalism and freedom.* Chicago, IL: University of Chicago Press.

Friedrich, D. (2014). "We brought it on ourselves": University-based teacher education and the emergence of boot-camp-style routes to teacher certification. *Education Policy Analysis Archives, 22*(2), 21.

Fukuyama, F. (1992). *The end of history and the last man.* New York, NY: Free Press.

Fullan, M., & Rincon-Gallardo, S. (2016). Developing high quality public education in Canada: The case of Ontario. In F. Adamson, B. Astrand, & L. Darling-Hammond (Eds.), *Global education reform: How privatization and public investment influence education outcomes* (pp. 169–193). New York, NY: Routledge.

Gabriel, R., & Paulus, T. (2014). Committees and controversy: Consultants in the construction of education policy. *Educational Policy,* pp. 1–28.

Gallup. (2014). *State of American schools.* Retrieved from www.gallup.com/ services/178709/state-america-schools-report.aspx

Gandin, L., & Apple, M. (2012). Can critical democracy last? Porto Alegre and the struggle over 'thick' democracy in education. *Journal of Education Policy, 27*(5), 621–639.

Gates, W. (2009). Speech at the National Conference of State Legislatures. Retrieved from www.gatesfoundation.org/media-center/speeches/2009/07/bill-gates-national-conference-of-state-legislatures-ncsl

Gay, G. (2002). Preparing for culturally responsive teaching. *Journal of Teacher Education, 53*(2), 106–116.

Gay, G. (2010). *Culturally responsive teaching: Theory, research, and practice* (2nd ed.). New York, NY: Teachers College Press.

Gee, J. P. (2005). *An introduction to discourse analysis.* New York, NY: Routledge.

Gee, J., Hull, G., & Lankshear, C. (1996). *The new work order: Behind the language of the new capitalism.* Boulder, CO: Westview Press.

Gelberg, D. (1997). *The "business" of reforming American schools.* Albany: State University of New York Press.

Gewirtz, S. (2002). *The managerial school: Post-welfarism and social justice in education.* London, UK: Routledge.

Gewirtz, S., Mahony, P., Hextall, I., & Cribb, A. (2009). *Changing teacher professionalism: International trends, challenges and ways forward.* London, UK: Routledge.

Gillies, D. (2011). Agile bodies: A new imperative in neoliberal governance. *Journal of Education Policy, 26*(2), 207–223.

Gilmore, R. (2007). In the shadow of the shadow state. In Incite! (Women of color against violence) (Ed.), *The revolution will not be funded: Beyond the non-profit industrial complex* (pp. 41–52). Cambridge, MA: South End Press.

Ginsberg, B. (2013). *The fall of the faculty: The rise of the all-administrative university and why it matters*. Oxford, UK: Oxford University Press.

Ginsberg, M., & Gorostiaga, J. (2001). Relationships between theorists/researchers and policy makers/practitioners: Rethinking the two cultures thesis and the possibility of dialogue. *Comparative Education Review, 45*(2), 173–189.

Gitlin, A., & Margonis, F. (1995). The political aspect of reform: Teacher resistance as good sense. *American Journal of Education, 103*, 377–405.

Glazerman, S., & Dotter, D. (2016). *Market signals: Evidence on the determinants and consequences of school choice from a citywide lottery*. Washington, DC: Mathematica Policy Research.

Gleason, P., Clark, M., Tuttle, C., & Dwyer, E. (2010). *The evaluation of charter school impacts: Final report* (NCEE 2010–4029). Washington, DC: National Center for Education Evaluation and Regional Assistance, Institute of Education Sciences, U.S. Department of Education.

Gleeson, D., & Knights, D. (2006). Challenging dualism: Public professionalism in 'troubled' times. *Sociology, 40*(2), 277-295.

Gobby, B., Keddie, A., & Blackmore, J. (2017). Professionalism and competing responsibilities: moderating competitive performativity in school autonomy reform. *Journal of Educational Administration and History*, pp. 1–15.

Godsey, M. (2015, March 25). The deconstruction of the K–12 teacher. *The Altantic*. Retrieved from www.theatlantic.com/education/archive/2015/03/the-deconstruction-of-the-k-12-teacher/388631/

Goldstein, D. (2014). *The teacher wars: A history of America's most embattled profession*. New York, NY: Anchor Books.

Goldstein, J. (2017). To increase productivity, UPS monitors drivers' every move. *National Public Radio Planet Money*. Retrieved from www.npr.org/sections/money/2014/04/17/303770907/to-increase-productivity-ups-monitors-drivers-every-move

Goldstein, J. (2010). *Peer review and teacher leadership: Linking professionalism and accountability*. New York, NY: Teachers College Press.

González, T. (2015). Socializing schools: Addressing racial disparities in discipline through restorative justice. In D. J. Losen (Ed.), *Closing the school discipline gap: Equitable remedies for excessive exclusion* (pp. 151–165). New York, NY: Teachers College Press.

Gonzalez, N., Moll, L., & Amanti, C. (2005). *Funds of knowledge: Theorizing practices in households and classrooms*. Mahwah, NJ: Lawrence Erlbaum.

Goodsell, C. T. (2004). *The case for bureaucracy: A public administration polemic*. Washington, DC: Congressional Quarterly Press.

Gould, E. (2016). *Austerity at all levels of government has created a teacher shortfall*. Retrieved from www.epi.org/publication/teacher-employment-and-the-number-of-jobs-needed-to-keep-up-with-enrollment-2003-2016/

Green, P., Baker, B., Oluwole, J., & Mead, J. (2016). Are we headed toward a charter school "bubble"? Lessons from the subprime mortgage crisis. *University of Richmond Law Review, 50*, 783, 796–799.

Green, T. (2017). "We felt they took the heart out of the community": Examining a community-based response to urban school closure. *Education Policy Analysis Archives, 25*(21), 1–26.

Gregory, A., Bell, J., & Pollock, M. (2014). *How educators can eradicate disparities in school discipline: A briefing paper on school-based interventions*. Bloomington: Indiana University. Retrieved from www.indiana.edu/~atlantic/wp-content/uploads/2014/03/Disparity_Interventions_Full_031214.pdf

Grissom, J. A., Rubin, M., Neumerski, C. M., Cannata, M., Drake, T. A., Goldring, E., & Schuermann, P. (2017). Central office supports for data-driven talent management decisions. *Educational Researcher, 46*(1), 21–32.

Gunter, H. (2012). *Leadership and the reform of education*. Bristol, UK: Policy Press.

Gunter, H., Grimaldi, E., Hall, D., & Serpieri, R. (Eds.). (2016). *New Public Management and the reform of education: European lessons for policy and practice.* London, UK: Routledge.

Gunter, H., Hall, D., & Mills, C. (2015). Consultants, consultancy and consultocracy in education policymaking in England, *Journal of Education Policy, 30*(4), 518–539.

Gunzenhauser, M. (2007). Resistance as a component of educational professionalism. *Philosophical Studies in Education, 38*(1), 23–36.

Gunzenhauser, M. (2012). *Active/ethical professional: A framework for responsible educators.* New York, NY: Continuum.

Haas, E. (2007). False equivalency: Think tank references on education in the news media. *Peabody Journal of Education, 82*(1), 63–102.

Habermas, J. (1987). *The theory of communicative action: Vol. 2. Lifeworld and system: A critique of functionalist reason* (T. McCarthy, Trans.). Boston, MA: Beacon Press.

Haney, W. (2000). The myth of the Texas miracle in education. *Educational Policy Analysis Archives, 8*(41). Retrieved from epaa.asu.edu/ojs/article/view/432

Hargreaves, A. (1994). *Changing teachers, changing times: Teachers' work and culture in the postmodern age.* New York, NY: Teachers College Press.

Hargreaves, A. (2003). *Teaching in the knowledge society: Education in the age of insecurity.* New York, NY: Teachers College Press.

Hargreaves, A., & Shirley, D. (2009). *The fourth way: The inspiring future for educational change.* Thousand Oaks, CA: Corwin Press.

Harvey, D. (2005). *A brief history of neoliberalism.* Oxford, UK: Oxford University Press.

Hashim, A. K., Strunk, K. O., & Dhaliwal, T. K. (2018). Justice for all? Suspension bans and restorative justice programs in the Los Angeles Unified School District. *Peabody Journal of Education.* doi.org/10.1080/0161956X.2018.1435040

Heclo, H. (1978). Issue networks and the executive establishment. In A. King (Ed.), *The new American political system* (pp. 87–124). Washington, DC: American Enterprise Institute.

Heffeman, A. (2017). The accountability generation: Exploring an emerging leadership paradigm for beginning principals. *Discourse: Studies in the Cultural Politics of Education.* dx.doi.org/10.1080/01596306.2017.1280001

Hemphil, C., & Mader, N. (2015). *Segregated schools in integrated neighborhoods: The city's schools are even more divided than our housing.* New York, NY: Center for New York City Affairs.

Herr, K. (2015). Cultivating disruptive subjectivities: Interrupting the new professionalism. *Education Policy Analysis Archives, 23*(86), 1–26.

Herr, K., & Anderson, G. (2008). Teacher research and learning communities: A failure to theorize power relations? *Language Arts, 85*(5), 382–391.

Herzer, K. R., & Pronovost, P. J. (2014). Motivating physicians to improve quality: Light the intrinsic fire. *American Journal of Medical Quality, 29*(5), 451–453.

Hinton, E. (2016). *From the war on poverty to the war on crime: The making of mass incarceration in America.* Cambridge, MA: Harvard University Press.

Hochschild, A. (2003). *The managed heart: Commercialization of human feeling.* Berkeley: University of California Press.

Hood, C. (1991). A public management for all seasons? *Public Administration, 69,* 3–19.

Hood, C., & Peters, G. (2004). The middle aging of New Public Management: Into the age of paradox? *Journal of Public Administration Research and Theory, 14,* 267–282.

Horn, J., & Libby, K. (2011). The giving business: Venture philanthropy and the New Schools Venture Fund. In P. Kovacs (Ed.), *The Gates Foundation and the future of U.S. public education* (pp. 168–185). New York, NY: Routledge.

Horsford, S. (2016). Social justice for the advantaged: Freedom from racial equality post-Milliken. *Teachers College Record, 118*(1), 1–18.

Howard, G. (2016). *We can't teach what we don't know: White teachers, multiracial schools.* New York, NY: Teachers College Press.

Howarth, D. (2010). Power, discourse, and policy: Articulating a hegemony approach to critical policy studies. *Critical Policy Studies, 3*(3–4), 309–335.

Huffington Post. (2012). *American public education: Gallup poll results show majority of Americans dissatisfied.* Retrieved from www.huffingtonpost.com/2012/08/31/gallup-poll-results-show-_n_1844774.html

Hursh, D. (2015). *The end of public schools: The corporate reform agenda to privatize education.* New York, NY: Routledge.

Hynds, A. (2010). Unpacking resistance to change within-school reform programmes with a social justice orientation. *International Journal of Leadership in Education, 13*(4), 377–392.

Ingersoll, R. (2006). *Who controls teachers' work: Power and accountability in America's schools.* Cambridge, MA: Harvard University Press.

Ingersoll, R., Nabeel, A.P., Quinn, P., & Bobbitt, S. (1997). *Teacher professionalization and teacher commitment: A multilevel analysis.* Washington, DC: DIANE Publishing.

Ishimaru, A. M. (2014). When new relationships meet old narratives: The journey towards improving parent-school relations in a district-community organizing collaboration. *Teachers College Record, 116*(2).

Jain, S. H., & Cassel, C. K. (2010). Societal perceptions of physicians. *Journal of the American Medical Association, 304*(9), 1009.

Johanek, M. C., & Puckett, J. (2007). *Leonard Covello and the making of Benjamin Franklin High School as if citizenship mattered.* Philadelphia, PA: Temple University Press.

Johnson, L. (2017). Culturally responsive leadership for community empowerment. In Y. Cha, G. Jagdish, S. Ham, & M. Lee (Eds.), *Multicultural education in global perspectives: Policy and institutionalization* (pp. 183–199). New York, NY: Springer.

Johnson, M. (2017). Organizing for North Carolina: Social movement unionism in a southern state. *Peabody Journal of Education, 92*, 127–140.

Johnson, S. (1998). *Who moved my cheese?* New York, NY: Putnam's Sons.

Jost, J. T., Federico, C. M., & Napier, J. L. (2009). Political ideology: Its structure, functions, and elective affinities. *Annual Review of Psychology, 60*(1), 307–337.

Juahar, S. (2017, October 10). Shouldn't doctors control hospital care? *New York Times.* Retrieved from www.nytimes.com/2017/10/10/opinion/shouldnt-doctors-control-hospital-care.html

Junemann, C., & Ball, S. (2015). *Pearson & PALF: The mutating giant.* Brussels, Belgium: Education International.

Kahneman, D. (2011). *Thinking fast and slow.* New York, NY: Farrar, Straus, and Giroux.

Kantor, H. A. (1988). *Learning to earn: School, work, and vocational reform in California, 1880–1930.* Madison: University of Wisconsin Press.

Kaplan, E. (2015, March). The spy who fired me: The human cost of workplace monitoring. *Harper's,* pp. 31–40.

Katz, M. B. (1987). *Reconstructing American education.* Cambridge, MA: Harvard University Press.

Kearns, C., Apollonio, D., & Glantz, S. (2017). Sugar industry sponsorship of germ-free rodent studies linking sucrose to hyperlipidemia and cancer: An historical analysis of internal documents. *PLoS Biology, 15*(11). doi.org/10.1371/journal.pbio.2003460

Keith, N. Z. (1996). A critical perspective on teacher participation in urban schools. *Educational Administration Quarterly, 32*(1), 45–79.

Keith, N. (2015). *Engaging in social partnerships: Democratic practices for campus-community partnerships.* New York, NY: Routledge.

Kelley, C., & Mead, J. (2017). Revolution and counter-revolution: Network mobilization to preserve public education in Wisconsin. *Peabody Journal of Education, 92*, 103–114.

Khalifa, M. (2012). A re-new-ed paradign in successful urban school leadership: Principal as community leader. *Educational Administration Quarterly, 48*(3), 424–467.

Kickert, W. (1995). Steering at a distance: A new paradigm of public governance in Dutch higher education. *Governance, 8*(1), 135–157.

Kingdon, J. W. (1984). *Agendas, alternatives, and public policies* (2nd ed.). New York, NY: Harper Collins.

Kirp, D. (2013). *Improbable scholars: The rebirth of a great American school system and a strategy for America's schools.* Oxford, UK: Oxford University Press.

Klein, N. (2007). *The shock doctrine: The rise of disaster capitalism.* New York, NY: Metropolitan Books.

Kliebard, H. M. (1995). *The struggle for the American curriculum, 1893–1958.* New York, NY: Routledge.

Klikauer, T. (2013). *Managerialism: A critique of an ideology.* New York, NY: Palgrave Macmillan.

Korten, A. (2009). *Change philanthropy: Stories of foundations maximizing results through social justice.* San Francisco, CA: Jossey-Bass.

Kovaks, P., & Christie, H.K. (2009). The Gates' Foundation and the Future of U.S. Public Education: A Call for Scholars to Counter Misinformation Campaigns. *Journal for Critical Education Policy Studies, 6*(2).

Koyama, J. (2011). Principals, power, and policy: Enacting "supplemental educational services". *Anthropology & Education Quarterly, 42*(1), 20–36.

Koyama, J. (2014). Principals as bricoleurs: Making sense and making do in an era of accountability. *Educational Administration Quarterly, 50*(2), 279–304.

Kumashiro, K. K. (2012, May/June). *When billionaires become educational experts.* Retrieved from www.aaup.org/article/when-billionaires-become-educational-experts

Labaree, D. (1997). *How to succeed in school without really learning: The credentials race in American education.* London, UK, & New Haven, CT: Yale University Press.

Labaree, D. (2004). *The trouble with ed schools.* New Haven, CT: Yale University Press.

Labaree, D. (2010). *Someone has to fail: The zero-sum game of public schooling.* Cambridge, MA: Harvard University Press.

Labaree, D. (2012). School syndrome: Understanding the USA's magical belief that schooling can somehow improve society, promote access, and preserve advantage. *Journal of Curriculum Studies, 44*(2), 143–163.

Ladson-Billings, G. (1994). *The dreamkeepers: Successful teachers of African American children.* San Francisco, CA: Jossey-Bass.

Ladson-Billings, G. (1995). Toward a theory of culturally relevant pedagogy. *American Educational Research Journal, 32*(3), 465–481.

Lafer, G. (2017). *The one percent solution: How corporations are remaking America one state at a time.* Ithaca, NY: Cornell University Press.

Lakoff, G. (2004). *Don't think of an elephant.* White River Junction, VT: Chelsea Green.

Lakoff, G. (2006). *Thinking points: Communicating our American values and vision.* New York, NY: Farrar, Straus and Giroux.

Lakoff, G. (2008). *The political mind: Why you can't understand 21st-century politics with an 18th-century brain.* New York, NY: Viking Books.

Lave, J. (1988). Situating learning in communities of practice. In L. Resnick, S. Levine, & L. Teasley (Eds.), *Perspectives of socially shared cognition* (pp. 63–82). Washington, DC: American Psychological Association.

Lawn, M., & Ozga, J. (1987). The educational worker? A re-assessment of teachers. In L. Barton & S. Walker (Eds.), *Schools, teachers and teaching* (pp. 45–64). Lewes, UK: Falmer.

Layton, L. (2014, June 7). How Bill Gates pulled off the swift common core revolution. *Washington Post*. Retrieved from www.washingtonpost.com/politics/how-bill-gates-pulled-off-the-swift-common-core-revolution/2014/06/07/a830e32e-ec34-11e3-9f5c-9075d5508f0a_story.html?utm_term=.c553a2ebc021

Lazerson, M., & Grubb, W. N. (1974). *American education and vocationalism: A documentary history 1870–1970*. New York, NY: Teachers College Press.

Lazzarato, M. (2009). Neoliberalism in action. *Theory, Culture & Society, 26*(6), 109–133.

Leachman, M., Masterson, K., & Figueroa, E. (2017, November 29). *A punishing decade for school funding*. Washington, DC: Center on Budget and Policy Priorities. Retrieved from www.cbpp.org/research/state-budget-and-tax/a-punishing-decade-for-school-funding

Leask, I. (2012). Beyond subjection: Notes on the later Foucault and education. *Educational Philosophy and Theory*. doi.org/10.1111/j.1469-5812.2011.00774.x

Lieberman, A. & Miller, L. (2008). *Teachers in professional communities: Improving teaching and learning*. New York, NY: Teachers College Press.

Lepore, J. (2014, June 23). The disruption machine: What the gospel of innovation gets wrong. *The New Yorker*. www.newyorker.com/magazine/2014/06/23/the-disruption-machine

Levine, A. (2006). *Educating school teachers*. Princeton, NJ: Education Schools Project.

Lipman, P. (2009). Paradoxes of teaching in neo-liberal times: Education 'reform' in Chicago. In S. Gewirtz, P. Mahony, I. Hextall, & Cribb, A. (Eds.), *Changing teacher professionalism: International trends, challenges and ways forward* (pp. 67–80). London, UK: Routledge.

Lipman, P. (2011). *The new political economy of urban education: Neoliberalism, race, and the right to the city*. New York, NY: Routledge.

Lipsky, M. (1980). *Street-level bureaucracy: Dilemmas of the individual in public services*. New York, NY: Russell Sage Foundation.

Locke, R., & Spender, J-C. (2011). *Confronting managerialism: How the business elite and their schools threw our lives out of balance*. New York, NY: Zed Books.

Lopez, I.H. (2014). *Dog whistle politics: How coded racial appeals have reinvented racism & wrecked the middle class*. Oxford, UK: Oxford University Press.

Lortie, D. (1977). *Schoolteacher: A sociological study*. Chicago, IL: University of Chicago Press.

Lubienski, C., & Brewer, T.J. (2018). Do impacts on test scores even matter? (American Enterprise Institute, March 2018). Boulder, CO: National Education Policy Center.

Lubienski, C., Brewer, T. J., & La Londe, P. L. (2016). Orchestrating policy ideas: Philanthropies and think tanks in US education policy advocacy networks. *The Australian Educational Researcher, 43*(1), 55–73.

Lubienski, C., & Lubienski, S. (2014). *The public school advantage: Why public schools outperform private schools*. Chicago, IL: University of Chicago Press.

Luke, A. (2003). Literacy and the other: A sociological approach to literacy research and policy in multilingual societies. *Reading Research Quarterly, 38*(1), 132–141.

Lustick, H. (2017). Administering discipline differently: A Foucauldian lens on restorative school discipline. *International Journal of Leadership in Education, 20*(3), 297–311.

Lynch, K., Grummell, B., & Devine, D. (2015). *New managerialism in education: Commercialization, carelessness and gender*. New York, NY: Palgrave Macmillan.

Maier, A., Daniel, J., Oakes, J., & Lam, L. (2017). *Community schools as an effective school improvement strategy: A review of the evidence*. Palo Alto, CA: Learning Policy Institute.

Malen, B., & Ogawa, R. (1988). Professional-patron influence on site-based governance councils: A confounding case study. *Educational Evaluation and Policy Analysis, 10*(4), 251–270.

Malsbary, C.B. (2016). The refusal: Teachers making policy in NYC. *International Journal of Qualitative Studies in Education, 29*(10), 1326–1338.

Mann, B., & Bennett, H. (2016). Integration without integrating: How gentrification and community socioeconomic trends relate to differences in charter and traditional schooling options in Washington D.C. Paper presented at the annual meeting of University Council on Educational Administration, Detroit, MI.

Markow, D., Macia, L., & Lee, H. (2013). *The MetLife survey of the American teacher: A survey of teachers and principals*. Retrieved from www.metlife.com/assets/cao/foundation/MetLife-Teacher-Survey-2012.pdf

Marshall, C., & Anderson, C. (Eds.). (2009). *Activist educators: Breaking past limits*. New York, NY: Routledge.

Martin, S., Snow, J., & Franklin Torrez, C. (2011). Navigating the terrain of third space: Tensions with/in relationships in school-university partnerships. *Journal of Teacher Education, 61*(3), 299–311.

Mausethagen, S., & Granlund, L. (2012). Contested discourses of teacher professionalism: Current tensions between education policy and teachers' union. *Journal of Education Policy, 27*(6), 815–833.

Mautner, G. (2010). *Language and the market society: Critical reflections on discourse and dominance*. London, UK: Routledge.

Mayer, J. (2017). *Dark money: The hidden history of the billionaires behind the rise of the radical right*. New York, NY: Anchor Books.

Mazzucato, M. (2015). *The entrepreneurial state: Debunking public vs. private sector myths*. New York, NY: Perseus Books.

McGhan, B. (2002, March 1). A fundamental education reform: Teacher-led schools. *Phi Delta Kappan, 83*(7), 538–540.

McLean, N. (2017). *Democracy in chains: The deep history of the radical right's stealth plan for America*. New York, NY: Viking Books.

McMillan Cottom, T. (2017). *Lower ed: The troubling rise of for-profit colleges in the new economy*. New York, NY: The New Press.

Mehan, H., Hubbard, L., & Villanueva, I. (1994, June). Forming Academic Identity: Accomodation without Assimilation Among Involuntary Minorites. *Anthropology and Education Quarterly, 25* (2), pp. 91–117.

Mehta, J. (2010). The varied roles of ideas in politics: From "whether" to "how". In D. Beland & R. H. Cox (Eds.), *Ideas and politics in social science research* (pp. 23–46). Oxford, UK: Oxford University Press.

Mehta, J. (2013). *The allure of order: High hopes, dashed expectations, and the troubled quest to remake American schooling*. Oxford, UK: Oxford University Press.

Meier, D. (1995). *The power of their ideas: Lessons from a small school in Harlem*. Boston, MA: Beacon Press.

Mendez, G. (2003). Bachillerato IMPA: Middle school education for adults at a recovered factory. In E. Rodriguez (Ed.), *Pedagogies and curriculums to (re)imagine public education* (pp. 97–111). New York, NY: Springer.

Meyer, H., & Rowan, B. (2006). Institutional analysis and the study of education. In H. Meyer & B. Rowan (Eds.), *The new institutionalism in education* (pp. 1–14). Albany: State University of New York Press.

Meyer, J. W., & Rowan, B. (1977). Institutionalized organizations: Formal structure as myth and ceremony. *American Journal of Sociology, 83*(2), 340–363.

Mickelson, R., Giersch, J., Stearns, E., & Moller, S. (2013). How (and why) NCLB failed to close the achievement gap: Evidence from North Carolina, 1998–2004. *ECI Interdisciplinary Journal for Legal & Social Policy, 3*(1). Retrieved from ecipublications.org/ijlsp/vol3/iss1/1

Miller, J. (1990). *Creating spaces and finding voices: Teachers collaborating for empowerment*. Albany: State University of New York Press.

Miller, P. M. (2008). Examining the work of boundary spanning leaders in community contexts. *International Journal of Leadership in Education, 11*(4), 353–377.

Minow, M. (2002). *Partners, not rivals: Privatization and the public good.* Boston, MA: Beacon Press.

Mirel, J. (1993). *The rise and fall of an urban school system: Detroit, 1907–1981.* Ann Arbor: University of Michigan Press.

Miron, G., & Gulosino, C. (2016, April). *Virtual schools report 2016.* Boulder, CO: National Education Policy Center.

Mirowski, P. (2013). *Never let a serious crisis go to waste: How neoliberalism survived the financial meltdown.* Brooklyn, NY: Verso Books.

Mitchell, L. (2007). *The speculation economy: How finance triumphed over industry.* San Francisco, CA: Berrett-Koehler.

Mitra, D., Mann, B., & Hlavacik, M. (2016). Opting out: Parents creating contested spaces to challenge standardized tests. *Education Policy Analysis Archives, 24*(31).

Mitra, S. (2003). Minimally invasive education: A progress report on the "hole-in-the wall" experiments. *British Journal of Educational Technology, 34*(3), 367–371.

Moe, T. (2011). *Special interest: Teachers Unions and America's public schools.* Washington, DC: Brookings Institution Press.

Moll, L. C., & Gonzalez, N. (1994). Lessons from research with language-minority children. *Journal of Reading Behavior, 26*(4), 439–456.

Molnar, A., Miron, G., Gulosino, C., Shank, C., Davidson, C. Barbour, M., . . . Nitkin, D. (2017). *Virtual schools in the U.S.* Boulder, CO: National Education Policy Center.

Mongeau, L. (2015, September 9). Teachers wanted: Passion a must, patience required, pay negligible. *The Atlantic.* Retrieved from www.theatlantic.com/education/archive/2015/09/teachers-wanted-passion-a-must-patience-required-pay-negligible/404371/

Moore, A., & Clarke, M. (2016). 'Cruel optimism': Teacher attachment to professionalism in an era of performativity. *Journal of Education Policy, 31*(5), 666–677.

Moreton, B. (2009). *To serve God and Walmart: The making of Christian free enterprise.* Cambridge, MA: Harvard University Press.

Muller, J. (2018). *The tyranny of metrics.* Princeton, NJ: Princeton University Press.

Mungal, A. S. (2015). Hybridizing teacher education programs in New York City: A missed opportunity? *Education Policy Analysis Archives, 23*(89). https://epaa.asu.edu/ojs/article/view/2096/1655

Mungal, A. S. (2016). Teach for America, Relay Graduate School, and the charter school networks: The making of a parallel education structure. *Education Policy Analysis Archives, 24*(17). dx.doi.org/10.14507/epaa.24.2037

Murphy, M. (1990). *Blackboard unions: The AFT and the NEA, 1900–1980.* Ithaca, NY: Cornell University Press.

Naison, M. (2014). *Badass teachers unite: Reflections on education, history, and youth activism.* Chicago, IL: Haymarket.

Nasir, N.S., McLaughlin, M., & Jones, A. (2009). What does it mean to be African-American? Constructions of race and academic identity in an urban public high school. *American Educational Research Journal, 46*(1), 73–114.

National Commission on Excellence in Education. (1983). *A nation at risk: The imperative for educational reform.* Washington, DC: Government Publishing Office.

National Superintendents Roundtable. (2018, January). *How high the bar?: How would other nations perform if their students were judged by Common Core or NAEP benchmarks?* (Rep.). Retrieved from www.superintendentsforum.org/the-roundtable-in-2018/how-high-the-bar-report

Naylor, C. (2015). Why and how a teacher union supports autonomous teacher professional development in an age of new managerialism. In N. Bascia (Ed.), *Teacher unions in public education* (pp. 139–154). New York, NY: Palgrave Macmillan.

Nespor, J., & Voithofer, R. (2016). "Failure" irrelevant: Virtual schools and accountability-immunity. *Teachers College Record, 118*(1), 1–28.

Nichols, S., & Berliner, D. (2007). *Collateral damage: How high-stakes testing corrupts America's schools.* Cambridge, MA: Harvard University Press.

Niesche, R. (2010). Discipline through documentation: A form of governmentality for school principals. *International Journal of Leadership in Education, 13*(3), 249–263.

Niesz, T. (2010). "That school had become all about show": Image making and the ironies of constructing a good urban school. *Urban Education, 45*(3), 371–393.

Nunez, I., Michie, G., & Konkol, P. (2015). *Worth striking for: Why education policy is every teacher's concern.* New York, NY: Teachers College Press.

O'Neil, C. (2016). *Weapons of math destruction: How big data increases inequality and threatens democracy.* New York, NY: Crown Books.

Oplatka, I. (2007). The principal's role in marketing schools: Subjective interpretations and personal influences. *Planning and Changing, 38*, 208–221.

Oregon Education Investment Board. (2011). *Equity lens* (Oregon Department of Education). Retrieved from www.ode.state.or.us/superintendent/priorities/final-equity-lens-draft-adopted.pdf

Ospina, S., & Foldy, E. (2010). Building bridges from the margins: The work of leadership in social change organizations. *The Leadership Quarterly, 21*, 292–307.

O'Sullivan, J. (2016, November 8). Mass. voters reject charter school expansion. *Boston Globe.* Retrieved from www.bostonglobe.com/metro/2016/11/08/mass-voters-consider-expanding-charter-schools-legalizing marijuana/HP0dyVrKYZYCLeNf8DCaUK/story.html

Palmer, D., & Rangel, V. S. (2011). High stakes accountability and policy implementation: Teacher decision making in bilingual classrooms in Texas. *Educational Policy, 25*(4), 614–647.

Payne, C. (2008). *So much reform, so little change.* Cambridge, MA: Harvard Education Press.

Peck, J. (2010). *Constructions of neoliberal reason.* Oxford, UK: Oxford University Press.

Pedroni, T. (2007). *Market movements: African-American involvement in school voucher reform.* New York, NY: Routledge.

Perez-Rocha, M. (Dec. 3, 2014). When corporations sue governments. *New York Times.* https://www.nytimes.com/2014/12/04/opinion/when-corporations-sue-governments.html

Peters, T., & Waterman, R. (1982). *In search of excellence: Lessons from America's best-run companies.* New York, NY: Harper & Row.

Phelps, R. (Ed.). (2005). *Defending standardized tests.* Mahwah, NJ: Erlbaum.

Phillips-Fein, K. (2009). *Invisible hands: The businessmen's crusade against the New Deal.* New York, NY: Norton.

Picower, B. (2011). Resisting compliance: Learning to teach for social justice in a neoliberal context. *Teachers College Record, 113*(5), 1105–1134.

Pizmony-Levy, O., & Saraisky, N. G. (2016). Who opts out and why? Results from a national survey on opting out of standardized tests. New York, NY: Columbia University Academic Commons.

Podair, J. (2002). *The strike that changed New York: Blacks, whites and the Ocean Hill-Brownsville crisis.* New Haven, CT: Yale University Press.

Pogue, J. (2018, January 19). The GOP's biggest charter school experiment just imploded: How a washed-up lobbyist built a charter school empire and siphoned millions from public schools. *Mother Jones.* Retrieved from www.motherjones.com/politics/2018/01/the-gops-biggest-charter-school-experiment-just-imploded/

Poole, W. (2008). Intersections of organizational justice and identity under the new policy direction: Important understandings for educational leaders. *International Journal of Leadership in Education, 11*(1), 23–42.

Posey Maddox, L. (2014). *When middle-class parents choose urban schools: Class, race, and the challenge of equity in public education.* Chicago, IL: University of Chicago Press.

Powell, L. (1971). *The Powell memo.* Retrieved from reclaimdemocracy.org/powell_memo_ lewis/

Power, M. (1999). *The audit society: Rituals of verification.* Oxford, UK: Oxford University Press.

Quiggin, J. (2003, July 2). Word for Wednesday: Managerialism. *Commentary.* Retrieved from johnquiggin.com/index.php/

Quinn, R., & Carl, N. M. (2015). Teacher activist organizations and the development of professional agency. *Teachers and Teaching, 21*(6), 745–758.

Quinn, R., Oelberger, C., & Meyerson, D. (2016). Getting to scale: Ideas, opportunities, and resources in early diffusion of the Charter Management Organization, 1999–2006. *Teachers College Record, 118,* 1–44.

Radin, B. (2006). *Challenging the performance movement: Accountability, complexity, and democratic values.* Washington, DC: Georgetown University Press.

Ranciere, J. (1991). *The ignorant schoolmaster: Five lessons in intellectual emancipation.* Stanford, CA: Stanford University Press.

Ratliff, M. (2016). *Wisconsin vs. Minnesota: What the data show.* Washington, DC: Center for Economic and Policy Research.

Ravitch, D. (2011). *The death and life of the great American school system: How testing and choice are undermining education.* New York, NY: Basic Books.

Ravitch, D. (2014). *Reign of error: The hoax of the privatization movement and the danger to America's public schools.* New York, NY: Knopf.

Reardon, S. (2013). *The widening income achievement gap. Educational Leadership, 70*(8), 10–16.

Reckhow, S. (2013). *Follow the money: How foundation dollars change public school politics.* New York, NY: Oxford University Press.

Reeves, R. (2017). *Dream hoarders: How the American middle class is leaving everyone else in the dust, why that is a problem, and what to do about it.* Washington, DC: Brookings Institution Press.

Rich, A. (2013). Think tanks and the war of ideas in American politics. In M. Kazin (Ed.), *In search of progressive America* (pp. 73–84). Philadelphia: University of Pennsylvania Press.

Riedl, B. (2018). *Another Omnibus spending bill loaded with pork.* The Heritage Foundation. Retrieved from www.heritage.org/budget-and-spending/report/another-omnibus-spending-bill-loaded-pork

Riep, C., & Machacek, M. (2016). *Schooling the poor profitably: The innovations and deprivations of Bridge International Academies in Uganda.* Brussels, Belgium: Education International.

Rist, R. (1973). *The urban school: Factory for failure: A study of education in American society.* Cambridge, MA: MIT Press.

Robertson, S., & Verger, A. (2012). Governing education through public private partnerships. In S. Robertson, K. Mundy, A. Verger, & F. Menashy (Eds.), *Public private partnerships in education* (pp. 21–42). Cheltenham, UK: Edward Elgar.

Robinson, G. (2015). NYC school that skip standardized tests have higher graduation rates. *The Hechinger Report.* Retrieved from hechingerreport.org/nyc-schools-that-skip-standardized-tests-have-higher-graduation-rate

Rogers, D. (2006). *110 Livingston Street: Politics and bureaucracy in the New York City school system.* Clinton Corners, NY: Eliot Werner. (Original work published 1968)

Rogers, J., & Terriquez, V. (2009). "More justice": The role of organized labor in educational reform. *Educational policy, 23*(1), 216–241.

Rose, N. (1993). Government, authority, and expertise in advanced liberalism. *Economy and Society, 22*(3), 283–300.

Rothstein, R. (2017). *The color of law: A forgotten history of how our government segregated America.* New York, NY: Liveright.

Rousmaniere, K. (2007). Go to the principal's office: Toward a social history of the school principal in North America. *History of Education Quarterly, 47*(1), 1–22.

Rousmaniere, K. (2013). *The principal's office: A social history of the American school principal.* Albany: State University of New York Press.

Ryan, J. E. (2004). The perverse incentives of the No Child Left Behind Act. *New York University Law Review, 79* N.Y.U. Rev.932.

Ryan, J. (1998). Critical leadership for education in a postmodern world: Emancipation, resistance and communal action. *International Journal of Leadership in Education, 1*(3), 257–278.

Sachs, J. (2000). The activist professional. *Journal of Educational Change, 1,* 77–95.

Sachs, J. (2003). *The activist teaching profession.* London, UK: Open University Press.

Sachs, J. (2016). Teacher professionalism: Why are we still talking about it? *Teachers and Teaching, 22*(4), 413–425.

Sallis, E. (1993). *Total quality management in education.* New York, NY: Routledge.

Saltman, K. (2010). *The gift of education: Public education and venture philanthropy.* New York, NY: Palgrave Macmillan.

Saltman, K. (2013). *The failure of corporate school reform.* Boulder, CO: Paradigm.

Saltman, K. (2016). *Capitalizing on disaster: Taking and breaking public schools.* New York, NY: Routledge.

Samier, E. A. (2013). Where have the disruptions gone? Educational administration's theoretical capacity for analysing or fomenting disruption. *International Journal of Leadership in Education, 16*(2), 234–244.

Santoro, D. A., & Morehouse, L. (2011). Teaching's conscientious objectors: Principled leavers of high-poverty schools. *Teachers College Record, 113*(12), 2670–2704.

Sasko, C. (2017, December 14). Now's your chance to tell Philly how to run our schools. *Philadelphia Magazine.* Retrieved from www.phillymag.com/news/2017/12/14/philadelphia-school-board-education/

Scheiber, N. (2016, January 9). Doctors unionize to resist the medical machine. *The New York Times.* Retrieved from www.nytimes.com/2016/01/10/business/doctors-unionize-to-resist-the-medical-machine.html?_r=1

Schmidt, V. A. (2008). Discursive institutionalism: The explanatory power of ideas and discourse. *Annual Review of Political Science, 11*(1), 303–326.

Schmidt, V. A. (2017). Britain-out and Trump-in: A discursive institutionalist analysis of the British referendum on the EU and the US presidential election. *Review of International Political Economy, 24*(2), 248–269.

Schmidt, V. A., & Thatcher, M. (2014). Why are neoliberal ideas so resilient in Europe's political economy? *Critical Policy Studies, 8*(3), 340–347.

Scott, J. (2009). The politics of venture philanthropy in charter school policy and advocacy. *Educational Policy, 23*(1), 106–136.

Scott, J. (2011). Market-driven education reform and the racial politics of advocacy. *Peabody Journal of Education, 86,* 580–599.

Scott, J., & DiMartino, C. (2009). Public education under new management: A typology of educational privatization applied to New York City's restructuring. *Peabody Journal of Education, 84*(3), 432–452.

Scott, J., & Fruchter, N. (2009). Community resistance to school privatization: The case of New York City. In R. Fisher (Ed.), *The people shall rule: ACORN, community organizing, and the struggle for economic justice* (pp. 180–205). Nashville, TN: Vanderbilt University Press.

Seddon, T., Ozga, J., & Levin, J. (2013). Global transitions and teacher professionalism. In T. Sedden & J. Levin (Eds.), *Educators, professionalism and politics: Global transitions, national spaces and professional projects* (pp. 3–24). London, UK: Routledge.

Selwyn, N. (2011). 'It's all about standardization'—Exploring the digital (re)configuration of school management and administration. *Cambridge Journal of Education, 41*(4), 473–488.

Selwyn, N., Nemorin, S., Bulfin, S., & Johnson, N. (2017). *Everyday schooling in the digital age: High school, high tech?* New York, NY: Routledge.

Sennett, R. (1998). *The corrosion of character: The personal consequences of work in the new capitalism.* New York, NY: Norton.

Sennett, R. (2006). *The culture of the new capitalism.* New Haven, CT: Yale University Press.

Sennett, R., & Cobb, J. (1972). *The hidden injuries of class.* New York, NY: Norton.

Sergiovanni, T. (2000). *The lifeworld of leadership: Creating culture, community, and personal meaning in our schools.* San Francisco, CA: Jossey-Bass.

Settlage, J., & Meadows, L. (2002). Standards-based reform and its unintended consequences: Implications for science education within America's urban schools. *Journal of Research in Science Teaching, 39*(2), 114–127.

Shaffer, D. W., Nash, P., & Ruis, A. R. (2015). Technology and the new professionalization of teaching. *Teachers College Record, 117*(1), 1–30.

Shipps, D. (2006). *School reform, corporate style: Chicago, 1880–2000.* Lawrence: University Press of Kansas.

Shipps, D. (2012). Empowered or beleaguered? Principals' accountability under New York City's diverse provider regime. *Education Policy Analysis Archives, 20*(1), 1–40. Retrieved from epaa.asu.edu/ojs/article/view/892/950.

Shirley, D. (2016). Entrenched enemies, tactical partners, or steadfast allies? Exploring the fault lines between teacher unions and community organizing in the United States. *Leadership and Policy in Schools, 15*(1), 45–66.

Shore, C., & Wright, S. (2015). Governing by numbers: Audit culture, rankings and the new world order. *Social Anthropology, 23*(1), 22–28.

Shutz, A. (2006). Home is a prison in the global city: The tragic failure of school-based community engagement strategies. *Review of Educational Research, 76*(4), 691–743.

Siddle Walker, V. (1996). *Their highest potential: An African American school community in the segregated south.* Chapel Hill: University of North Carolina Press.

Singer, N., & Ivory, D. (2017, May 13). How Google took over the classroom. *The New York Times.* Retrieved from www.nytimes.com/2017/05/13/technology/google-education-chrome-books-schools.html

Singer, P. W. (2007). *Corporate warriors: The rise of the privatized military industry.* Ithaca, NY: Cornell University Press.

Sizer, T. (1984). *Horace's compromise.* New York, NY: Mariner Books.

Skiba, R. J., Horner, R. H., Chung, C., Rausch, M. K., May, S. L., & Tobin, T. (2011). Race is not neutral: A national investigation of African American and Latino disproportionality in school discipline. *School Psychology Review, 40*(1), 85–107.

Skrla, L., & Scheurich, J. (2004). *Educational equity and accountability.* New York, NY: Routledge.

Slaughter, S., & Rhoades, G. (2009). *Academic capitalism and the new economy: Markets, state, and higher education.* Baltimore, MD: Johns Hopkins University Press.

Sleeter, C. E. (2012). Confronting the marginalization of culturally responsive pedagogy. *Urban Education, 47*(3), 562–584.

Smith, E. J., & Harper, S. R. (2015). *Disproportionate impact of K–12 school suspension and expulsion on black students in southern states.* Philadelphia: University of Pennsylvania, Center for the Study of Race and Equity in Education.

Smith, M., & Pandolfo, N. (2011, November 27). For-profit certification for teachers is booming. *The New York Times.* p. A33.

Smith, M. L., Miller-Kahn, L., Heinecke, W., & Jarvis, P. (2004). *Political spectacle and the fate of American schools.* New York, NY: Routledge/Falmer.

Soja, E. (1996). *Thirdspace: Journeys to Los Angeles and other read-and-imagined places.* New York, NY: Blackwell Pub.

Sondel, B. (2015). Raising citizens or raising test scores? Teach for America, "no excuses" charters, and the development of the neoliberal citizen. *Theory & Research in Social Education,* *43*(3), 289–313.

Sondel, B. (2017). The new teachers' roundtable: A case study of collective resistance. *Critical Education, 8*(4), 1–22.

Star, K. (2011). Principals and the politics of resistance to change. *Educational Management, Administration & Leadership, 39,* 646–657.

State Higher Education Executive Officers Association (2017). SHEF: FY2017 State Higher education finance. Retreived from www.sheeo.org/sites/default/files/SHEF_FY2017.pdf

Steele, J. L., Slater, R. O., Zamarro, G., Miller, T., Li, J., Burkhauser, S., & Bacon, M. (2017). Effects of dual-language immersion programs on student achievement. *American Educational Research Journal, 54*(1), 282–306.

Stevenson, H., & Gilliland, A. (2016). In J. Evers & R. Kneyber (Eds.) The teachers' voice: Teacher unions at the heart of a new democratic professionalism. In *Flip the system: Changing education from the ground up* (pp. 108–119). London, UK: Routledge.

Stone-Johnson, C. (2014). Parallel professionalism in an era of standardization. *Teachers and Teaching: Theory and Practice, 20*(1), 74–91.

Strathern, M. (Ed.). (2000). *Audit cultures: Anthropological studies in accountability, ethics, and the academy.* London, UK: Routledge.

Strauss, V. (2013, June 14). Teachers' letters to Bill Gates. *The Washington Post.* Retrieved from www.washingtonpost.com/news/answer-sheet/wp/2013/06/14/teachers-letters-to-bill-gates/?utm_term=.68450d84420b

Strauss, V. (2017, May 14). In Arizona, teachers can now be hired with absolutely no training in how to teach. *The Washington Post.* Retrieved from www.washingtonpost.com/news/answer-sheet/wp/2017/05/14/in-arizona-teachers-can-now-be-hired-with-absolutely-no-training-in-how-to-teach/?utm_term=.f46abd240b97

Strauss, V. (December 28, 2017). Federal judge tells Arizona it can't ban Mexican American studies. *The Washington Post.* Retrieved from www.washingtonpost.com/news/answer-sheet/wp/2017/12/28/federal-judge-tells-arizona-it-cant-ban-mexican-american-studies/?utm_term=.f8a1bb32c0e7

Sullivan, W. (2004). *Work and integrity: The crisis and promise of professionalism in North America.* San Francisco, CA: Jossey-Bass.

Superville, D. (2015, November 3). Principals go to school to learn management savvy: New wave of principal-prep programs emphasize business practices. *Education Week.* Retrieved from www.edweek.org/ew/articles/2015/11/04/principals-go-to-school-to-learn-management.html

Superville, D. R. (2016, May 31). Oregon's 'equity lens' frames schools' take on bias. *Education Week.* Retrieved from www.edweek.org/ew/articles/2016/06/01/oregons-equity-lens-frames-schools-take-on.html

Tarlau, R. (2013). Coproducing rural public schools in Brazil: Contestation, clientelism, and the Landless Workers' Movement. *Politics & Society, 41,* 395–424.

Taylor, F. (2009). *The principles of scientific management.* Ithaca, NY: Cornell University Press. (Original work published 1911)

Theoharris, G. (2007). Social justice educational leaders and resistance: Toward a theory of social justice leadership. *Educational Administration Quarterly, 43,* 21–58.

Thomas, M., & Mockler, N. (2018). Alternative routes to teacher professional identity: Exploring the conflated sub-identities of Teach for America corps members. *Education Policy Analysis Archives, 26*(6). Retrieved from epaa.asu.edu/ojs/article/view/3015/1997

Thomas, R., & Davies, A. (2005). Theorizing the micro-politics of resistance: New Public Management and managerial identities in the UK public services. *Organization Studies, 26*(5), 683–706.

Thomas, W. B., & Moran, K. J. (1991). The politicization of efficiency concepts in the progressive period, 1918–1922. *Journal of Urban History, 17*(4), 390–409.

Thomson, P. (2008). Headteacher critique and resistance: A challenge for policy, and for leadership/management scholars. *Journal of Educational Administration and History, 40*(2), 85–100.

Thomson, P., Hall, C., & Jones, K. (2013). Towards educational change leadership as a discursive practice—or should all school leaders read Foucault? *International Journal of Leadership in Education, 16*(2), 155–172.

Torres, A. C., & Weiner, J. (2018). The new professionalism? Charter teachers' experiences and qualities of the teaching profession. *Education Policy Analysis Archives, 26*(19). Retrieved from epaa.asu.edu/ojs/article/view/3049/2010

Trujillo, T. (2014). The modern cult of efficiency: Intermediary organizations and the new scientific management. *Educational Policy, 28*(2), 207–232.

Tucker, M. (2011). *Surpassing Shanghai: An agenda for American education built on the world's leading systems.* Cambridge, MA: Harvard Education Press.

Tummers, L., Bekkers, V., & Steijn, B. (2009). Policy alienation of public professionals. *Public Management Review, 11*(5), 685–706.

Tumulty, K., & Layton, L. (2014, October 5). Changes in AP history trigger a culture clash in Colorado. *The Washington Post.* Retrieved from www.washingtonpost.com/politics/2014/10/05/fa6136a2-4b12-11e4-b72e-d60a9229cc10_story.html

Turner, E. (2014). Districts' responses to demographic change: Making sense of race, class, and immigration in political and organizational context. *American Educational Research Journal, 20*(10), 1–36.

Tyack, D. B. (1974). *The one best system: A history of American urban education.* Cambridge, MA: Harvard University Press.

Uetricht, M. (2014). *Strike for America: Chicago teachers against austerity.* Brooklyn, NY: Verso Books.

Valencia, R. *Dismantling contemporary deficit thinking: Educational thought and practice.* New York, NY: Routledge.

Valenzuela, A. (Ed.). (2004). *Leaving children behind: How "Texas style" accountability fails Latino youth.* Albany: State University of New York Press.

Yates, M. & McChesney, R. (2012). *Wisconsin uprising: Labor fights back.* New York, NY: Monthly Review Press.

Vellanki, M. (2015, September). *How startups are shaping the future of the $2 trillion education industry.* Mahesh VC [Web log post]. Retrieved from www.mahesh-vc.com/blog/how-startups-are-shaping-the-future-of-the-2-trillion-education-industry

Veltri, B. (2010). *Learning on other people's kids: Becoming a Teach for America teacher.* Charlotte, NC: Information Age.

Wacquant, L. (2016) Revisiting territories of relegation: Class, ethnicity and state in the making of advanced marginality. *Urban Studies, 53*(6), 1077–1088.

Wang, Y. (2017). The social networks and paradoxes of the opt-out movement amid the common core state standards implementation: The case of New York. *Education Policy Analysis Archives, 25*(34), 1–23.

Ward, S. (2011). The machinations of managerialism: New Public Management and the diminishing power of professionals. *Journal of Cultural Economy, 4*(2), 205–215.

Ward, S. (2012). *Neoliberalism and the global restructuring of knowledge and education.* New York, NY: Routledge.

Watkins, W. (2001). *The white architects of black education: Ideology and power in America, 1865–1954.* New York, NY: Teachers College Press.

Wayman, J., & Springfield, S. (2006). Technology-supported involvement of entire faculties in examination of student data for instructional improvement. *American Journal of Education, 112*(4), 549–571.

Weatherly, R., & Lipsky, M. (1977). Street-level bureaucrats and institutional innovation: Implementing special education reform. *Harvard Education Review, 47,* 171–197.

Weiner, L. (2018). Labor renaissance in the heartland. *Jacobin.* Retrieved from jacobinmag. com/2018/04/red-state-teachers-strikes-walkouts-unions

Weiner, L. (2012). *The future of our schools: Teachers unions and social justice.* Chicago, IL: Haymarket Books.

Welch, A.R. (1998). The cult of efficiency in education: Comparative reflections on the reality and the rhetoric. *Comparative Education, 34*(2), 157–175.

Westheimer, J. (2015). *What kind of citizen? Educating our children for the common good.* New York, NY: Teachers College Press.

Whitfield, D. (2001). *Public services or corporate welfare.* London, UK: Pluto Press.

Wilkins, C. (2011). Professionalism and the post-performative teacher: New teachers reflect on autonomy and accountability in the English school system. *Professional Development in Education, 37,* 389–409.

Wilkinson, R., & Pickett, K. (2010). *The spirit level: Why greater equality makes societies stronger.* New York, NY: Bloomsbury.

Willie, C., Edwards, R., & Alves, M. (2002). *Student diversity, choice, and school improvement.* New York, NY: Praeger.

Wills, J., & Sandholtz, J. H. (2009). Constrained professionalism: Dilemmas of teaching in the face of test-based accountability. *Teachers College Record, 111*(4), 1065–1114.

Wilson, W.J. (1997). *When work disappears: The world of the new urban poor.* New York, NY: Alfred A. Knopf.

Wilson, W.J. (2009). *More than just race: Being Black and poor in the inner city.* New York, NY: W.W. Norton.

Wolff, R. (2012). *Democracy at work: A cure for capitalism.* Chicago, IL: Haymarket Books.

Wood, D. R. (2011). And then the basals arrived: School leadership, learning communities and professionalism. *International Journal of Leadership in Education, 14*(4), 475–497.

Woods, P. (2005). *Democratic leadership in education.* London, UK: Sage.

Woods, P. (2011). *Transforming education policy: Shaping a democratic future.* Bristol, UK: Policy Press.

Wright, D. (2015). *Active learning: Social justice education and participatory action research.* New York, NY: Routledge.

Wright, K. B., Shields, S. M., Black, K., Banerjee, M., & Waxman, H. C. (2018). Teacher perceptions of influence, autonomy, and satisfaction in the early Race to the Top era. *Education Policy Analysis Archives, 26*(62).

Yates, M. (2012). *Wisconsin uprising: Labor fights back.* New York, NY: New York University Press.

Ylimaki, R. M. (2012). Curriculum leadership in a conservative era. *Educational Administration Quarterly, 48*(2), 304–346.

Zeichner, K. (2010). Competition, economic rationalization, increased surveillance, and attacks on diversity: Neo-liberalism and the transformation of teacher education in the U.S. *Teaching and Teacher Education, 26,* 1544–1552.

Zeichner, K. (2014). The struggle for the soul of teaching and teacher education in the USA. *Journal of Education for Teaching: International Research and Pedagogy, 40*(5), 551–568.

Zeichner, K., & Pena-Sandoval, C. (2015). Venture philanthropy and teacher education policy in the U.S.: The role of the New Schools Venture Fund. *Teachers College Record, 117*(6). Retrieved from www.tcrecord.org/content.asp?contentid=17539

Zilversmit, A. (1993). *Changing schools: Progressive education theory and practice, 1930–1960.* Chicago, IL: University of Chicago Press.

Index

NAMES

Abramovitz, M., 83
Abrams, S., 54, 58, 79
Achievement Reporting and
    Innovation System
    (ARIS), 16
Achinstein, B., 3, 24, 76, 122
Adamson, F., 2, 8, 53, 104
Addison, J., 59
Alexander, Michelle, 124
Allegretto, S., 136
Alves, M., 119
Amanti, C., 131
American Legislative Exchange
    Council (ALEC), 78
Amrein-Beardsley, A., 17
Anderson, C., 115
Anderson, G. L., 11, 12, 62, 64,
    66, 75, 79, 82, 97, 105,
    114, 121, 123, 131
Anderson, James D., 46
Anderson, J.D., 12
Anderson, J. D., 47, 125
Ansari, Zakiyah, 137
Anyon, J., 25, 97, 109, 113
Anyon, Y., 133, 134
Apollonio, D., 82
Apple, Michael, 12, 13, 26, 73,
    74, 76, 115, 124
Ashby, S., 130
Astrand, B., 2, 135
Au, W., 16, 31, 85
Ayers, W., 129

Baker, B., 10, 54
Baldridge, B., 7
Baldwin, William H., 48
Ball, S., 1, 2, 63, 72, 77, 84,
    85, 91, 98, 99, 100, 101,
    107, 124

Bancroft, K., 53
Banerjee, M., 15
Bannon, Steve, 68
Barnum, M., 64
Barrow, C. W., 7
Barton, P. E., 136
Basken, P., 105
Bastow, S., 22
Bates, R., 99
Beardsley, S., 85
Beck, U., 18, 19
Beilke D., 79
Bekkers, V., 8
Bell, D., 124, 133
Bennett, H., 54, 74
Berliner, D., 16, 17, 52, 53, 55,
    63, 73, 124
Bhaba, H., 3, 132
Bhanji, Z., 84
Biddle, B., 52, 63
Biesta, G. J., 9, 120, 124, 128
Black, K., 15
Blackmore, J., 23
Blake, A., 115
Blanco Bosco, E., 53
Blasio, Bill de, 103
Bloomberg, M., 16, 23, 103,
    111
Blount, J. M., 35
Blowfield, M., 3
Blyth, M., 104
Bobbitt, Franklin, 12, 32, 38
Boggs, C., 23
Bonilla-Silva, E., 72
Bottery, M., 21
Bowles, S., 52
Brantlinger, A., 12
Brantlinger, E., 74
Braun, A., 124

Breneman, D., 10
Brewer, T. J., 50, 53
British Revised Code of 1860,
    30
Broad, Eli, 45
Bronfenbrenner, U., 16
Brook, R. H., 89
Brown, E., 54, 74
Brown, J., 38
Bruno, R., 130
Buchanan, James, 137
Buffett, Warren, 134
Bulfin, S., 119
Bundy, McGeorge, 44
Buntrock, LeAnn M., 56
Buras, K., 63
Burch, P., 11, 20, 64, 75, 115
Bush, G. W., 67, 68, 75
Butler, J. S., 36
Byers, Brook, 87

Cabrera, N., 132
Callahan, R., 25, 31, 32
Cammarota, J., 131
Campbell, D., 9
Capper, C., 65
Carnegie, D., 86
Carnoy, M., 14, 135
Carpenter, S., 116
Carstensen, M. B., 104
Cassel, C. K., 90
Center for Research on Educa-
    tion Outcomes, 22, 53
Chamber of Commerce, U.S.,
    46
Chen, P. G., 89
Christie, H. K., 80
Chubb, J., 64, 118
Clark, M., 22

Clarke, M., 17, 98
Coalition for Community
    Schools, 127
Coalition of Essential Schools,
    128
Cobb, J., 17
Cochran-Smith, M., 13
Codd, J., 13
Cohen, M., 57, 66, 94, 97, 98,
    101, 107
Cohen, S., 33, 125
Coley, R. J., 136
Collyer, F. M., 77
Connell, K. W., 54
Corcoran, S., 54
Costigan, A., 15, 100, 104, 131
Cottom, McMillan, 70
Counts, George, 25
Courtney, S., 70, 101
Cox, Archibald, 41
Crary, J., 14
Cremin, I. A., 46
Cribb, A., 8
Crocco, M. S., 15, 131
Crosson, F. J., 89
Cuban, L., 3, 8, 26, 38, 39, 40,
    52, 64, 65, 112
Cubberley, Ellwood P., 32, 34,
    35, 36, 38

Daniel, J., 125
Darling-Hammond, L., 2, 8,
    123
Datnow, A., 16
Davies, A., 99
Davis, Angela, 124
Davis, G. F., 59
Dayton, Mark, 136
De Bie, m., 124
Debray, E., 72
Defense Advanced Research
    Projects Agency (DAR-
    PA), 59
De La Cruz, P., 82
Denhardt, J., 2, 13, 14
Denhardt, R., 2, 13, 14
Derber, C., 61
Devine, D., 56
DeVos, Betsy, 68, 135
Dewey, J., 25, 38, 111
Dhaliwal, T. K., 134
DiMartino, C., 11, 20, 75, 84,
    86, 103

Dodge, Mary Abigail, 38
Doerr, John, 87
Domina, T., 116, 117
Donchik, Montoro, 11, 62, 79
Dotter, D., 54
Drame, E., 131
Driscoll, M. E., 24, 42, 116
Drutman, L., 62, 75
Ducey, Doug, 86
Dunleavy, P., 22
Dwyer, E., 22
Dzur, A., 97, 115, 119, 133

Economic Policy Institute, 8
Edelman, M., 4, 52, 63
Edmonds, R., 52
Education Industry Associa-
    tion (EIA),, 75
Education International, 129
Education Technology Indus-
    try Network, 75
Edwards, M., 81, 119
Ellis, V., 115
Elmore, R., 14
Every Student Succeeds Act
    (ESSA), 86
Evetts, J., 2, 13, 62, 115
Exworthy, M., 2, 13

Faber, Nick, 127
Fairclough, N., 65
Federico, C. M., 93
Fenwick, T., 114, 121
Ferguson, K., 43, 44
Ferrare, J., 85
Figueroa, E., 135
Fine, M., 131
Fitzgerald, T., 98
Ford Foundation, 44, 49, 86
Foroohar, R., 57, 59
Forsey, M., 14
Foucault, M., 91, 92, 94, 96,
    101, 109, 121
Fournier, V., 121
Frankenberg, E., 54
Fraser, J. A., 18
Fraser, J. W., 52
Fraser, N., 109
Frederickson, H. G., 51
Freire, P., 103, 130
Friedberg, M. W., 89
Friedman, M., 8, 10, 23, 61, 64,
    73, 75, 82, 137

Friedrich, D., 24, 87
Fruchter, N., 76
Fukuyama, F., 73
Fullan, M., 135
Fuller, Howard, 75

Gabriel, R., 20
Gandin, L., 124
Gates, Bill, 45, 71, 84
Gay, G., 114, 131
Gee, J., 102, 103
Gelberg, D., 40, 41, 42
Gewirtz, S., 8, 62
Giersch, J., 22
Gillies, D., 1, 100
Gilliland, A., 129
Gilmore, R., 7
Ginsberg, B., 85
Ginsberg, M., 131
Gintis, H., 52
Gitlin, A., 99
Glantz, S., 82
Glazerman, S., 54
Gleeson, P., 22, 105
Gobby, B., 23
Godsey, M., 69
Goldstein, D., 12, 43, 44
Goldstein, J., 13, 128, 129
Gonzalez, N., 128, 131
Gonzalez, T., 134
Goodsell, C. T., 10
Gorostiaga, J., 131
Gould, Elise, 8
Gove, Aaron, 31
Granlund, L., 130
Green, P., 10
Green, T., 114, 116
Gregory, A., 133
Grimaldi, E., 22
Grinberg, J., 121
Grossman,, 61
Grubb, W. N., 46
Grummell, B., 56
Gulosino, C., 79
Gunter, H., 20, 22, 91, 101
Gunzenhauser, M., 90, 114

Haas, E., 82
Habermas, J., 3, 14
Haley, Margaret, 31
Halford, S., 2, 13
Hall, D., 20, 22, 103
Haney, W., 22

Hanselman, P., 116
Hargreaves, A., 16, 22, 123
Harper, S. R., 133
Harvey, D., 10, 11, 22, 68, 72
Hashim, A. K., 134
Heffeman, A., 17
Heinecke, W., 63
Hemphil, C., 112
Heritage Foundation, 134
Herr, K., 75, 98, 105
Herzer, K. R., 89
Hextall, I., 8
Hinton, E., 72
Hlavacik, M., 76
Hochschild, A., 56
Hodge, Andrea, 56
Hood, C., 21
Horn, J., 87
Horsford, S., 52
Howard, G., 113
Howarth, D., 91
Hubbard, L., 124, 132
Huffington Post, 76
Hursh, D., 28
Hwang, N., 116
Hynds, A., 122

Ingersoll, R., 8, 12, 19
Irby, D., 131
Ishimaru, A. M., 116
Ivory, D., 82

Jain, S. H., 90
Jamison, M., 65
Jaquette, O., 132
Jarvis, P., 63
Jessen,, S. B., 20
Johanek, M. C., 36, 121
Johnson, L., 36, 121
Johnson, M., 129
Johnson, S., 18, 72, 119
Jones, A., 103, 132
Jost, J. T., 93
Juahar, S., 85
Junemann, C., 84, 85
Jungck, S., 115

Kahneman, Daniel, 93
Kantor, Harvey A., 45, 46
Kaplan, E., 101
Katz, M. B., 30, 31
Kearns, C., 82
Keddie, A., 23

Keith, N., 115, 121
Keller, Franklin, 47, 48
Khalifa, M., 114
Kickert, W., 14
King, Samuel, 30
Kingdon, J. W., 124
Kirp, David, 112
Klein, Naomi, 63
Kliebard, H. M., 39, 46
Klikauer, T., 9
Knights, D., 105
Konkol, P., 4, 129
Korten, A., 81, 137
Kovaks, P., 80
Koyama, J., 75, 90
Kumashiro, K. K., 45, 50

Labaree, D., 37, 38, 39, 40, 87,
     113, 116, 119, 135
Ladson-Billings, G., 114, 132
Lafer, G., 55
Lakoff, George, 4, 52, 63, 66,
     67, 80, 91, 93, 104
Lam, L., 125
Lankshear, C., 102
Laura, C., 129
Lave, J., 13
Lawn, M., 115
Layton, L., 84, 98
Lazerson, M., 46
Lazzarato, M., 100
Leachman, M., 135
Learning to Earn, 46
Leask, I., 98
Lee, H., 20
Lepore, J., 20
Levin, J., 2
Levine, A., 24
Libby, K., 87
Lieberman, A., 15
Lipman, P., 76, 102
Lipsky, M., 40
Locke, R., 9, 57, 58, 60, 73
Lopez, I. H., 82, 137
Lortie, D., 122
Lubienski, C., 2, 8, 22, 50, 53,
     54, 104
Luke, A., 102
Lustick, H., 134
Lynch, K., 56
Lytle, S., 13

Machacek, M., 10, 22, 68

Macia, L., 20
Maguire, M., 124
Mahony, P., 8
Maier, A., 125, 126, 127
Makris, M. V., 54, 74
Malen, B., 115
Malsbary, C. B., 104
Mann, B., 54, 74, 76
Margetts, H., 22
Margonis, F., 99
Markow, D., 20
Marshall. C., 114
Martin, S., 3
Marx, R., 132
Masterson, K., 135
Mausethagen, S., 130
Mautner, G., 65, 66, 103
Mayer, J., 81
Mazzucato, Mariana, 10, 59,
     60, 65
McChesney, R., 4
McCoy, Rhoady, 43
McEachin, A., 116
McGhan, B., 124
McLaughlin, M., 132
McLean, N., 11, 137
McNally, J., 115
McNicholl, J., 115
Mead, J., 10
Meadows, L., 53
Mehan, H., 124, 132
Mehta, J., 13, 49, 53, 93, 98
Meier, D., 24
Mendez, G., 124
Mexican-American Legal
     Defense Fund, 75
Meyer, J. W., 65
Meyerson, D., 54
Michie, G., 4, 129
Mickelson, R., 22
Milem, J., 132
Miller, J., 116
Miller, P.M., 131
Miller-Kahn, L., 63
Milliken v. Bradley, 52
Mills, C., 20
Minow, M., 10, 64, 83
Mirel, J., 42, 44
Miron, G., 54, 79
Mirowski, P., 123
Mitchell, L., 59
Mitra, D., 70, 76
Mitra, Sugata, 69

Mittenfelner, C., 106, 107
Mockler, N., 85
Moe, T., 42, 64, 118
Moll, L. C., 128, 131
Moller, S., 22
Molnar, A., 70
Mongeau, L., 95
Moore, A., 17
Moran, K. J., 38
Morehouse, L., 100
Moreton, B., 74
Muller, J., 100
Mungal, A. S., 3, 22, 56, 68, 81, 85, 86
Murphy, M., 42, 43
Murray, A., 3

Nabeel, A. P., 12
Naison, M., 137
Napier, J. L., 93
Nash, P., 70
Nasir, N. S., 132
National Association for the Advancement of Colored People (NAACP), 75
National Association of Manufacturers (NAM), 38, 46
National Commission on Excellence in Education, 49, 57, 63
National Education Policy Center, 132
Nation at Risk, A (National Commission on Excellence in Education), 13, 72
Naylor, C., 130
Nemorin, S., 119
Nespor, J., 3
New Schools Venture Fund, 45, 87
New Teachers' Roundtable, 106
Nichols, S., 53
Niesche, R., 104
Niesz, T., 107
Nixon, Richard, 10
Nunez, I., 4, 129, 130

Oakes, J., 125
Obama administration, 68, 93
Oelberger, C., 54
Ogawa, R., 3, 24, 76, 115, 122
Ogden, Robert C., 48

Olmedo, A., 98, 99, 100, 101
Oluwole, J., 10
O'Neil, Cathy, 9
Oplatka, I., 20
Oregon Education Investment Board, 133
O'Sullivan, J., 54
Ozga, J., 2, 115

Palmer, D., 104
Pandolfo, N., 86
Paulus, T., 20
Payne, C., 24, 52, 122
Peck, J., 91
Pedroni, T., 52, 75, 119
Peer Assistance and Review (PAR), 128
Pena-Sandoval, C., 3, 12, 24
Perez-Rocha, M., 62
Peters, T., 21, 23
Phelps, R., 52
Phillips-Fein, K., 49, 137
Pickett, K., 67, 118
Picower, B., 105, 106
Pizmony-Levy, O., 53
Podair, J., 24, 41, 75, 116
Pogue, J., 70
Pollock, M., 133
Poole, W., 2, 100, 102
Posey Maddox, L., 74
Powell, Lewis, 10, 49
Power, M., 13
Pronovost, P. J., 89
Puckett, J., 36, 121
Pusser, B., 10

Quiggin, J., 9
Quinn, R., 12, 54, 106, 107

Race to the Top, 93
Radin, B., 2, 13
Ranciere, J., 70
Rangel, V. S., 104
Ratliff, M., 136
Ravitch, Diane, 8, 74
Reagan, Ronald, 72
Reardon, S., 54
Reckhow, S., 86
Reeves, R., 117
Rhoades, G., 8, 56, 85
Rich, A., 82
Rideau, S., 17
Riedl, B., 134

Riep, C., 10, 22, 68
Rigler, Frank, 30
Rincon-Gallardo, S., 135
Rist, R., 113
Ritchell, Amy, 126, 127
Robertson, S., 10, 20
Robinson, G., 128
Rockefeller Foundation, 86
Rogers, D., 24, 111
Rogers, J., 129
Rose, N., 14
Rosenwald, Julius, 47
Rosenwald Fund, 47
Rothstein, R., 72, 118, 136
Rousmaniere, Kate, 12, 33, 34, 35, 36, 37
Rowan, B., 65
Ruis, A. R., 70
Ryan, J., 53, 66, 101

Sachs, J., 17, 114, 122, 124, 130
Sallis, E., 23
Saltman, K., 28, 45, 53, 63
Samier, E. A., 100
Sandholtz, J. H., 14, 76
Santoro, D. A., 100
Saraisky, N. G., 53
Sasko, C., 76
Savage, J., 98
Scheiber, N., 89
Scheurich, J., 53
Schmidt, V. A., 93, 103, 104
Scott, J., 1, 8, 11, 12, 45, 71, 72, 75, 76, 77, 81, 84, 86, 103
Seddon, T., 2
Selwyn, N., 119
Sennett, R., 17, 18, 19, 20, 21, 55, 56, 100
Sergiovanni, T., 3, 14
Serpieri, R., 22
Settlage, J., 53
Shaffer, D. W., 70
Shanker, Albert, 43
Shields, S. M., 15
Shipps, D., 7, 23, 28
Shirley, D., 123, 129
Shore, C., 13
Shutz, A., 116
Siddle Walker, V., 37, 121
Siegel-Hawley, G., 54
Singer, N., 82
Singer, P.W., 10
Siskin, L., 14

Sizer, Ted, 128
Skiba, R. J., 133
Skrla, L., 52
Slaughter, S., 8, 56, 85
Sleeter, C. E., 3, 131
Smith, B., 12
Smith, E. J., 133
Smith, Kim, 87
Smith, M., 86
Smith, M. L., 63
Snow, J., 3
Soja, E., 3
Sondel, B., 100, 105, 106
Speiglman, A., 3
Spender, J.-C., 9, 57, 58, 60, 73
Springfield, A., 15, 16
Star, K., 122
State Higher Education Exec-
    utive Officers Associa-
    tion, 7
State Innovation Exchange
    (SIX), 80
State Policy Network (SPN), 78
Stearns, E., 22
Steele, J. L., 124
Steijn, B., 8
Stevenson, H., 129
Stoddard, C., 54
Stone-Johnson, C., 17
Strathern, M., 13
Strauss, V., 13, 45, 86, 132
Strunk, K. O., 134
Students in Free Enterprise
    (SIFE), 74
Sullivan, W., 120
Superville, D., 56, 57, 133

Tarlau, R., 124
Tashima, A. Wallace, 132
Taylor, Frederick, 31, 57
Taylor, George, 41
Terriquez, V., 129
Thatcher, Margaret, 73, 99, 104
Theoharris, G., 122
Thomas, M., 85
Thomas, W. B., 38, 99
Thomson, P., 100, 103
Thorndike, Edward, 38, 39
Tinkler, J., 22
Torres, A. C., 17
Torrez, Franklin, 3
Trujillo, T., 31
Trump, Donald, 134, 137
Tucker, M., 53
Tummers, L., 8
Tumulty, K., 98
Turner, E., 10, 66
Tuttle, C., 22
Tutty, M., 89
Tyack, D. B., 30, 31, 32, 33, 34,
    35, 39, 45

Uetricht, M., 129, 130

Valencia, R., 113
Valenzuela, A., 22
Vellanki, M., 74
Veltri, B., 3
Verger, A., 10, 20
Villanueva, I., 124, 132
Voithofer, R., 3

Wacquant, L., 113

Walker, Scott, 136
Wang, Y., 54, 76
Ward, S., 2, 11, 21, 91
Waterman, R., 23
Watkin, William H., 48
Watkins, W., 12, 48, 116
Waxman, H. C., 15
Wayman, J., 15, 16
Weatherly, R., 40
Weiner, L., 11, 17, 76, 129
Welch, A. R., 30
Westheimer, J., 118, 124
Whitfield, D., 63
Wildemeersch, D., 124
Wilkins, C., 17
Wilkinson, R., 67, 118
Willie, C., 119, 124
Wills, J., 14, 76
Wilson, W. J., 67, 119
Wolff, R., 3
Wood, D. R., 105, 123
Woods, P., 13, 115
Wright, K. B., 15
Wright, S., 13, 131

Yates, M., 4
Ylimaki, R. M., 102, 103

Zeichner, K., 3, 8, 12, 24, 87,
    100
Zelnik, J., 83, 84
Zilversmit, A., 39
Zuckerberg, Mark, 69

SUBJECTS

Accountability, 26, 49. *See also* Responsibility
    alternative systems of, 128–129
    corporate, 62, 84–85
    forms of, 14–15
    managerial meaning of, 9
    norms and, 93
    performance and, 107–108
    in public sector, 7, 8
    vs. responsibility, 119–120
    system world vs. lifeworld in, 14
Accumulation by dispossession, 11, 22, 68
Achievement gap, 136
Activism, 1, 4, 38, 83, 136
Activism/advocacy dimension, 26
Activists, Black, 42, 43
Activist state, 23
Administrative progressives, 39
Administrative state, 68
Administrators. *See also* Leadership; Principals
    in bureaucracy, 32
    career ladder for, 34
    certification requirements, 12–13, 35, 36
    of charter schools, 86
    efficiency as goal of, 32
    as expert managers, 33–34
    gender and, 35
    preparation of, 32, 45, 56, 100
    as professional, 12–14, 33
    professionalization of, 32
    resistance and, 101
Advocacy, 121–123. *See also* Activism
Advocacy Leadership (Anderson), 123
African Americans. *See* Activists, Black; Communities of color; Low-income communities of color; Low-income students of color
Agency, professional, 107
Agency, strategic, 104
ALEC (American Legislative Exchange Council), 11, 62, 88, 135, 136
Alliance for Quality Education, 137
American Educational Research Association, 64
American Enterprise Institute, 53
American Legislative Exchange Council (ALEC), 11, 62, 88, 135, 136
Analytics, predictive, 9
Arizona, 132
Arts-testing initiative, 93–94
Assessment, alternative, 128
Assessment, formative, 28
Assimilation of immigrants, 31

Audit culture, 13, 16–17, 108
Austerity, 8, 83–84, 108, 135, 136–137
Austin, Texas, 112
Authority, 34, 104
Automation, 20
Autonomy, 13–14, 15, 23, 38–40

Bain Capital, 27
Bannon, Steve, 22
Benefits, 55
Big data, 9, 15–16
Black education, 46–48, 116. *See also* Low-income students of color; Students of color
Blended-learning schools, 70
Brown v. Board of Education, 35–36, 49
Bureaucracy
    vs. centralization, 42
    centrally governed, 29–31
    communities of color and, 42–43
    low-income neighborhoods, 42
    principals in, 34–37
    professionalism in, 32–42
    teachers in, 32–33, 37–42
Bureaucrats, street-level, 40
Business. *See also* Corporations; Reforms, business-oriented
    influence of, 33, 49–50, 51
    over-regulation of, 3
    perceived attack on, 10
    shift to new managerialism, 51
    support of public schools and, 3
    transfer of principles to public sector, 7
Business associations, 77
Business Council, 77
Business leaders
    curriculum and, 46
    historical influence of, 28–32
    influence on Black education, 46–48
    policymaking and, 27, 28, 45–48
Business model
    appeal of, 52
    failure of, 58–61
    popularity of, 55
Business Roundtable, 11, 77
Business schools, 56–57, 58, 60, 96

Campaign for Fiscal Equity, 137
Campbell's law, 9
Capital accumulation by dispossession, 11, 22, 68

Capitalism
    academic, 56
    educational, 56
    fast/late, 11, 18. *See also* neoliberalism
    new, 21
Capitalism and Freedom (Friedman), 10, 82–83
Capitalists, venture, 45
Case method, 58
Center for Education Reform, 135
Certification, alternative. *See* Teacher preparation
Certification requirements, 12–13
Chamber of Commerce, U.S., 10–11, 49
Character, 19, 21
Charter management organizations (CMOs), 54, 85
Charter schools, 1, 53, 64, 74, 107 108. *See also* New Public Management (NPM)
    leaders of, 86
    low-income communities of color and, 76
    oversight of, 70
    performance of, 53–54
    philanthropists' support for, 81
    segregation and, 54
Chicago, activism in, 4
Child-centered philosophy, 38, 46
Choice, 7. *See also* School choice
Citizens United, 62, 80
City University of New York (CUNY), 136
Civil rights, 49, 72, 116, 136
Class, professionalism and, 12
CMOs (charter management organizations), 54, 85
Coalition for Community Schools, 126–127
Cognitive framing, 66–67
Cohen, Michael, 27
Cold War, 44
Collective-bargaining rights, 41
Commodification, 63, 82
Common Core State Standards, 64, 74, 84
Common sense, NPM as, 91
Communities of color. *See also* Low-income communities of color; Low-income students of color
    bureaucracy and, 42–43
    support for NPM, 75–76
Community
    vs. bureaucracy, 42–45
    linking schools with, 112, 116
    vs. professionalism, 42–45
Community control, 43–44
Community schools, 124–128

Compensation, 13, 41, 136
Competition, in public sector, 7
Conservatives, 73–74
Constitution, U.S., 79
Consultants, 19
Contact zones, 118
Contracting, 84
Contracts, 50
Corporate accountability, 84–85
Corporate culture, 17
Corporate discourses, 64–66
Corporate sector, reform from, 21. *See also* Reforms, business-oriented
Corporations
    flexible, 55
    history of, 61–62
Corporatism, vs. managerialism, 61
Corrosion of Character, The (Sennett), 19
Counter-conduct, 97, 104–108
Counter-discourses, 97, 102–104
Counter-networks, 79–80, 137–138
Counter-publics, 109
Cowles Commission, 58
Crises, 52, 63, 83
Criteria, 12
Critical vigilance, 97, 98–101
Cultural shifts, business-oriented reforms and, 30
Curriculum
    for Black students, 46–48
    business leaders' influence on, 46
    culturally relevant, 43
    culturally responsive, 131–133
    double, 100

Data. *See also* Outcome measures; Testing, high-stakes
    in early reforms, 30
    emphasis on, 15–16
Deceptive frames, 66–67
Decisionmaking
    control over, 13
    data-driven, 16
    inclusion in, 115
    managers involved in, 57
    mathematical models for, 58
    use of quantitative social indicators, 9
Susan and Michael Dell Foundation, 27
Democracy
    neoliberalism and, 9
    threats to, 2
    in workplace, 3

Democracy at Risk (Forum for Education and Democracy), 123
Democratic dimension, 26
Democratic practices, enacting, 124
Democratic professionalism, 42, 97, 109, 115–119
Democrats, 25
Democrats for Education Reform, 25
Destabilization, 82
Destabilization of public sector, 63
Detracking, 116
DeVos, Betsy, 123
Dewey, John, 38, 46
Disciplinary power, 92
Disciplinary practices, 121
Discipline, of professionals, 14
Discipline, student, 133–134
Discourse critique, 102–104
Discourses, 66–67, 97, 102–104
Discretion, 40. *See also* Autonomy
Disembedding, 73
Disinvestment
    from higher education, 7
    from K–12 education, 8
    from public sector, 8, 63, 82, 137
Doctors, 89–90, 96
Domination, 96
Due process, 100

Economy, education and, 46, 50, 57, 72
Edubusinesses, 10, 71, 72, 75, 79
Education
    as commodity, 55–56
    linked to economy, 50, 57
    minimally invasive, 70
    private parallel system, 22
    as profit center, 74–75, 82
Education, U.S. Department of, 12, 68, 123
Educational Researcher (journal), 64
Education and the Cult of Efficiency (Callahan), 31–32
Education industry, 64, 79, 113. *See also* Edubusinesses
Education International, 129
Education management organizations (EMOs), 79
Efficiency, 7, 31, 32, 34
Electronic Classrooms of Tomorrow, 70
Elementary and Secondary Education Act, 49, 136
Emancipatory knowledge framework, 131
EMOs (education management organizations), 79

Entrepreneurial culture, 18
Entrepreneurial ethos, in schools, 23
Entrepreneurialism, 10, 59
Entrepreneurial State, The (Mazzucato), 59
Equal educational opportunity, 49, 72, 116–118, 125. *See also* Integration; Segregation
Equity language, 66
Evaluation, 27, 50, 92
Every Student Succeeds Act, 112

Factory model, 24, 31
Faculty, education, 131
Finance, 60
Financialization, 18, 68, 84
First Amendment, 62
Flexibility, 20, 21
Ford Foundation, 43–44, 58
Formative assessments, influence of philanthropists on, 28
For-profit universities, effectiveness of, 70
Forum for Education and Democracy, 123
Foucault, Michel, 99
Fourteenth Amendment, 61
Framing, 66–67
Franklin Institute, 78
Freedom, neoliberalism and, 9
Friedman, Milton, 18, 54
Functionaries, 32–33
Funding, 52
    alternative sources of, 108
    decrease in, 7
    equitable, 52

Gates, Bill, 28
Gates, Melinda, 28
Gates Foundation, 27, 28, 45
Gender
    administrators and, 35
    professionalism and, 12
Germany, 58–59
Gig economy, 55
Governance
    digital-era, 22
    inclusion in, 26, 115–116
Government, 61
Governmentality, 92
Graduate programs, online, 68
Grants, requirements for participating in, 108
Grassroots organizations/activism, 4, 137. *See also* Activism
Great Society, 72, 136

Harvard School of Business Administration, 58

Healthcare, 89–90, 96
Heritage Foundation, 78
Hidden Injuries of Class, The (Sennett and
    Cobb), 17–18
Higher education, 7–8, 136. *See also* Teacher
    preparation
Hospitals, corporatization of, 85
Human capital, 13, 46, 49, 135
Human rights, 116

Ideas, normalizing power of, 93
Identities, new professional, 96
Identities, professional, 1, 2, 50, 85
Identity, power and, 95
Ideology, overturning, 104
Ignorant Schoolmaster, The (Ranciere), 70
Immigrants, 31, 33
Impression management, 20
Improbable Scholars (Kirp), 112
Incarceration, 124
Incarceration,, 72
Incentives, 2, 8, 53, 89
Inclusion, 26, 115–116
Industrial economy, 29
Industry, poor performance of, 58
Inequality, effectively maintained, 116–117
Inequities, 113
Innovation, 59–60, 61
Inquiry, 15–16, 130–131
In Search of Excellence (Peters and Waterman),
    23
Integration, 36, 43, 118–119
Intensification, 14, 18, 19, 23
Investment, public, in education, 134–137
Issue networks, 77–83
IT industry, 59

Japan, 58
Job satisfaction, 15, 20, 89
Job security, 18, 37, 41, 55, 84, 100

Keynesian welfare state, 8, 72
KIPP, 86
Krasner, Larry, 76

Labor. *See also* Unions
    costs, in education, 11
    distance from management, 58
Language
    corporate discourses, 64–66
    counter-discourses, 102–104
    deceptive frames, 66–67
    legitimacy and, 65

Laws, anti-labor, 78
Leadership. *See also* Administrators; Principals
    distributed, 115
    graduate degree programs in, 96
    masculine, 35
Learning process, 32, 39
Legislation. *See* Policy
Liberalism, embedded, 72
Libertarians, 73
Lifeworld, 14–15
Lobbying, 62
Low-income communities, 33
    relation with teachers' unions, 43–44
    support for NPM, 75–76
    teacher gap in, 8
Low-income communities of color
    centralized governance and, 42
    resistance to NPM, 76
    unions and, 130
Low-income parents, 75–76
Low-income students, 14
Low-income students of color
    educator turnover and, 19
    philanthropists and, 81
    reforms and, 3
    schools serving, 52
Loyalty, 56

Males, White, 12
Management, 31, 58
Management science, 58
Managerialism, 1, 84. *See also* New Public Man-
    agement (NPM); Professional, new
    beginnings of, 57
    vs. corporatism, 61
    in private sector, 18
    reforms from, 1
    shift to, 51
    transferred to education, 62–67
    transfer to public sector, 10
    use of term, 9, 57, 58
Managerial school, 62
Managers, expert, 33–34
Market, 1
    discipline by, 14
    reforms and, 2. *See also* New Public Manage-
        ment (NPM)
    relation with state, 23
Marketization, 83
Market regime, effects of, 8
Mathematical models, 60
Meritocracy, 67
Merit pay, 50

Mexican-American Studies program, 132
Middle-class professionals, 74
Migration, Black, 47
Minnesota, 136
Minoritized communities. *See* Activists, Black;
    Communities of color; Low-income
    communities; Low-income communities
    of color; Low-income students of color;
    Students of color
Motivation, 15

NAM (National Association of Manufacturers),
    49
National Assessment of Educational Progress
    (NAEP), 22
National Association of Manufacturers (NAM),
    49
National Superintendents Roundtable, 22
Nation at Risk, A, 46, 49, 63, 123
NCLB (No Child Left Behind), 15, 49, 52, 53, 75,
    123, 133
Neoclassical model. *See* Neoliberalism
Neoliberalism, 7, 9, 10–11, 18, 73. *See also*
    Managerialism
    as backlash against women/minorities, 12
    Foucault's study of, 92
    job security and, 100
    as new normal, 91
    use of term, 8–9
New managerialist logic. *See* New Public Man-
    agement (NPM)
New Orleans, 106
New Public Management (NPM), 2
    accumulation by dispossession and, 22
    activist state and, 23
    appeal of, 66
    desire to eliminate teachers' unions, 129
    education industry and, 113
    entrance into public education, 23
    failure of reforms, 53
    goal of, 22, 68
    higher education and, 136
    impact on everyday teaching, 38
    influence on thinking, 95
    lack of benefits from, 22
    as new normal, 91–96
    opening for, 52
    opposition to, 76
    overview of, 21–23
    popularity of, 52
    power of ideology, 54–55
    private-sector service workers and, 4
    promotion of, 22, 71
    public choice theory and, 11
    rejection of, 112
    resistance to, 76, 91, 96–110
    response to, 17
    support for, 73–76, 123
    unintended consequences of, 53
    use of term, 9
New York City
    under Bloomberg, 23
    demand for community control in, 43
    New York Performance Standards Consor-
        tium, 128
    public school system, 103
New York Performance Standards Consortium,
    128
Nihilism, 19
No Child Left Behind (NCLB), 49, 52, 53, 75,
    123, 133
Normal, new, 96
Normalization, recognizing, 100
Normal schools, 37
Norms, 91–94, 95–96, 98
NPM (New Public Management). *See* New
    Public Management (NPM)

Obama administration, 67
Observation rubrics, 92
Opportunity, inclusion in, 116–118
Opportunity hoarding, 117
Opt-out movement, 74, 76
Oregon Department of Education, 132–133
Outcome measures, 1, 9, 13, 30, 108

Parents, low-income, 75–76. *See also* Low-in-
    come communities
Parents of color, 75–76. *See also* Low-income
    communities of color
Participatory Action Research, 130–131
Paternalism, 81, 124
Pay-for-performance, 67
Pedagogical progressives, 39
Pensions, 55
Performance, accountability and, 107–108
Philadelphia schools, 76
Philanthropists, 81. *See also Individual founda-
    tions*
    charter schools and, 54
    control of education technology, 71
    influence of, 46
    policymaking and, 27, 28, 81
    privatization of teacher/administrator prepa-
        ration and, 87
    promotion of neoliberal regime, 72
    in public school reform, 44–45
    resistance to, 45

think tanks and, 81–83
views of roles of, 45
white male, 81
PISA (Program for International Student Assessment), 22
PLC (professional learning community), 105
Policy
    business leaders' influence on, 45–48
    capitalists and, 45
    controlling discourse and, 102
    educators' voice in, 72
    implementing, 40
    neoliberal education, 53
    philanthropists' influence on, 46, 81
    political implications of, 98–99
Policy actors, 27–28, 71, 72
Policy alienation, 8
Policy analysis, 102–103
Policy networks, 71, 72, 77–83
Political spectacle, 52, 63
Politics
    rightward shift in, 49, 73–74, 77
    in schools, 33
Portland, Oregon, 30
Power
    concept of, 91–96
    constant vigilance and, 99
    distribution of, 115
    identity and, 95
    individuals as vehicles of, 101
    norms and, 91–94, 98
    technologies of, 3
PPP (public–private partnerships), 83
Principals. See also Administrators; Leadership
    in bureaucracy, 34–37
    education for, 56–57
    efficiency-minded, 34
    gender and, 35
    identity of, 95
    licensing requirements for, 35, 36
    race of, 35–36
    relation with teachers, 36, 37
    relation with upper administration, 36–37
Principals, Black, 36
Principals, female, 35
Principles of Scientific Management, The (Taylor), 57
Privatization
    in Britain, 63
    in education, 51
    effects on teachers, 55
    financialization, 84
    managerialism, 84
    philanthropists' support for, 81

of public sector, 8, 68, 83
of teacher/administrator preparation, 87
Professional, democratic, 24–25
    as advocate/activist, 121–123
    characteristics of, 114–123
    dimensions of, 26
    responsibility and, 119–121
Professional, new, 55, 62
Professional, new education, 85–87
Professional development, 13
Professional ethos, 24
Professionalism
    attempts to control, 96
    audit culture in, 16–17
    in bureaucracy, 32–42
    vs. community, 42–45
    creating new model of, 96
    criteria of, 12
    defending, 96. *See also* resistance
    diminished by reforms, 17
    modes of, 113, 114
    new model of, 109
    shifts in, 7, 13–14
Professionalism, democratic, 42, 97, 109, 115–119
Professionalism, new, 2
    appeal of, 2
    corporate characteristics of, 2
    impact on everyday teaching, 38
    resistance to, 3, 90, 96–110
    shift to, 13
Professionalism, occupational, 13, 14
Professionalism, organizational, 13, 14
Professionalism, parallel, 17
Professionalism, teacher, 12, 33, 37–42
Professionalization, 32
Professional learning, 130–131
Professional learning community (PLC), 105
Professionals
    middle/upper-class, 74
    over-regulation of, 3
    private-sector, 1, 17
    public-sector, 7. *See also* teachers
Profit centers
    education as, 82
    new, 11
    public sector as, 10, 25
Profitization, of public sector, 8
Profits
    of edubusiness, 10
    focus on, 59, 79
Profit-seekers, 74–75, 123
Program for International Student Assessment (PISA), 22

Progressive Policy Institute, 25
Progressives, administrative, 39
Progressives, pedagogical, 39
Public, meaning of, 118
Public choice theory, 11
Public education. *See also* Education; Schooling
    assault on, 24
    democratic mission of, 90
    linked to economy, 72
    NPM's entrance into, 23
    private parallel system to, 68
Public ethos, erosion of, 24
Public–private partnerships (PPP), 83
Public sector
    assault on, 24
    business principles in, 7
    creative destruction of, 63
    disinvestment from, 8, 63, 137
    efforts to eliminate, 22
    innovation in, 60
    marketizing, 11
    privatization of, 7, 68, 83
    as profit center, 10, 25
Public sphere, inclusion in, 118–119

Quantitative social indicators, 9

Race
    administrators and, 35–36
    Black education, 46–48
    professionalism and, 12
Race to the Top, 67, 84
Racism, 72, 130
Rand Corporation, 58
Reagan administration, 49
Reaganomics, 83
Reforms. *See also* Managerialism
    barriers to, 38
    business-oriented, 2, 29–32. *See also* New
        Public Management (NPM)
    from corporate sector, 21
    failures of, 51, 53–55, 112
    neoliberal education, 51, 53–55
    professionalism and, 17
    reappropriation of, 105–108
    responsibility for, 28
    standards-based, 49
    whole-school, 52
Relationality, 56
Religious right, 74
Resistance. *See also* Democratic professionalism
    contemporary theory of, 90
    counter-conduct, 97, 104–108
    counter-discourses, 97, 102–104
    critical vigilance, 97, 98–101
    education movement, 109
    to neoliberal reform model, 25
    to new professionalism, 3, 90
    to NPM, 76, 91, 96–110
    principled, 24
    principled leavers, 100
    productive, 97, 109
    to reforms, 40
    reports of, 109
Responsibility, 26, 127. *See also* Accountability
    vs. accountability, 119–120
    alternative systems of, 128–129
    democratic professional and, 119–121
Responsibility, professional, 9
Restorative justice practices, 133–134
Revenue, alternative sources of, 108
Rockefeller family, 48
Rosenwald Fund, 46–47

Sacred Heart Medical Center, 89–90, 96
School choice, 1, 52, 53, 74. *See also* New Public
        Management (NPM)
    cognitive frames and, 67
    low-income communities of color and, 76
    philanthropists' support for, 81
    segregation and, 54, 112
Schooling. *See also* Education; Public education
    disembedded from out-of-school factors, 73
    goal of, 13
    purpose of, 46, 48, 49, 135
    white males and, 12
School in the Cloud, 70
School leadership. *See* Administrators; Leader-
        ship; Principals
School performance framework, 92–93
Schools
    linking communities with, 112, 116
    support for, 3
Scientific Management, 31–32
Segregation, 36, 43, 54, 112, 117
Self-determination, 42, 43–44. *See also* Autono-
        my; Community control
Service Employees International Union (SEIU),
        129
Sexism, 72
Sharing economy, 70
Smith, Adam, 58
Social justice, 121–122, 125
Social justice discourse, 66
Social movements, 103
South (region), 46

Springfield, Oregon, 89–90, 96
Standards. *See* Common Core State Standards
Standards-based reforms, 31, 49
Startup culture, 20
Startups, 59
State
    activist, 23
    administrative, 68
    relation with market, 23
State Policy Network, 78
Steering, 14
Stock prices, 18, 19
Stress, 8, 20
Strikes, 1, 4, 83, 130. *See also* Activism
    healthcare, 136
Students, as human capital, 13, 46, 135
Students, low-income. *See* Low-income students
    of color
Students of color. *See also* Low-income students
    of color
    Black education in south, 116
    discipline and, 133–134
    education for, 46–48
Student supports, integrated system of, 127
Supply-side economics, 11. *See also* Neoliberalism
Surveillance, 100–101
System world, 14

Taxes, 60
Taylor, Frederick, 32
Teacher Activist Group, 107
Teacher gap, 8
Teacher Incentive Fund (TIF), 108
Teacher preparation, 12–13, 37, 85, 130, 131
    alternative, 1, 50, 56, 100
    opportunities to question NPM and, 100
    privatization of, 68, 87
Teachers
    in bureaucracy, 32–33, 37–42
    certification requirements, 37
    deprofessionalization of, 42–45
    effects of organizational conditions on, 19
    effects of privatization on, 55
    job satisfaction and, 20
    job security of, 37
    marginalization of, 33, 69–70
    NPM and, 17
    principled leavers, 100
    relation with principals, 37
    as technicians/factory hands, 32, 38
    threats to, 1
Teach for America, 86

Teaching
    everyday, 39
    oversimplification of, 32
    as profession, 12–14
    proletarization of, 115
Tech industry, 82
Technology. *See also* Virtual schools
    control of, 71
    isolation and, 119
    marginalization of teachers and, 70
    promotion of, 70–71
Technology companies, 55
Tenure, 37, 100
Testing, high-stakes, 1, 52, 53, 93–94. *See also*
        New Public Management (NPM)
    arts-testing initiative, 93–94
    benchmarks, 22
    opt-out movement, 53, 74, 76
    validity of, 53
Test scores, 13, 16, 53–54. *See also* Outcome
        measures
Think tanks, 11, 52, 72, 76, 81–83
Third spaces, 106–107, 132
Tracking, 116
Training, of new education professional, 85–87.
        See also Teacher preparation
Trump administration, 68, 123
Trust, 56
Tucson Unified School District, 132

UFT (United Federation of Teachers), 43, 44
Uniformity, obsession with, 30
Union City, NJ, 112
Unionism, reform, 129
Unions
    anti-labor laws, 78
    doctors', 89–90
    public-sector, 3, 78
    teachers', 4, 11, 13, 41, 42, 43–44, 50, 55, 129,
        130
United Federation of Teachers (UFT), 43, 44
Universities, corporatization of, 85

Value-added measures, 50, 53
Vigilance, 97, 98–101
Virtual schools, 70, 79, 119
Vocational education, 46–48, 116
Vouchers, 1, 54

Walkouts, 1, 4, 83, 136. *See also* Activism
Wall Street meltdown, 60–61
Walmart, 74
Walton Foundation, 27

War on poverty, 72, 83
Washington Post, The, 45
Weapons of Math Destruction (O'Neil), 9
White Architects of Black Education, The (Watkins), 48
White males, 81
White northern philanthropists, 48
Who Moved My Cheese? (Johnson), 18
Wisconsin, 4, 136

Workers
    controlling, 100–101
    division with management, 31
Work ethic, 19
Workplace
    corporate, shifts in, 18
    democracy in, 3
    flexible, 19

About the Authors

Gary L. Anderson is a professor in the Steinhardt School of Culture, Education, and Human Development at New York University. A former high school teacher and principal, he has published on many topics, including critical ethnography, participatory action research, school micropolitics, new policy networks, and the new professional. His most recent books are *Advocacy Leadership: Toward a Post-Reform Agenda*; *The Action Research Dissertation: A Guide for Students and Faculty, Second Edition* (with Kathryn Herr); and *The Politics of Education Policy in an Era of Inequality: Possibilities for Democratic Education* (with Sonya Horsford and Janelle Scott).

Michael Ian Cohen is an assistant professor in the College of Education and Behavioral Sciences at the University of Northern Colorado. He has served as a high school English teacher and in various administration positions at the school and district levels in New Jersey and Colorado. His research focuses on new public management, public educator professionalism, and critical policy studies.